The Seventy Weeks
& The Great Tribulation

GREAT CHRISTIAN BOOKS
LINDENHURST, NEW YORK

THE SEVENTY WEEKS

& THE GREAT TRIBULATION

PHILIP MAURO

Great Christian Books
is an imprint of Rotolo Media
160 37th Street Lindenhurst, New York 11757
(631) 956-0998

©2015 Rotolo Media / Great Christian Books

All rights reserved under International and Pan-American Copyright Conventions. No part of this book maybe reproduced in any form, or by any means, electronic or mechanical, including photocopying, and informational storage and retrieval systems without the expressed written permission from the publisher, except in the case of brief quotations embodied in articles or reviews or promotional/advertising/catalog materials. For additional information or permissions, address all inquiries to the publisher.

Mauro, Philip, 1859-1952
The Seventy Weeks and The Great Tribulation / by Philip Mauro
p. cm.
A "A Great Christian Book" book
GREAT CHRISTIAN BOOKS an imprint of Rotolo Media
ISBN 978-1-61010-006-9
Recommended Dewey Decimal Classifications: 200, 202, 230, 236
Suggested Subject Headings:
1. Religion—Christianity & Christian theology—Eschatology
2. Christianity—Bible—Theology
I. Title

Book and cover design are by Michael Rotolo, www.michaelrotolo.com. This book is typeset in the Minion typeface by Adobe Inc. and is quality-manufactured on acid-free paper stock. To discuss the publication of your Christian manuscript or out-of-print book, please contact us.

Manufactured in the United States of America

Contents

Principles That Govern in Interpretation of Prophecy	7
The Commandment to Restore, And to Build	17
Details of the Seventy Weeks	39
Unto Messiah the Prince	51
Messiah Cut Off	65
The Seventieth Week	73
Are the Seventy Weeks Consecutive?	83
Daniel's Last Vision	109
The King	127
Michael the Great Prince—The Time of Trouble—Many Awakening—Many Running To and Fro—Knowledge Increased—How Long the End?	155
"The Wise Shall Understand"—Have These Prophecies A Future Application?	173
The Lord's Prophecy on Mount Olivet	181
Outline of the Olivet Prophecy	193
Such As Never Was	203
The Siege of Jerusalem As Described by Josephus	223
Concluding Comments	241
Appendix	259
Endnotes	265

CHAPTER 1

Principles That Should Govern in the Interpretation of Prophecy

Our object in the present series of papers is to bring before our readers some results of recent studies of the prophecy of The Seventy Weeks (Daniel 9), and of the Lord's discourse on Mount Olivet (Matthew 24, Mark 13, Luke 21), in which He applied and expanded a part of that prophecy.

Writings and addresses on prophecy always excite interest, because they appeal to the element of curiosity which is prominent in human nature. But such writings and addresses are of benefit only so far as they rightly interpret the Scripture. In the case of unfulfilled prophecy this is oftentimes a matter of difficulty; while on the other hand writers on prophetic themes are under constant temptation to indulge in Surmises and speculations, and even in flights of imagination. Much has been put forth as interpretation of prophecy which is utterly unproved, but which could not be disproved except, as in cases where dates have been set for the coming of Christ, by the event itself.

Another fact which has been impressed upon us in this connection is that there has been no progress in the interpretation of unfulfilled prophecy for a good many years. At "prophetic conferences", and in books and magazines, the same things are being repeated today, with little variation, that were said two decades ago. It would seem that, for some reason, the Lord has not been, of late, shedding fresh light upon this part of His precious Word. Our own thought about the matter is that writers on prophecy have gone so far in advancing, and the people of God in accepting, mere conjectures, unproved theories, or at best mere probabilities, as interpretations of the prophetic Scriptures, that there must needs be a surrender of our speculative ideas, and a retracing of some of our steps (which have diverged from the truth), ere there can be any real advance in the understanding of this part of the Word of God.

Having these things in mind, we purpose, in entering upon the present line of studies, to be governed by certain principles which, we believe, should control at all times those who assume to expound the Word of God to their fellow saints.

The first of these controlling principles is, neither to accept nor to give forth as settled interpretation anything that rests upon surmise or mere probability; but only what is supported either by direct proof from Scripture, or by reasonable deduction therefrom. We maintain that it is far better to have no explanation at all of a difficult passage than to accept one which may turn out to be wrong. For it is not easy to give up an idea when once we have committed ourselves to it.

In fact, that which chiefly stands in the way of the acceptance of fresh light and truth from the Scriptures is the strong (in some cases almost invincible) reluctance of the human mind to surrender, or even to examine the ground of, opinions which possibly were originally accepted upon human authority only, and without any inquiry as to the support which can be found for them in the Word of God.

Another guiding principle is that the proof adduced in support of any interpretation should be taken from the Scripture itself. Our conviction is that, whatever information is essential for the interpretation of any and every passage of Scripture is to be found somewhere in the Bible itself. Were it not so the Holy Scriptures would not be able to make the man of God perfect, that is to say, complete, and thoroughly furnished unto every good work (2 Timothy 3:16–17). We must, of course, appeal to history in order to show the fulfillment of prophecy; for it cannot be shown in any other way. But the interpretation of Scripture is another matter.

Furthermore, wherever we offer a statement or opinion to the reader for his acceptance, we feel bound to give along with it the proofs by which we deem it to be established. This should be demanded of every writer. But, most unhappily, there are now in circulation many books dealing with Bible subjects, whose authors deem themselves to be such high "authorities" that they habitually make assertions of the most radical sort without citing in support thereof any proof whatever. We earnestly caution our readers to beware of all such. It is not according to the mind of God that His people should rest upon any human "authorities" whatever. His own Word is the only authority.

These papers are prepared for the benefit of "the common people". What we undertake by the grace of God to do is to make every statement and conclusion so plain, and to support it by such clear proof from the Scriptures alone, that the ordinary reader will be able both to see for himself the meaning of the passage, and also to comprehend perfectly the scriptural evidence by which that meaning is established. Thus he will be entirely independent of all human "authority".

This is an exceedingly important point. For, as matters now stand, it would be difficult or impossible to find any one whose view of the Seventy Weeks prophecy does not rest, as to some one or more essential features thereof, upon mere human authority. In our own case, when we began these studies (about May 1921) our opinion (in regard especially to the Chronology of the prophetic period) had no better basis than that such were the views of certain eminent writers on Bible topics; and this was most unsatisfactory, because we knew that there were other equally eminent students of the Bible who held an entirely different view. But now we are in no uncertainty. We have solid ground under our feet; for every conclusion rests upon the unshakable rock of God s own testimony. This is as it should be.

We wish particularly to impress upon our readers that the proofs furnished by the Scriptures for our comprehension of this great and marvelous prophecy are not hard to understand or to apply. On the contrary they are quite simple. On a moment s reflection it will be seen that it could not be otherwise. For the Scriptures were written, not for the erudite, but for the simple minded. Our Lord said, speaking of this very prophecy, "Whoso readeth, let him understand" (Matthew 24:15); and it should not surprise us to find that all the materials needed for our understanding of the matter are contained in the Bible itself.

Bible Chronology

Prior to the publication of Martin Anstey's great work in 1913, all the existing systems of Bible Chronology were dependent, for the period of time embraced by the Seventy Weeks, upon sources of information outside the Bible, and which are, moreover, not only unsupported by proof, but are in conflict with the Scriptures. Anstey's system has the unique merit of being based on the Bible alone. Therefore it is capable of being verified by all Bible readers. But for the prophecy of the Seventy Weeks there is no need to resort to any system of chronology, seeing that the prophecy contains its own chronology. In fact the difficulties and confusion which have arisen in connection with this prophecy are due in large measure to the attempt to make it conform to an incorrect chronology.

A Prophecy of Transcendent Interest

The Scripture we are now about to study is one of the most marvelous and most transcendently important in the Word of God. That which is of supreme interest in it is the divinely revealed time measure, starting from the return of the Israelites out of Babylonian historical event second in importance only to the Exodus from Egypt—down to the culminating event of all prophecy and all history, even "unto Messiah," and to His being "cut off and having nothing."

The very nature of the things here revealed is a guaranty that, in the Scriptures themselves, will be found everything that is needed for a right and clear understanding thereof; and further that the whole matter lies within the comprehension of ordinary saints. All we ask of our readers is their prayerful attention to the Scriptures to which we shall refer. Upon that sole condition we can confidently promise them that they will be well able to understand every matter advanced, and to see for themselves whether it be supported by the Word of God or not.

Finally we desire to say that the conclusions we have reached involve nothing (unless in respect to some minor details) that has not been pointed out by sound Bible expositors of other days. This, however, we were (in some important particulars) unaware of until our studies were completed; for while they were in progress we consulted no human authorities except Anstey's Bible Chronology, mentioned above.

If any of our readers should find themselves in disagreement as to any of the matters set forth herein, we would ask of such only a patient examination of the proofs advanced, together with that measure of kindly toleration which is to be expected in such cases amongst those who are, with equal sincerity, seeking to know the mind of God.

"Daniel The Prophet" (Matthew 24:15)

The book of Daniel differs in marked particulars from all others. The miraculous element abounds in it; and because of this it has been within recent years an object of venomous attack by the enemies of truth. Furthermore, the communications found in it are not, like other prophecies, in the nature of exhortations and warnings to the people of that time; for Daniel was not (like the other prophets), the messenger of God to the people of Daniel s own day. They are, on the contrary, in the nature of Divine revelations, given to Daniel, either in the form of visions, or of messages direct from heaven. It does not appear that they were communicated to the people of that day. Thus the book is seen to be not for the people of Daniel s own time, but for those of a later period or periods. Here is a very marked difference between the prophecies of Daniel, and all others.

Moreover, the book of Daniel has to do in a very special way with Christ; and to this feature we would call particular attention. Christ Himself is distinctly seen in it, once in earth in the midst of the burning fiery furnace, delivering the men who trusted in their God (3:25); and once in heaven, receiving an everlasting Kingdom (7:13-14). And beyond all else in interest and importance is the fact that to Daniel was given the exact measure of time from an event clearly marked in his own day—an event for which he had fervently prayed—to the coming of Christ, and to His being "cut off". Moreover, in this connection God revealed to Daniel the marvelous things which were to be accomplished through the crucifixion of Christ, as well as the overwhelming judgments—the "desolations"—far surpassing anything of like nature theretofore—which were to fall upon the City, the Sanctuary and the People, in consequence of their rejection and crucifixion of Christ.

In respect to these remarkable and immensely important features the book of Daniel stands in a class by itself.

Moreover, this book contains, not only predictions that were to be fulfilled at the first coming of Christ, but also predictions relating to the end of the present age. For we have in the vision of the great image of gold, silver, brass, iron and clay, recorded in Chapter 2, an outline of the course of human history from Daniel's own time down to the second coming of Christ in power and glory; and the breadth of the prophecy is such that it embraces the chief political changes of the whole world.

It is doubtless because of the unique character and importance of this book that it has been so fiercely attacked within recent times, and that every attempt has been made to raise a doubt as, to its authenticity; for great efforts have been made to convince the people in general that it was not written by Daniel, or in his day. Those attempts have conspicuously failed; but the efforts of the adversary to discredit this book are still to be seen in the crude interpretations, miscalculations, and fantastical views which have been poured forth in this day, now that it has become a matter of importance to "understand" these prophecies.

An intimation of the efforts that would be made to becloud the prophecy of Daniel is found in the words of Christ when, in referring directly to that prophecy, he said, "Whoso readeth let him understand" (Matthew 24:15). But those words may also be taken as an encouragement to seek a right understanding of that wonderful series of prophecies.

The chief interest of our study centers in the revelation given to Daniel in the first year of the MedoPersian empire, and found in the ninth Chapter; and it is to this prophecy of prophecies that we wish to direct attention at the present time. It is generally known as the prophecy of the Seventy Weeks (Daniel 9:24–27).

The setting of this prophecy should first be carefully noted. Daniel had learned, through Jeremiah 25:11; 29:10, that the period which God had set for the "desolations of Jerusalem" was just seventy years (Daniel 9:1). That period was then about to expire; for the decree, whereby the captivity was ended and the Jews were allowed (and even exhorted) to return to their land and city, was issued by, Cyrus within two years (Ezra 1:1). That this was the fulfillment of Jeremiah's prophecy is certainly known, because it is recorded in Ezra 1:1, that the Lord stirred up the spirit of Cyrus to issue that decree, for the express purpose that "the word of the Lord by the mouth of Jeremiah might be fulfilled". This is surpassingly wonderful and impressive.

The effect upon Daniel of receiving this revelation was to send him to his knees in confession and prayer. His prayer should be carefully examined. It will be seen that it has to do entirely with the city, the sanctuary, and the people of God, with special reference to the "desolations" of the city. It will be seen also that these same subjects are what occupy the prophecy which the angel Gabriel brought to Daniel in response to his prayer. We call special attention to this, and also to the following points of interest:

1. God's response to Daniel's prayer was in the form of a revelation brought to him by the angel Gabriel, who stated, as the first item of information, that the seventy years of captivity were to be followed by a period of seventy sevens (of years). The word here rendered "weeks" is literally "sevens"; so there is no doubt that the period designated in this prophecy is seventy sevens of years—490 years.

2. The decree which was to bring the captivity to an end by freeing the Jews, granting them liberty to return to their own land and to rebuild the city and sanctuary, was to be also the starting point of the "determined" period of seventy sevens of years. This is clearly seen from the prophecy itself in connection with Ezra 1:1 and other Scriptures hereafter referred to; and it is important—indeed necessary in order to avoid being misled—that we grasp this fact and keep it in mind. So we repeat that the epoch-making decree of Cyrus in the first year of his reign (as sole king), in virtue of which the city and temple were rebuilt under Zerubbabel and Joshua, was both the termination of the 70 years captivity and also the starting point for the prophetic period of 70 sevens, which had been "determined", or measured out, in the councils of heaven,

upon the people and the holy city. Where the one period was to end, the other (just seven times as long) was to begin. Again we ask that this point be carefully noted. Full proof of its correctness will be given in our next chapter.

3. Daniel had, in his player, confessed the sins of his people, for which sins God had brought upon them the "desolations" of their city and sanctuary. But, to his intense grief no doubt, the angel Gabriel revealed to him that a far more terrible sin, the very culmination of the sins of the people, was yet to be committed by them. This was to happen within the period "determined" by the prophecy; and moreover, in consequence thereof, a judgment far more severe was to fall upon them, even the utter destruction of the city and sanctuary, the sweeping away of the nation as "with a flood", and "desolations" of age-long duration. No wonder eve find Daniel, in the third year of Cyrus, still mourning and fasting three full weeks, and lamenting that his comeliness was turned in him into corruption (10:2–3, 8). Daniel had said in his prayer, "Yea, all Israel have transgressed" (verse 11). An evident response to this is seen in the words of Gabriel, "seventy weeks are determined upon thy people to finish the transgression." With this we may compare the words of Christ, spoken to the leaders of Israel, just before the Olivet discourse: "Fill ye up then the measure of your fathers" (Matthew 23:32). They did so by rejecting and crucifying Him.

4. The most important feature of the revelation brought by Gabriel to Daniel was the precise measure of time (69 sevens, or 483 years) "to Messiah, THE PRINCE"; and the time when Messiah was to be "cut off and have nothing". This is the wonder of wonders, the prophecy of prophecies.

5. The angel Gabriel, who brought these marvelous predictions to Daniel, is the same who announced the approach of the fulfillment of them to Zachariah and to Mary (Luke 1:11–19; 26).

6. The expression used by Gabriel to Daniel, "thou art greatly beloved", is the exact equivalent of the word addressed by the same messenger to Mary—"thou art highly favored" (Anstey's Bible Chronology, p. 276). Mr. Anstey says of this expression: "It is used three times to Daniel, and never to anyone else except Mary; and Gabriel is the only angel employed to make known to men the revelation of the mystery of redemption."

7. The revelation embraces two main subjects (a) the coming and cutting off of the Messiah, (b) the destruction and "desolation" of the City and Sanctuary. It is a fact very familiar to all readers of the Bible, that Christ Jesus called this prophecy to the minds of His disciples on the eve of His being "cut off," and definitely announced to them at that time the approaching destruction and "desolation" of Jerusalem and the Temple (Matthew 24:1–22; Luke 21:20-24).

In these seven points we have the main elements for a right understanding of the prophecy.

CHAPTER 2

"The Commandment to Restore, and to Build."

"From the going forth of the commandment to restore and to build Jerusalem unto Messiah the Prince" (Daniel 9:25)

The prophecy begins at, verse 24. The angel informs Daniel that seventy sevens of years were "determined" (or marked out) upon his people, and upon his holy city, to finish the transgression, to make an end of sins, to make reconciliation for iniquity, to bring in everlasting righteousness, to seal up the vision and prophecy, and to anoint the most holy (place). Here are six things which were to be accomplished within the definitely determined period of 490 years of Jewish history. Into those six things we purpose to look later on. But there is one important question that should be settled first. When does the stretch of 490 years begin? The next verse gives this needed information. We read, "Know therefore, and understand, that from the going forth of the commandment to restore and to build Jerusalem unto the Messiah, the Prince, shall be seven weeks and three score and two weeks." From this we learn that there was to be a total of 69 weeks (7 weeks plus 62 weeks) or 483 years from the given starting point unto the Messiah.

We must therefore determine with certainty the event from which the count of the seventy weeks was to begin; for it is manifest that the measuring line, notwithstanding it was given directly from heaven, and notwithstanding it is recorded for our benefit in the inspired Scriptures, will be of no use to us whatever unless the starting point be certainly known. It is equally manifest that the starting point cannot be certainly known unless it be revealed in the Scriptures and in such wise that the ordinary reader can "know and understand" it beyond a doubt. This essential matter, however, is revealed in the Word of God; and moreover the information is given in a manner so plain and so simple that the wayfaring man need not err therein. To this we will come in a moment. But first it is desirable to speak of the various and conflicting ideas on this vital point that are found in current writings on prophecy. For, strange to say, there is the greatest disagreement and contrariety of opinion as to the particular "commandment" or "word" referred to by the angel as the starting point of the 70 weeks. There are no less than four different decrees, or royal commands, which have been brought forward as the point from which the seventy weeks are to be counted. Some able and learned expositors choose one, and others equally able and learned choose another. Yet the Word of God speaks as clearly as to this as it speaks concerning where Christ should be born.

Why then this difference of opinion? The explanation is that those who, in recent years, have turned their attention to this prophecy, have gone about the interpretation of it in the wrong way. They have pursued a method which cannot do other than lead to an erroneous conclusion. This should be understood by the reader (and we will seek to make it quite clear) before proceeding further.

The right way of getting at the chronology of the prophecy is so simple and obvious that a child can readily comprehend it. All we need to do is to ascertain from the Word of God the two events specified by the angel, (1) the going forth of the "commandment" and (2) the manifestation of "Messiah the Prince." Having definitely fixed these two events (which the Scriptures enable us to do with certainty) we know from the prophecy itself that from the one to the other is just 483 years. By this method we have no need of a system of chronology.

But our expositors have proceeded in a very different way. First they have made choice of one or another of the various systems of chronology which have been compiled by various chronologists—as Ussher's, Lloyd's, Clinton's or Marshall's. Then, having assigned the correctness of the selected chronology, they have sought first for a decree of some Persian king, and second for some event in the lifetime of Christ, which would be as near as possible to 483 years apart, according to the selected chronology.

It will be clear upon the briefest consideration that, according to this method, the interpretation of the prophecy is controlled by whatever chronology the expositor may have selected; for he needs must reject every interpretation which does not agree with his assumed chronology.

Now, not only is this method of procedure fundamentally wrong in that it tries to make events of Bible history fit in with a man-made chronological scheme, but the fact is that every chronological System covering the period we have to do with (i.e., from the beginning of the Persian monarchy down to Christ) is largely a matter of guesswork. All those systems, without any exception, are based upon the "canon" of Ptolemy, that is to say, a list of supposed Persian kings, with the supposed length of the reign of each, which list was compiled by Ptolemy, a heathen astronomer and writer of the second century AD But Ptolemy does not even pretend to have had any facts as to the length of the Persian period (that is to say, from Darius and Cyrus down to Alexander the Great). Ptolemy estimates or guesses this period to have been 205 years long. And this is what has caused all the trouble and uncertainty; for every one who has attempted to construct a Bible chronology has based himself on Ptolemy's estimate. In a word then, there is no chronology in existence of the period from Cyrus to Christ except in the Bible.

In order to show how great is the uncertainty as to the length of the Persian empire, we have only to mention the fact that, according to Jewish traditions in the days of Christ (which surely are as much to be trusted as heathen traditions of a later date), the period of the Persian kings was only 52 years. Here is a difference of 153 years, and that in regard to a matter which is essential to an understanding of this prophecy. Sir Isaac Newton says that "some of the Jews took Herod for the Messiah, and were called 'Herodians'. They seem to have grounded their opinion on the 70 weeks." Inasmuch as the accession of Herod was 34 years before Christ, it is evident that the opinion of the Herodians required a comparatively short Persian period. On the other hand, the opinions of certain modern expositors are based upon a Persian era of supposedly long duration.

In order that the reader may clearly understand the situation, and its hearings upon our study, we would point out that Ussher's chronology (whose dates are given at the head of the "margin" of our Bibles) makes it 536 years from the first year of Cyrus to the year 1 AD (four years after the birth of Christ). Add to this 26 years to the Lord's manifestation to Israel at His baptism and we have 562 years. But, according to the Word of God it was to be only 483 years from the commandment to restore Jerusalem "unto Christ." If, therefore, one begins by taking Ussher's chronology (or any of the others) as the basis of his interpretation, he is forced to select a starting point about eighty years subsequent to King Cyrus, who (according to Scripture) was the true restorer, the man whom God specially raised up, and of whom He said, "He shall build My city". (To this we will come shortly.)

The Commandment to Restore and to Build 21

But we are not left to choose between Jewish traditions and heathen traditions, or to base our conclusions upon either. For the Word of God shows us plainly what was the beginning of the prophetic period; and with that information in our possession, we know certainly that it was just 483 years "unto Christ." Therefore, we are bound to reject any and every chronological scheme, whether from Jewish or heathen sources, and any and every system of interpretation based thereon) which conflicts with the facts revealed in the Scriptures.

This important matter of the defective character of all existing chronologies is fully discussed, and the facts clearly set forth, in Martin Anstey's Bible Chronology, published in 1913, to which we must refer such of our readers as wish to study the matter exhaustively. Mr. Anstey's work commands our confidence and respect because he disregards all heathen sources, and all guesswork, and derives his information solely from the Scriptures.

Concerning the dates given in Ptolemy's table of Persian Kings, Anstey says: "They rest upon calculations or guesses made by Eratosthenes, and on certain vague floating traditions, in accordance with which the period of the Persian Empire was mapped out as a period of 205 years." And he shows, by a great variety of proofs taken entirely from the Scriptures, that the period which Ptolemy assigns to the Persian Empire is about eighty years too long. It follows that all who adopt Ptolemy's chronology, or any system based upon it (as all modern chronologists prior to Anstey do) would inevitably be led far astray. It is impossible to make the real Bible events agree, within 80 years, with the mistaken chronology of Ptolemy. This single fact makes many modern books on Daniel utterly worthless, so far as their chronology is concerned; and the chronology is the main thing.

Concerning Eclipses

An attempt has been made to call Astronomy to the aid of the defective Chronology of Ptolemy, by utilizing certain incidental references, contained in fragmentary historical records, to eclipses of the sun or moon. But such references are of no value whatever for the purpose, seeing that it is impossible to determine, in any given case, which one of a number of eclipses—within say fifty or a hundred years—was the one referred to. For example, one of the clearest of these historical references is that of the "Eclipse of Thales," mentioned by Herodotus. This eclipse is located by one astronomer as occurring in 625 B. C.; by another as late as 585 B. C. (a difference of 40 years); and by others at different dates in between (Anstey, p. 286).

We see then first that the method adopted in current expositions of the Seventy Weeks prophecy is fundamentally wrong; and second that the chronological system on which they are all based is formed largely by guesswork, and is certainly very wide of the mark as regards the length of the Persian Empire.

An accurate and complete secular chronology exists from the conquest of Persia by Alexander the Great down to the present time. It is only as regards the period from Cyrus to Alexander that there is uncertainty.

The Decree of Cyrus The Great

We will now proceed to show that the point of beginning of the seventy weeks is that great epoch-making and divinely prompted decree of Cyrus the Great, whereof a record is given in 2 Chronicles 36:22-23, and also in Ezra 1:1-4. The proof is not only clear, simple and absolutely conclusive for all who believe the Word of the Lord, but it was given under circumstances which were designed to inspire wonder and admiration at the marvelous ways of God in bringing to pass that which He has purposed and promised to perform.

The Commandment to Restore and to Build

Turning to Isaiah, Chapters 44 and 45, we find there God's promise that Jerusalem should be rebuilt and its captives restored to their home, and not only so but we find that God mentioned by name the very man, "Cyrus", by whom that promise was to be accomplished. The proof that King Cyrus was the one who should give the commandment (or word). for the restoring and rebuilding of Jerusalem, is doubly forceful and impressive, and designedly so as the Scripture itself declares, because it was spoken by the mouth of the Lord two hundred years before Cyrus came to the throne.

The passage begins with the words, "Sing, O ye heavens, for the Lord hath done it" (Isaiah 44:23). Evidently God is here calling attention to a work of great importance and one in which He takes special delight. It was to be a work, moreover, by which the tokens of the liars (those who consulted omens) were to be frustrated, and the "diviners" made mad, and the "wise men" turned backward, and their knowledge made foolish (verse 25). Notwithstanding all that opposed His will, the high walls and strong gates of Babylon, and the wisdom of the astrologers, soothsayers and Chaldeans, God would "confirm the word of His servant, and perform the counsel of His messengers"; for it was He "that saith to Jerusalem, Thou shalt be inhabited, and to the cities of Judah, Ye shall be built, and I will raise up the decayed places thereof; that saith to the deep, Be dry, and I will dry up thy rivers; that saith of CYRUS, He is My shepherd, and shall perform all my pleasure, EVEN SAYING TO JERUSALEM, THOU SHALT BE BUILT; AND TO THE TEMPLE, THY FOUNDATION SHALL BE LAID" (verses 26–27).

We pause at this point to call to the reader's mind that when the time for the fulfillment of this prophecy by Isaiah was at hand, the last Babylonian King, Belshazzar, was carousing with a thousand of his courtiers in fancied security behind the strong walls of Babylon, while the armies of Darius and Cyrus were besieging the city. Then appeared the part of a man's hand, tracing upon the wall those four words which declared the doom of Babylon, though the magicians and astrologers and soothsayers were confounded by them, and their wisdom turned to foolishness. Moreover, secular history has preserved for us the fact that the engineers of Cyrus' army dug a new channel for the River Euphrates which ran through the city (thus fulfilling the words, "and I will dry up thy rivers") and Cyrus entered by way of the dry bed of the stream. Thus were the "two-leaved gates" of Babylon opened to God's appointed conqueror, who was to be a "shepherd" and a deliverer to His people. The next verse of the prophecy speaks of this:

> "Thus saith the Lord to His anointed, to Cyrus, whose right hand I have holden, to subdue nations before him; and I will loose the loins of kings—see Daniel 5:6, where it is said of Belshazzar, when he saw the handwriting on the wall, "so that the joints of his loins were loosed"—"to open before him the two-leaved gates, and the gates shall not be shut" (Isaiah. 45:1).

Here is God's own testimony that King Cyrus, and not one of his successors, was to give the "commandment" whereby Jerusalem was to be rebuilt and its inhabitants restored. Nothing could be plainer than the words, "He (Cyrus) shalt perform all My pleasure, even saying to Jerusalem, Thou shalt be built, and to the temple, Thy foundation shalt be laid." This proof cannot be overthrown. Indeed none who believe the Scriptures to be inspired will even question it. Having this to guide us we must needs decline to follow those who, with a faulty heathen chronology as their only guide, grope for some event, long after Cyrus was laid in his grave, which can be taken as "the commandment to restore and to build Jerusalem."

No further evidence is needed. But in this exceedingly important matter God has been pleased to give proof upon proof. Thus in Isaiah 46:13 we have this further word concerning Cyrus:

> "I have raised him up in righteousness, and I will direct all his ways; HE SHALL BUILD MY CITY, AND HE SHALL LET GO MY CAPTIVES."

No one who believes the Word of God will, with this Scripture before him, dispute for a moment that it was by Cyrus that Jerusalem was rebuilt and its captives restored to it. Here are two things which God distinctly foretold were to be done by Cyrus (and this was 200 years before he came to the throne); first he was to rebuild the city, and second he was to restore the captive Jews to their home. These are the very things mentioned by the angel to Daniel; for he said, "from the commandment to restore and to build Jerusalem." And the Scriptures make it plain that Cyrus made haste to fulfil this Word of God; and moreover that he knew just what he was doing, and why.

There is truth here which, with a little attention, we can get hold of, and which, when understood, will both clear all uncertainties away, and also will fill us with admiration because of the wonders and perfections of the Word of God.

Observe then that, when the angel mentioned "the commandment to restore and to build," Daniel would have known from the prophecy of Isaiah (which was familiar to him, as we shall see) that it was Cyrus who would issue that command. Now Cyrus was at that time co-ruler with, and subordinate to, "Darius the Mede" (Daniel 9:1). But in less than two years Cyrus became the sole ruler; and it was in the very first year of his reign that he issued the foundations decree which gave new existence to the Jewish nation.

That Daniel knew the prophecy of Jeremiah which gives the length of the captivity is expressly stated in Daniel 9:2. But that he also knew the prophecy of Isaiah, which foretold that the captivity would be ended by the decree of Cyrus, appears by reference to the decree of that monarch, which is partly quoted by Ezra. These are the words: "Thus saith Cyrus, King of Persia, The Lord God of heaven hath given me all the kingdoms of the earth, and He hath charged me to build Him an house at Jerusalem, which is in Judah" (Ezra 1:2).

It is clear that this "charge" came to Cyrus, not through the book of Jeremiah, but through that of Isaiah; for it is in Isaiah that God, speaking to Cyrus who was yet unborn, charged him to build the city and temple and to release the captive Jews. It will thus be seen that God has given to Cyrus a remarkable place in His Word and in the execution of His plans.

Daniel had not learned about the ending of the captivity by a direct revelation from God, but "by books"—evidently not the book of Jeremiah only, but that of Isaiah also. We too have the same "books" that Daniel had; and we have also the book of Ezra, which contains a record of the great decree of Cyrus; and these several "books" give all the light that is needed to make the matter perfectly clear.

Concerning Cyrus

This wonderful prophecy of Isaiah concerning Cyrus, and its bearing upon the purposes of God as a whole, have not received by any means the attention this, importance deserves; and while ii is not within the scope of this volume to treat it exhaustively, yet it is appropriate that we should direct attention to some of its striking features.

We note then that the restoration of the captive Jews and the rebuilding of the temple was evidently a matter of great importance in the eyes of God. The frequent references to it in the messages of the prophets are proof enough of that. But here is the extraordinary case of a distinct prophecy, in plain words, of what God purposed to do, coupled with the name of the man by whom God purposed to do it. The only like case where an action is described and the name of the man who was to perform it is given before he was born, is that of King Josiah (1 Kings 13:2, fulfilled 2 Kings 23:15–17).

When the time for the ending of the captivity (given by another prophet, Jeremiah) was on the point of expiring, God put into the hands of the man He had called by name two hundred years before, "all the kingdoms of the world," so that he had the needed power to fulfil God's Word and to "do all His pleasure"; and beside all that, God himself "stirred up the spirit of Cyrus, that be made a proclamation throughout all his kingdom, and put it also in writing" (Ezra 1:1). And thereupon, in virtue of that command, over forty-two thousand Jews, headed by Zerubbabel, Joshua and Nehemiah, returned forthwith to Jerusalem (Ezra 2:1–6); and with them more than seven thousand servants and maids (verse 65). It was a new beginning for Israel; and Cyrus was God's "shepherd," chosen long beforehand, for bringing His sheep back to their proper fold.

The entire passage concerning Cyrus (Isaiah 44:23–45:14) should be carefully read. We quote a part:

> "I will go before thee and make the crooked places straight. I will break in pieces the gates of brass, and cut in sunder the bars of iron." (This refers to the defences of Babylon.) "And I will give thee the treasures of darkness, and hidden riches of secret places" (the treasures of Babylon), "that thou mayest know that I the Lord, which call thee by thy name, am the God of Israel. For Jacob My servant's sake, and Israel mine elect, I have even called thee by thy name; I have surnamed thee, though thou hast not known me. I am the Lord, and there is none else. There is no God beside me. I girded thee, though thou hast not known me; that they may know, from the rising of the sun, and from the west, that there is none beside me: I am the Lord and there is none else."

In this remarkable passage God calls attention again and again to the fact that He had called Cyrus by name, long before he was born; yet this fact receives but scant attention, and its significance has been lost sight of by many who have undertaken to expound the prophecy of the Seventy Weeks. This must needs be the case with all who reject the decree of Cyrus as the starting point of the seventy weeks.

Furthermore, God speaks not about Cyrus but directly to him. From this we can understand how Cyrus would say: "The Lord God of heaven hath given me all the kingdoms of the world, and He hath charged me", etc.

Finally, God declares that He had "girded" Cyrus for this work in order that, from the east to the west, that is to say, in all the world, it might be known that He is the Lord, and there is none else. Manifestly, this purpose of God, in His marvelous dealings with King Cyrus, is virtually frustrated when, in the interpretation of the Seventy Weeks' prophecy, the decree of Cyrus is set aside, and the word of some other king is chosen as that whereby Jerusalem was rebuilt and its captives restored.

May the contemplation of God's marvelous dealings in the case of Cyrus lead us to adore Him Who is perfect in knowledge, and Who worketh all things after the counsel of His own will.

It was to be expected that, inasmuch as God has been pleased to give in His Word, an exact time measure from a given event unto Christ, He would also make it clear beyond a doubt what the event is from which the count of years was to begin. And this expectation is fully met.

Upon the plain and simple facts stated above it is evident that every expositor who sets aside this decree of Cyrus as the starting point of the 70 weeks, and substitutes some other event, must either be unaware of the testimony of Isaiah 44 and 45 (and of other Bible testimony to which we will refer presently) or else he prefers the guesses of a heathen astronomer (who had no means of knowing the facts which occurred over five hundred years before his time) to the evidence of Scripture.

This is a case where a mistake in regard to the starting point is fatal to an understanding of the prophecy as a whole. If we make a wrong start, we shall be in error throughout.

It is interesting in this connection to see how this matter was understood by learned Jews in ancient times. Thus we find recorded in the history of Josephus[1] that Cyrus wrote throughout all his dominions that "God Almighty hath appointed me to be king of the habitable earth" and that "He indeed foretold my name by the prophets, and that I should build Him a house at Jerusalem which is in the country of Judea." Josephus goes on to say that, when Cyrus had read the words of the prophet Isaiah, "He called for the most eminent Jews in Babylon and said to them, that he gave them leave to go back to their own country, and TO REBUILD THEIR CITY JERUSALEM AND THE TEMPLE OF GOD."

Josephus also gives a copy of a letter written by Cyrus to the governors that were in Syria, which letter begins as follows:

"King Cyrus to Sisinnes and Sathrabuzzanes, sendeth greeting. I have given leave to as many of the Jews that dwell in my country as please [to do so) to return to their own country, and TO REBUILD THE CITY, AND TO REBUILD THE TEMPLE, OF GOD AT JERUSALEM on the same place where it was before" (Ant. Bk. XI, Ch. 1, sec. I and 3).

The proof that the rebuilding of the city was done by the commandment of Cyrus is so conclusive that Prideaux (one of the leading commentators on Daniel) frankly admits that "Jerusalem was rebuilt by virtue of the decree granted by Cyrus in the first year of his reign." Yet this learned man rejects the decree of Cyrus as the starting point of the seventy weeks, simply because he shared the mistaken idea (for which there is no proof of any sort) that 490 years would not reach from that decree to the days of Christ. But if the fact be, as Prideaux admits, then to take any other event as the starting point is to falsify the prophecy. It is a choice between the clear statements of the Word of God and the guesses of heathen historians and astronomers. We are writing for the benefit of those who accept the Word of God as conclusive.

It is true that Ezra, in the very brief statement he gives of the decree of Cyrus, does not specifically mention the building of the city. But that emission affords no ground whatever for assuming that the decree of Cyrus did not provide for the rebuilding of the city, much less does it afford reason for setting aside the word of the Lord spoken by Isaiah. In fact the decree of Cyrus, under which the Jews were, one and all, permitted to return to Jerusalem, and under which over forty-two thousand did return at once, necessarily implied permission to build houses to dwell in. The building of the temple is the most important matter, and that is why it is specifically mentioned in Ezra's brief reference to the decree of Cyrus. But, according to the prophecy of Isaiah "the commandment to rebuild the city was to be joined with that to rebuild the temple. Hence when we have found the commandment to rebuild the temple we have found that to rebuild the city.

It should be observed that the words of Gabriel call for the going forth of a commandment to restore and to build Jerusalem. Those words fit the decree of Cyrus which was promulgated throughout his dominions, and which is expressly called by Ezra a "commandment" (Ezra 6:14).

Furthermore, that the building of Jerusalem did actually proceed under the decree of Cyrus, appears from the fact that, at a time when only the foundation of the temple had been laid, the adversaries complained that the Jews were "rebuilding the rebellious and bad city, and have set up the walls thereof, and have joined the foundations" (Ezra 4:12).

That statement of the adversaries was not a fabrication; for it is fully corroborated by Haggai, who (prophesying during that same period of the cessation of work on the temple) said that the people were dwelling in their own panelled-up houses, and that they ran every one to his own house (Haggai 1:4, 7).

Moreover, it will be observed, in reading the book of Ezra, that he speaks throughout of Jerusalem as an existing city, and in Chapter 9:9 be gives thanks to God that He had given them "a wall in Judah and in Jerusalem." Some expositors have selected as the point of beginning for the 70 weeks the decree mentioned in

Ezra 7:11–28. But that cannot be; for, in the first place, to assume it would contradict the Word of the Lord spoken by Isaiah, which bore witness that the "commandment" to restore the captives, to rebuild the city, and to lay the foundation of the temple, should be given by Cyrus; whereas the decree mentioned in Ezra 7 was made by "Artaxerxes" (Darius Hystaspes) who was one of the successors of Cyrus.

Upon a careful reading of Ezra, chapters 6 and 7, it will be seen that what is there recorded agrees with and fully supports the Scriptures heretofore cited, showing that the work then in progress at Jerusalem, and which the enemies of the Jews sought to hinder, was based entirely upon the decree of Cyrus. For when those adversaries complained by letter to King Darius concerning the work of rebuilding the temple (which the Jews had resumed under the stimulus of the prophesying of Haggai and Zechariah), Darius caused search to be made amongst the archives in the house of rolls (Ezra 6:1), and he found the decree of Cyrus commanding that the temple be rebuilt; and upon the authority of that decree of Cyrus, his successor Darius issued the decree mentioned in Ezra 6:6–12.

It should be observed that, at that time, it wasn't a question of the rebuilding of the city. That had already been done, at least to an extent sufficient to accommodate those who had returned. About 50,000 people had returned in the first company, with wives and children, and others subsequently; and their first occupation was to provide themselves homes. We have already called attention to the statement of Ezra 4:12 that the Jews had "come unto Jerusalem, building the rebellious and bad city, and have set up (margin, finished) the walls thereof, and joined the foundations."

The completion of the temple is mentioned in Ezra 6:14–15, and it is said that it had been done "according to the commandment of Cyrus, and Darius"—that of Darius being merely a reaffirmation of the decree of Cyrus, which had given the authorization for the entire work of restoration.

The decree mentioned in Ezra 7:11–28 was some years later still. It had nothing whatever to do with the rebuilding of either the city or the temple. It could not have been the "commandment" for the building of either; for that commandment had already been given. It was simply a "letter" which the king gave to Ezra, for we read that "the king granted him all his request" (Ezra 7:6). That "letter" provided, first, that all the people of Israel, the priests and Levites, who were so minded of their own free will, might go to Jerusalem; second, that they might carry silver and gold to buy animals for sacrifice, and whatsoever else might be needful for the house of God; and third, that no taxes or tribute were to be imposed upon any priests, Levites, singers, porters, Nethinims or ministers of the house of God. So far from there being, in this "letter", if any "commandment" for the building of the city or temple, its contents show that both city and temple were already in existence.

Nehemiah's Work on Temple Wall

We come now to the latest in date of all the supposed "decrees" which have been selected by any expositor as that to which the angel Gabriel referred as "the commandment to restore and to build Jerusalem." This is the "letter" given by the king to Nehemiah, at his request, as stated in Nehemiah 2:4–8.

This letter or written permit given to Nehemiah by the then monarch, or "Artaxerxes", being the latest in date of all, is the farthest of all from the truth. Nevertheless it is the favorite of certain learned expositors of our day, and for the very reason that it is the latest in date, and hence agrees best with the mistaken chronologies which have been derived from the canon of Ptolemy. But even so, if this "Artaxerxes" was, as Mr. Anstey shows by satisfactory proof, the same king "Darius" is mentioned by Ezra, then the twentieth year (Nehemiah 2:7) of his reign would be too early by at least fifty years to agree with any of the before-mentioned chronologies. Consequently it has been further assumed that the king of Nehemiah's day was Artaxerxes Longimanus. But that monarch's twentieth year would be approximately 100 years subsequent to the return front Babylon in the days of Cyrus; and hence it would be too close to the days of Christ to fit in with any of the existing chronologies. Therefore, to force an agreement in this case it is necessary to make the "seventy sevens" a period shorter than 490 years. The ingenuity of our expositors has been quite equal to this; for, to meet this difficulty, they have supposed, that the "sevens" were not sevens of years, but of nondescript periods of 360 days each, which are not "years" at all. Thus, the acceptance of a false chronology (instead of basing conclusions on the Scriptures alone) leads even able and learned men to adopt one false assumption after another, and thus to go further and further astray.

But we need not go outside the book of Nehemiah itself for conclusive proof that the "letter" which the king gave to that devoted man was not "the commandment" in virtue of which Jerusalem was rebuilt. Indeed, we have only to read chapters 1, 2 and 3 of Nehemiah with ordinary care to perceive that the city had been already rebuilt, with walls and gates, at the time referred to in those chapters; that the tidings brought to Nehemiah, as recorded in Chapter 1, were tidings of damage freshly done by the enemies of the Jews to the walls and gates of the rebuilt city; that the letter given by the king to Nehemiah was simply a permit to repair that damage; and that the work done by Nehemiah, as recorded in Chapter 3, was the "repairing" of the wall, and the "repairing" of the gates, and the setting up the doors; the locks, and the bars thereof. For proof of these statements it is only necessary to read the chapters referred to.

The tidings from Jerusalem. In Chapter 1 Nehemiah relates that, while he was attending to his customary duties in the palace of the king certain brethren came from Jerusalem with tidings to the effect that those in the province of Judah, who had been left of the captivity, were in great affliction and reproach. Further they reported, saying, "the wall of Jerusalem also is broken down, and the gates thereof are burned with fire" (Nehemiah 1:1-3).

The effect of this report upon Nehemiah shows clearly that it was of a fresh and unexpected calamity they were speaking. For he relates that, when he heard those words, he sat down, and wept, and mourned certain days, and fasted and prayed before the God of heaven. The record makes it plain that the cause of his distress was not the condition of the Jews in the province, but the tidings of the damage which had been done to the walls and gates of the holy city. That could not possibly have been the destruction wrought by Nebuchadnezzar, for that had taken place more than a hundred years previously. Nehemiah had known about that all his life. His brethren, when he asked them "concerning Jerusalem, " could not have told him, as a piece of news, of the damage that had been done a century before. That would not have been news to him, nor would the hearing of it have plunged him into deep distress. He states that he had not been sad beforetime in the king's presence (2:7); but now his sorrow was so great that he could not banish the evidences of it from his countenance even in the king's presence. There must have been a cause for this; and nothing but unexpected tidings of a fresh calamity to the beloved city could account for his acute distress. With the walls damaged and the gates burned with fire, the city was exposed to her enemies, and the new temple itself was in danger of being again destroyed.

In this report we have an indication of the "troublous times" foretold by the angel Gabriel (Daniel 9:25).

In Chapter 2 we have the account of Nehemiah's request to the king, and of the "letter" given to him. There is no decree, no "commandment," nothing what, ever about rebuilding the city. And how could there be in view of the word of the Lord concerning Cyrus, saying, "He shall build My city"? It is true that Nehemiah made request that the king would send him to the city of his father's sepultures, that he might "build it." But the word here rendered "build" is of very broad meaning, and would be appropriate to describe the repairing of the damage to the walls and gates, which in fact is what it does mean in this instance. Nehemiah only sought permission to restore the parts that had been freshly destroyed. This will be shown below.

What Nehemiah meant by his request appears in verses 7–8, namely, letters to the governors beyond the river to give him safe passage (in other words a passport), and also a letter to the keeper of the king's forest to supply "timber to make beams for the gates of the palace which appertained to the house, and for the wall of the city, and for the house that I shall enter into." These requests the king granted. Manifestly those letters do not constitute a commandment to rebuild the city.

Finally, it clearly appears by Chapter 3 that the work which Nehemiah did during his stay in Jerusalem was the repairing of the wall and of the gates of the city. The word "repaired" is used over twenty times in that chapter to describe that work. It was a small work (comparatively to the work of rebuilding the city and temple) for it was completed, notwithstanding all hindrances, in the short space of 52 days, less than two months (6:15). In the third and fourth chapters of Nehemiah we find frequent incidental references to houses already existing in Jerusalem, and occupied by the owners thereof, but not a word as to any building of houses at that time. Thus we read in 3:20–21 of "the house of Eliashib, the high priest." In verse 23 we read that Benjamin and Hasshub repaired "over against their house," and Azariah "by his house." In verse 25 mention is made of "the king's high house." In verse 28 it is stated that the priests repaired, "every one over against his house." In verse 29 we read that Zadok repaired "over against his house."

In Chapter 4:7 the character of the work is shown by the words "the walls of Jerusalem were made up; and the breaches began to be stopped." Verses 1, 6, 15, 17 and 21 of the same Chapter; also

Chapter 6:1, 15 and Chapter 7:1 show that the work was only on the wall. The words of 6:15, "So the wall was finished in the twenty-fifth day of the month of Elul, in fifty and two days" record the completion of the entire work.

In Chapter 7:3 we read that Nehemiah appointed "watches of the inhabitants of Jerusalem, every one in his watch, and every one over against his house." This again shows that the inhabitants of the city had houses to dwell in; though we should hardly need to be informed of a matter so obvious. The next verse appears at first glance to be inconsistent, though of course it is not. It says: "Now the city was large and great (or broad in spaces); but the people were few, and the houses were not built." The meaning plainly is that there were yet large spaces within the walls which had not been rebuilt. Only a relatively small proportion of the population of the city had returned ("the people were few"), and hence the entire city had not yet been rebuilt.

What we gather from this verse, taken in connection with the statements of the preceding chapters, tends still further to show that the work Nehemiah was charged with was not the building of the city. The account of what he did, which is quite detailed and minutes giving both the several workers and the work done by them, contains no reference at all to the city. It clearly appears that when the wall was finished in fifty-two days, the work was finished (6:15). It further appears that the people all had houses to live in (7:3). And finally, after all had been done which Nehemiah came to do, there remained yet a large part of the city rebuilt (7:4).

In order then to force the record of the Book of Nehemiah into agreement with a scheme of interpretation based upon the canon of Ptolemy, it is necessary to make the following assumptions, all of which are either unsupported by proof, or contrary thereto: first, that Ptolemy's chronology, when "corrected" according to the ideas of some modern chronologists, is right; second, that the

"Artaxerxes," spoken of by Nehemiah, is Longimanus; third, that in all the century previous, since the ending of the captivity, no decree had gone forth to restore and build Jerusalem; fourth, that the "letters" given to Nehemiah were the decree going forth; fifth, that God's word concerning Cyrus was not fulfilled; sixth, that the "seventy weeks" were not weeks of true calendar years, but of periods of 360 days each. Obviously any conclusion, which rests upon these assumptions, and which would be overthrown if any one of them should be proved erroneous, is utterly worthless.

We have discussed this whole matter at length go that no question might be left unanswered; but it should be kept in mind that it is of little importance to determine when the rebuilding of the city began. For the starting point of the prophecy was not the rebuilding of the city, but the commandment to restore and to build it. That commandment was, beyond the shadow of a doubt, given by Cyrus. The Word of the Lord by Isaiah settles that beyond all controversy.

It is not necessary for our purposes to inquire which of the Persian' kings was this "Artaxerxes." But it is interesting to notice, as pointed out by Anstey, that, if this Nehemiah is the same as the one who went up with Zerubbabel, and whose name appears third on the list (Ezra 2:2), then the king could not be Artaxerxes Longimanus, as supposed by certain expositors; for in that case it would make Nehemiah at least 120 years at the time he repaired the wall, and 132 at the time of Chapter 13:6.

CHAPTER 3

Details of the Seventy Weeks

Having made sure of the true starting point, we can now proceed with confidence to an examination of the details of the prophecy. But it will be needful, as we go on, to test every conclusion by the Scriptures, and to exercise care that we accept nothing that is not supported by ample proof.

The prophetic part of the angel's message begins at verse 24, which, in our AV reads as follows:

> "Seventy weeks are determined upon thy people and upon thy holy city, to finish the transgression, and to make an end of sins, and to make reconciliation for iniquity, and to bring in everlasting righteousness and to seal up the vision and prophecy, and to anoint the most holy (place)."

Here are six distinct things which were to happen within a definitely marked off period of seventy sevens of years (490 years). These six specified things are closely related one to the other, for they are all connected by the conjunction "and."

This verse, which is a prophecy complete in itself, gives no information in regard to either the starting point of the 490 years, or the means whereby the predicted events were to be accomplished. That information, however, is given in the verses which follow. From them we learn that the prophetic period was to begin to run "from the going forth of the commandment to restore and to build Jerusalem"; also that sixty-nine weeks (seven plus sixty-two) would reach "unto Messiah, the Prince"; and further that "after the three-score and two weeks shall Messiah be cut off." It was by the cutting off of the Messiah that the six predictions of verse 24 were to be fulfilled. This should be carefully noted.

Thus we have before us a prophecy of transcendent interest, a predicted stretch of time from the rebeginning of the Jewish nation and the rebuilding of the holy city, down to the culminating event of all history, and of all the ages of time the crucifixion of the Divine Redeemer. These are things which the angels desire to look into (1 Peter 1:12); and surely our hearts should move us to inquire into them, not in a spirit of carnal curiosity, and not with any purpose to uphold a favorite scheme of prophetic interpretation, but with the reverent desire to learn all that God has been pleased to reveal touching this most important and most sacred matter.

Verses 25–27 also foretell the overwhelming and exterminating judgments—the "desolations" that were to fall upon the people and the city, and which were to last throughout this entire dispensation.

The first words of verse 25, "Know therefore," show that what follows is explanatory of the prophecy contained in verse 24 This too should be carefully noted.

It is essential to a right understanding of the prophecy to observe, and to keep in mind, that the six things of verse 24 were to be fulfilled (and now have been fulfilled) by Christ being "cut off," and by what followed immediately thereafter, namely, His resurrection from the dead, and His ascension into heaven. With that simple fact in mind it will be easy to "understand" all the main points of the prophecy.

These are the six predicted items:

1. *To finish the transgression.* The "transgression" of Israel had long been the burden of the messages of God's prophets. It was for their "transgression" that they had been sent into captivity, and that their land and city had been made a "desolation" for seventy years.

Daniel himself had confessed this, saying, "Yea, all Israel have transgressed Thy law. even by departing that they might not obey Thy voice. Therefore the curse is poured upon us" (verse 11). But the angel revealed to him the distressing news that the full measure of Israel's "transgression" was yet to be completed; that the children were yet to fill up the iniquity of their fathers; and that, as a consequence, God would bring upon them a far greater "desolation" than that which had been wrought by Nebuchadnezzar. For "to finish the transgression" could mean nothing less or other than the betrayal and crucifixion of their promised and expected Messiah.

We would call particular attention at this point to the words of the Lord Jesus spoken to the leaders of the people shortly before His betrayal; for there is in them a striking similarity to the words of the prophecy of Gabriel. He said: "Fill ye up then the measure of your fathers...that upon you may come all the righteous blood shed upon the earth" (Matthew 23:32). In these words of Christ we find first, a declaration that the hour had come for them "to finish the transgression"; and second, a strong intimation that the predicted desolations were to come, as a judgment, upon that generation, as appears by the words "that upon you may come."

Our Lord's concluding words at that time have great significance when considered in the light of this prophecy. He said, "Verily I say unto you, all these things shall come upon this generation"; and then, as the awful doom of the beloved city pressed upon His heart, He burst into the lamentation, "O Jerusalem, Jerusalem," ending with the significant words, "Behold, your house is left unto you desolate."

The terrible and unparalleled character of the judgments which were poured out upon Jerusalem at the time of its destruction in AD 70 has been lost sight of in our day. But if we would learn how great an event it was in the eyes of God, we have only to consider our Lord's anguish of soul as He thought upon it. Even when on the way to the Cross it was more to Him than His own approaching sufferings (Luke 21:28–30).

The apostle Paul also speaks in similar terms of the transgressions of that generation of Jews, who not only crucified the Lord Jesus, and then rejected the gospel preached to them in His Name, but also forbade that He be preached to the Gentiles. Wherefore the apostle said that they "fill up their sins always; for the wrath is come upon them to the uttermost" (1 Thessalonians 2:15–16). For they were indeed about to undergo God's wrath "to the uttermost" in the approaching destruction of Jerusalem, and in the scattering of the people among all the nations of the world, to suffer extreme miseries at their hands. These Scriptures are of much importance in connection with our present study, and we shall have occasion to refer to them again.

It is not difficult to discern why the list of the six great things comprised in this prophecy was headed by the finishing of the transgression; for the same act, which constituted the crowning sin of Israel, also served for the putting away of sin (Hebrews 9:26), and the accomplishing of eternal redemption (Hebrews 9:12). They did indeed take Him, and with wicked hands crucified and slew Him; but it was done "by the determinate counsel and foreknowledge of God" (Acts 2:23). The powers and authorities of Judea and of Rome, with the Gentiles and the people of Israel, were indeed gathered together against Him; but it was to do what God's own hand and counsel had determined before to be done (Acts 4:26–28). There is nothing more wonderful in all that has been made known to us, than that the people and their rulers, because they knew Him not, nor the voices of their own prophets which were read every Sabbath day, should have fulfilled them in condemning Him (Acts 13:27). Therefore, among the many prophecies that were then "fulfilled," a promise be given to that which forms the subject of our present study.

2. *To make an end of sins.* On this item we need not dwell at length; for we have already called attention to the marvellous workings of God's wisdom in causing that the extreme sin of man should serve to accomplish eternal redemption, and so provide a complete remedy for sin for the crucifixion of Christ, though it was truly a deed of diabolical wickedness on the part of man, was on His own part the offering of Himself without spot to God as a sacrifice for sins (Hebrews 9:14). It was thus that He "offered the one Sacrifice for sins forever" (Hebrews 10:12).

We understand that the sense in which the death of Christ made "an end of sins" was that thereby He made a perfect atonement for sins, as written in Hebrews 1:3, "when He had by Himself purged our sins'" and in many like passages. It is to be noted however, that the Hebrew word for "sins" in this passage means not only the sin itself, but also the sacrifice therefore. Hence it is thought by some that what the angel here foretold was the making an end of the sin offering required by the law. That was, indeed, an incidental result, and it is mentioned expressly in verse 27. But the word used in that verse is not the word found in verse 24, which means sin or sin offering It is a different word, meaning sacrifice. We conclude, therefore, that the words, "to make an end of sins", should be taken in their most obvious sense.

3. *To make reconciliation for iniquity.* The word here translated "reconciliation" is usually rendered "*atone*", but according to Strong's Concordance it expresses also the thought of appeasing or reconciling. We shall, therefore, assume that our translators had good reason for using the word "reconciliation." If, however, it be taken that "atonement" is the better rendering, the conclusion would not be affected; for both atonement and reconciliation were made by the death of Christ upon the cross.

The need of reconciliation arises from the fact that man is by nature not only a sinner, but also an enemy of God (Romans 5:8,

10). Moreover, it is because he is a sinner that he is also an enemy. As a sinner he needs to be justified; and as an enemy he needs to be reconciled. The death of Christ as an atoning sacrifice accomplishes both in the case of all who believe in Him. In Romans 5:8–10 these two distinct, but closely related, things are clearly set forth. For we there read, first, that "while we were yet sinners Christ died for us", and second, that "when we were enemies we were reconciled to God by the death of His Son".

Reconciliation has to do directly with the kingdom of God, in that it signifies the bringing back of those who were rebels and enemies into willing and loyal submission to God. In this connection attention should be given to the great passage in Colossians 1:12–22, which shows that, as the result of the death of Christ, those who have "redemption through His blood, the forgiveness of sins" (verse 14), are also translated into the kingdom of God's dear Son (verse 13), Christ "having made peace for them through the blood of His cross, by Him to reconcile all things unto Himself"; and the apostle adds, "And you, who were sometime alienated and enemies in your mind, yet now hath He reconciled in the body of His flesh, through death" (verses 20–22).

It is certain, therefore, that, when Christ Jesus died and rose again, atonement for sin and reconciliation for the enemies of God were fully and finally accomplished as a matter of historic fact. It is important, and indeed essential, to a right interpretation of this prophecy, to keep in mind that atonement and reconciliation were to be accomplished, and actually were accomplished, within the measure of seventy weeks from the going forth of the decree of King Cyrus.

It is thus seen that the prophecy has to do with the great and eternal purpose of God to establish His kingdom—and to bring pardoned and reconciled sinners into it as willing and loyal subjects of Christ, the King. And when the time drew near the kingdom was proclaimed by the Lord and by His forerunner as "at hand." The Lord's own words, when taken in connection with the prophecy of Gabriel, are very significant. He said: "The time is fulfilled, and the kingdom of God is at hand" (Mark 1:15). The time whereof He spoke was that declared in this great prophecy; which is the only prophecy which gives the time of His coming. Hence His words were really the announcement of His approaching death, resurrection and enthronement in heaven, as the heavenly King of God's heavenly kingdom.

4. *To bring in everlasting righteousness.* Righteousness is the most prominent feature of the kingdom of God. To show this we need only cite those familiar passages: "Seek ye first the kingdom of God and His righteousness" (Matthew 6:33); "the kingdom of God is righteousness and peace, and joy in the Holy Ghost" (Romans 14:17). One characteristic of God's righteousness, which He was "to bring in" through the sacrifice of Christ ((Romans 3:21–26), is that it endures forever; and this is what is emphasized in the prophecy. A work was to be done, and now has been done, which would bring in everlasting righteousness—everlasting because based upon the Cross, as foretold also through Isaiah, "My righteousness shall be forever" (Isaiah 51:8). Jesus Christ has now been made unto US "righteous" (1 Corinthians 1:30); and this is in fulfillment of another great promise: "behold the days come, saith the Lord, that I will raise Unto David a righteous Branch, and a King reign and prosper And this is His Name whereby He shall be called JEHOVAH OUR RIGHTEOUSNESS" (Jeremiah 23:5-6).

5. *To seal up vision and prophecy.* This we take to mean the sealing up of God's word of prophecy to the Israelites, as part of the punishment they brought upon themselves. The word "seal up" sometimes means, in a secondary sense, to make secure, since what is tightly sealed up is made safe against being tampered with. Hence some have understood by this item merely that vision and

prophecy were to be fulfilled. But we are not aware that the word "sealed up" is used in that sense in the Scriptures. For when the fulfillment of prophecy is meant, the word "to fulfill" is used. We think the word should be taken here in its primary meaning; for it was distinctly foretold, as a prominent feature of Israel's punishment that both vision and prophet—i.e., both eye and ear—were to be closed up, so that seeing they would see not, and hearing they would hear not (Isaiah 6:10).

Moreover, this very sealing up of vision and prophecy as a part of the chastening of Israel was foretold by Isaiah in that great passage where he speaks of Christ as the Foundation Stone (Isaiah 28:16). Following this is a prediction of "woe" to the city where David dwelt (29:1). So we have here a prophecy which is parallel to that of Gabriel. The latter spoke of the cutting off of Messiah to be followed by the destruction of Jerusalem; and Isaiah also spoke of Christ as God's Foundation Stone, laid in Zion (resurrection) and then of the overthrow of the earthly Zion. As to this overthrow God speaks through Isaiah very definitely saying, "And I will camp against thee round about and will lay siege against thee with a mount, and raise a fort against thee, and thou shalt be brought down" (Isaiah 29:1-4). Then the prophet speaks of a coming storm and tempest and devouring fire and also of the multitude of the nations that were to fight against the city (verses 6-9). And then come these significant words: "For the Lord God hath poured out upon you the spirit of deep sleep, and hath closed your eyes, the prophets' and your rulers, the seers, hath He covered. And the vision of all is become unto you as the words of a book that is sealed" (verses 10-11). This manifestly corresponds with Gabriel's words "to seal up vision and prophet." Moreover, the word "sealed," in Isaiah 29:11, is the same as in Daniel 9:24. These words of Isaiah also give a remarkably accurate description of the spiritual blindness of the people and their rulers in Christ's day, who, though they read the prophets every Sabbath day, yet because they knew not their voices, fulfilled them in condemning Him (Acts 13:27).

The fulfillment of Isaiah 6 also comes in here. For the Lord Himself declared that, in His day, was fulfilled the word "Go and tell this people, Hear ye indeed but understand not; and see ye indeed, but perceive not. Make the heart of this people fat, and make their ears heavy, and shut their eyes; lest they see with their eyes, and hear with their ears, and understand with their heart, and convert, and be healed" (Isaiah 6:9–10; Matthew 13:14–15). John also quotes this prophecy and applies it to the Jews of his day (John 12:39–41); and Paul does the same (Acts 28:25–27).

Hence we should note with deep interest the question which this sentence of judgment prompted Isaiah to ask, and the answer he received. Evidently the prophet understood that the judgment pronounced in the words quoted above was to be one of terrible severity, for he at once inquired anxiously, "How long" the period of judicial blindness was to last. The answer was, "Until the cities be wasted without inhabitant, and the houses without man, and the land be utterly desolate, and the Lord have removed men far away, and there be a great forsaking in the midst of the land" (Isaiah 6:11–12).

Here we have a clear prediction of that which Christ Himself prophesied when the desolation of Judea, and the scattering of the Jews among all nations (Luke 21:24).

6. *To anoint the most holy place.* When these papers were first written and published in serial form, we were of opinion that this prediction had its fulfillment in the entrance of the Lord Jesus Christ into the heavenly sanctuary (Hebrews 9:23–24). But subsequently a copy of Dr. Pusey's work on Daniel the Prophet came into our hands, and we were much impressed by the exposition of this passage given by that great Hebrew scholar, who so ably defended the Book of Daniel from the assaults of the destructive

critics. He pointed out that the word anoint had acquired a settled spiritual meaning, citing the words of Isaiah 61:1–2, which our Lord applied to Himself as He Whom God had "anointed." Dr. Pusey also pointed out that, inasmuch as the same word is used in the very next verse of Daniel "unto the Anointed, the Prince" it is to be assumed that words so closely united must be used with the same meaning. This gives the idea of an "anointing of an All Holy place" by the pouring out of the Holy Spirit thereon. Dr. Pusey cites much evidence in support of this idea; but without going into the discussion of the matter at length, we will simply state that we were led thereby to the conclusion that the coming of the Holy Spirit upon the disciples of Christ, on the day of Pentecost, thereby anointing (see 2 Corinthians 1:21) a spiritual temple "the temple of the living God" (2 Corinthians 6:16), furnishes a fulfilment of this detail of the prophecy, a fulfilment which is not only in keeping with the other five items, but which brings the whole series to a worthy climax.

These six predicted events, which we have now considered in detail, were, according to the words of God by Gabriel, to be accomplished within the "determined" (or limited, or "marked off") period of seventy sevens of years; and we have shown—indeed it is SO clear as hardly to be open to dispute—that all six items were completely fulfilled at the first coming of Christ, and in the "week" of His crucifixion. For when our Lord ascended into heaven and the Holy Spirit descended, there remained not one of the six items of Daniel 9:24 that was not dully accomplished.

Furthermore, by even a cursory reading of verses 25–26 we see that the coming of Christ and His being "cut off" are announced as the means whereby the prophecy was to be fulfilled; and that there is added the foretelling of the destruction of Jerusalem by Titus the Roman "prince," and the "desolations" of Jerusalem, and the wars that were to continue through this entire age "unto the end."

We do not speak at this point of verse 27. That part of the prophecy will require a particularly careful examination which we purpose to give it later on.

Prophetic events are often described in veiled language and highly figurative terms, so that it is a matter of much difficulty to identify the fulfillment of them. But in this instance it seems to us we have the exceptional case of a prophecy whose terms are plain and the identifying marks are numerous. If it were possible to fix with certainty only one of the six predictions of Daniel 9:24, that would suffice to locate the entire series. But the indications given to us enable us to identify five of the six with certainty, and the other with a high degree of probability. We have no doubt then that the entire prophecy of verve 24 was fulfilled in the death, resurrection and ascension of the Lord Jesus Christ and in the coming of the Holy from heaven. And the settlement of the fulfillment of verse 24 carries with it the location of the seventieth week, which is referred to specifically in verse 27. This will be shown later on.

CHAPTER 4

"Unto Messiah the Prince"

"From the going forth of the commandment to restore and to build Jerusalem, unto the Messiah, the Prince, shall be seven weeks, and threescore and two weeks" (Daniel 9:26)

We have seen that the first part of this passage gives the starting point of the seventy weeks. The passage also gives the measure of time (7 weeks and 62 weeks, or 69 weeks in all) from that starting point "unto the Messiah". We shall postpone to a later chapter the question why the total measure of time here mentioned is divided into two parts. The question which is of immediate importance for us to determine is, what was the precise occasion or event in the earthly lifetime of the Lord Jesus Christ, to which this stretch of 483 years; from the decree of Cyrus brings us? We will now seek the answer to this question.

Assuming, as we do, that God intended this prophecy to be understood (for verse 25 says, "Know therefore, and understand," and our Lord said, "Whoso readeth let him understandeth we confidently expect to find both the starting point and the terminal point clearly revealed in the Scriptures. We have already found this to be the case as regards the starting point, and we shall now find that the Scriptures also indicate clearly the event to which the measure of 483 years reaches, and to which the angel referred in the words "unto the Messiah, the Prince."

Had we followed the usual custom in beginning our study with a chronology selected from the various ones that are available, we should be forced thereby, as others have been, to pick out the event lying nearest to the 483 year mark on our adopted scale of years. We should have been obliged moreover to manipulate the materials, so far as necessary (either stretching the measuring line, or taking up the slack, according as it was too short or too long), and then to present the best arguments we could find for the conclusions arrive at. But, being untrammeled by a chronological scheme, we are entirely free to inquire of the oracles of God as to the meaning of the Words "unto Messiah, the Prince," and as to the occasion or event to which those words specifically refer. If we can, from the Scriptures, identify that event (which, we believe, can be clearly done) then we know, from the prophecy itself, that it is precisely 69 weeks (483 years) from the going forth of the decree of Cyrus, and that but one week of the seventy remains; and we know further that the fulfilment of the six predictions of verse 24 must be found within that remaining week.

We must, of course, look to the words themselves to guide us to the information we are seeking; and those words are all we need. We are accustomed to regard the term "the Messiah" as merely a name or a title, but in fact it is a descriptive Hebrew word meaning "the anointed (one)". In Greek the word Christos has the same meaning. Therefore, we have, only to ask, when was Jesus of Nazareth presented to Israel as the Anointed One? As to this we are not left in any doubt whatever, for it was an event of the greatest importance in the life of Jesus our Lord, as well as in the dealings of God with Israel, and in the history of the world, an event which is made prominent in all the four Gospels It was at His baptism in Jordan that our Lord was "anointed" for His ministry; for then it was that the Holy Spirit descended upon Him in bodily shape its a dove. The apostle Peter bears witness that "God anointed Jesus of Nazareth with the Holy Ghost and with power" (Acts 10:38). This is clear and explicit to the point that, when the years of Israel's history had unrolled to that marvelous day on which Father, Son and Holy Spirit were simultaneously manifested to the senses of men, it brought them "unto the Messiah." There is no day in all history like that. The event is marked in a way to distinguish it most conspicuously. The Lord's own testimony in regard to the matter is even more definite and impressive. For, after His return to Galilee in the power of the Spirit, He came to Nazareth where He had been brought up, and going into the synagogue on the Sabbath day, He read from the prophet Isaiah these striking words: "The Spirit, of the Lord is upon Me, because He hath ANOINTED Me to preach the gospel to the poor";—and after He had closed, the book He said, "This day is this Scripture fulfilled in your ears" (Luke 4:16-21). Thus the Lord declared Himself to be, at that time, the "Anointed" One, that is, "the Messiah".

The testimony of God the Father is to the same effect. For the Voice from heaven bore witness to Him, saying, "This is My Son, the Beloved." This declares Him to be the One of Whom David prophesied in the Second Psalm (verse 7). But that same Psalm sets Him forth as God's "anointed" (verse 2).

But we have a special witness in John the Baptist, who was a man sent from God to bear witness of Christ, and to make Him manifest, to Israel; for John himself declared this to be his mission, saying, "that He should be made manifest to Israel, therefore am I come baptizing with water" (John 1:6-7, 31). When, therefore, the Lord Jesus had been "anointed" with the Holy Ghost and had been "made manifest to Israel" by the testimony of John the Baptist, then, the words of the prophecy "unto the Anointed One" were completely fulfilled. From that great and wonderful event down to the day of His death, He was constantly before the people in His Messianic character, fulfilling His Messianic mission, going about, doing good, healing all that were oppressed of the devil, preaching the glad tidings of the Kingdom of God, manifesting the Father's Name, speaking the words His Father gave Him to speak, and doing the works the Father gave Him to do. Indeed, even before He announced Himself in the synagogue of Nazareth as God's "Anointed One," He had plainly said to the woman of Samaria (after she had spoken of "Messiah, who is called Christ"), "I that speak unto thee am He" (John 4:25–26). Moreover, to the Samaritans who came out to see Him on the woman's report, He so fully revealed Himself that they were constrained to confess Him, saying, "We have heard Him ourselves, and know that this is indeed the Christ (the Anointed One), the Saviour of the world" (verse 42).

Furthermore, the nature, as well as the effect of John the Baptist's public testimony to the Lord Jesus, is clearly revealed by the words of those who, on hearing his testimony, followed Jesus. It is recorded that "One of the two who heard John speak and followed Him (Jesus) was Andrew, Simon Peter's brother. He first findeth his own brother and saith unto him, We have found the Messiah, which is, being interpreted, the Christ" (John 1:40–41).

In these scriptures the Holy Spirit has caused the important fact that Jesus was the Anointed One to be stated in both Hebrew and Greek, so that the significance of it should not be missed. That "this Jesus is the Christ" is the great point of apostolic testimony (Acts 17:3); and it is the substance of "our faith"; for "Whosoever believeth that Jesus is the Christ is born of God" (1 John 5:1, 4–5). It is likewise the rock foundation on which He is building His church (Matthew 16:18; 1 Corinthians 3:11).

We have cited the foregoing scriptures to make it clear beyond all doubt that, from the Lord's baptism and His manifestation to Israel, He was in the fullest sense "the Messiah" or the "Anointed", of God. To this fact, the inspired records bear, as we have seen, the clearest testimony. Manifestly there is no previous event in the earthly lifetime of our Lord which could be taken as meeting in any way the words of Gabriel. And it is equally clear that no subsequent event could be taken as the fulfillment of those words; for there is no subsequent occasion when the Lord was any more "the Anointed One" than He was when the Holy Spirit descended upon Him at His baptism. Thus the Scriptures absolutely shut us up to the Lord's baptism as the terminal point of the 483 years; for it was then that "God anointed Him with the Holy Ghost, and with power."

Another fact which has an important bearing on this part of our study is the great particularly with which the date of the beginning of John's ministry is given in the Gospel by Luke (3:1–3). There we read that the preaching of John the Baptist began in the fifteenth year of Tiberius Caesar, Pontius Pilate being governor of Judea, Herod (Antipas) tetrarch of Galilee, his brother Philip tetrarch of Iturea, Lysanias tetrarch of Abilene, and Annas and Caiaphas being high priests. Thus the new era, which was that of the Messiah-God manifest in the flesh—is marked with extraordinary precision. And this is the more remarkable because it is the only event whereof the date is thus recorded in the New Testament.

This is highly significant; for just as the date of the decree of Cyrus, marking the beginning of the Seventy Weeks, is stated with great definiteness, so likewise the preaching of John, which marked the termination of the 483 years, is stated with extraordinary minuteness. It is a reasonable inference that God has given prominence to these dates in His Word because they mark the beginning and the ending of this prophetic period.

It is also worthy of special notice that the dates of both these events are given by reference to the reigns of Gentile rulers. One is given as Occurring "in the first year of Cyrus, King of Persia," the other "in the fifteenth year of the reign of Tiberius Caesar." This is an indication that the things which were to be consummated within the time limit of 70 weeks were not matters which concerned the

Jews only, but were of world wide interest, having to do with the welfare of all mankind. God's dealings, therefore, had been matters of Jewish history. But now, beginning with the voice of one crying in the wilderness, "Prepare ye the way of the Lord," a now era was beginning, one in which God's dealings were to be matters of world history. It is appropriate, therefore, that we should find at this point in the Word of God (Luke 3:1–3) a change from terms of Jewish to terms of Gentile chronology.

The prophets had foretold the ministry of John the Baptist in words which show that his appearance was to mark the beginning of a new and wonderful era, the preparation for the coming of Christ and His gospel (Isaiah 40:3–11; Malachi 3:1; 4:5–6). Moreover, just as the prophets had pointed forward to John's ministry as the beginning of this new era, so likewise the apostles pointed back to it. Thus, when one was to be chosen to fill the place of Judas, it was required that the choice should be limited to those who had companied with the apostles all the time that the Lord Jesus had gone in and out among them, "beginning from the baptism of John" (Acts 1:21–22). Again, when Peter preached to the Gentiles in the house of Cornelius, telling them of "the word which God sent to the children of Israel, preaching peace by Jesus Christ," he declared that the preaching of this message (or "word"), which was "published throughout all Judea," had begun "from Galilee after the baptism which John preached" (Acts 10:36–37). And Paul likewise, in proclaiming the fulfillment of God's great promise of a "Savior" to Israel, referred to John's preaching as the beginning of the era of this fulfillment (Acts 13:24).

It is clear, therefore, in the light of Scripture, that the 483 years "unto the Messiah" terminated at the Lord's baptism, when His ministry as "the Messiah" began. Moreover, the prophecy itself furnishes a means whereby we can check up our conclusions thus far, and test their correctness. To this we will refer later on. The terms of the prophecy make it plain that the expiration of the sixty-ninth week would bring the fulfillment, of the greatest of all promises, the manifestation of Christ to Israel; and we have now shown that the records of the New Testament mark the era of His manifestation with the utmost precision.

Thus we have the coming of Christ plainly announced, and the time of His manifestation to Israel definitely fixed by the measure of years from His decree to restore and build Jerusalem. But for what purpose was He to come? And what was He to accomplish for the deliverance and welfare of His people Israel? The Jews would, of course, look for an era of triumph over all their foes, of great national prosperity and glory, and of supremacy for them over all the nations of the world. In the light of their expectations the prophecy would seem most strange. It would be utterly irreconcilable with their hopes in regard to what their promised Messiah was to do for them. For the only thing Said of Him was that He would be "he cut off and have nothing"; and while there was some hope in the promise that He should "confirm the covenant with many," yet there was also the dreadful prediction of a prince whose people should destroy the rebuilt city and sanctuary, and the further prophecies that the land should be devastated as by a flood, and that to the end there should be wars land desolations. A more depressing prophecy, Or one more in conflict with the Messianic expectations of the Jews, could not well be imagined.

But, our immediate concern is not with the character of the message but With the time of the several events foretold in it. The chief thing said of the Messiah is that He should "be cut off and have nothing" (Daniel 9:25); and this was to be "after the threescore and two weeks." Thus we have our attention focussed its it were upon the cutting off of the Christ. That transcendent event, the Cross, is thus made the central feature of the Prophecy. And this feature becomes the more grandly prominent when we take notice of the facts: (1)

that it was by the cutting off of the Messiah that the six predicted things of verse 24 where to be accomplished; (2) that it was by the cutting off of the Messiah that the covenant with many (verse 27) was to be confirmed and the sacrifice and oblation caused to cease (as will be shown later on); and (3) that it was because of the cutting off of the Messiah that the devastating judgments foretold in the prophecy were to fall upon the city, the temple, and the people.

Thus it is seen that the prophecy is one of marvelous unity, and that all its details center around the Cross.

Now as to the time of this transcendent event, it is expressly stated that it was to be "after the threescore and two weeks." That part of the determined period was to bring us only "unto the Messiah." None of the predicted events were to happen within the sixty-nine weeks. The expiration thereof left only "one week" (verse 27) of the appointed seventy. Hence, within that one remaining week Messiah must be cut off if the predictions of verse 24 were to be fulfilled within 490 Years from the beginning of the prophetic period. For it should be carefully noted, in view of certain interpretation which have been put forth within recent years, that, we have not yet come to the fulfillment of any one of the six things foretold in Daniel 9:24. The expiration of the 483 years has brought us only "unto" the One in Whom those six things, which involve the whole purpose of God in redemption, were to be accomplished. Sixty-nine weeks of the determined seventy have passed. Only one week remains. It follows, therefore, of necessity, that the predictions of verse 24 must be fulfilled in that week. Within the next seven years the transgression of Israel must be finished, reconciliation must be made for iniquity, and everlasting righteousness must be brought, in, else the prophecy would utterly fail.

But this is just what might, have been understood from verse 24 alone. The words "seventy weeks are determined" are enough to inform us that the seventieth week was the one which would see the accomplishment of the predicted events; for if they, or some of them at least, were not to fall in that last week, then the prophetic period would not have been announced as one of seventy weeks, but as one of a lesser number. In fact, the very manner in which the prophecy is given to us—the last week being set off from the rest for special and separate mention indicates the exceptional importance of that, week. And this is easily seen; for if we look attentively at the terms of the prophecy we perceive that our Lord's personal ministry lay entirely within the seventieth week. We ask our readers to lay firm hold of this fact. The prophecy plainly says there should be 69 weeks "unto the Anointed One." Then, to make this clear beyond all doubt, it says, "And after the threescore and two weeks shall Messiah be cut off." This definitely places His whole ministry within the seventieth consecutive week from the decree of Cyrus. This is of the highest importance to an understanding of the prophecy.

In this connection, and by way of anticipation of what we propose to consider more fully hereafter, we briefly call attention to several points which bear directly upon this part of our study:

1. It is clear front what is recorded in John's Gospel (and this has been often pointed out from the earliest days of our era) that our Lord's ministry was approximately, if not exactly, three years and a half in duration. Hence front His anointing to His death would be half a "week?" and His crucifixion would be "in the midst of the (70th) week."

2. Glancing now for a moment at Daniel 9:27 we note the words "and in the midst of the week he shall cause the sacrifice and the oblation to cease." If, as we expect to show hereafter by ample proof, the "he" of this verse is Christ, and the words quoted refer to His causing the sacrifices of the law to cease by His offering of Himself its a sacrifice for sin once for all, then we have a perfect agreement, in the finished work of Christ, with all the terms of the

prophecy, and particularly in regard to the length of time assigned to His earthly ministry both by the prophecy and by the Gospel according to John.

We need to exercise much care in this part of our study, because it has to do with matters regarding which there has been great uncertainty and wide difference of opinion. The difficulties, however, have been largely imported into the subject. They tire due in great measure to the wrong method which has been pursued (its we have shown in a previous chapter), and to the choice of a wrong starting point. For manifestly, the consequences of a mistake at the beginning will appear all along the way. On the other band, it will be easy to keep from error and confusion if we bear in mind these simple facts (1), that, at the baptism of Christ 69 weeks had elapsed; (2) that the beginning of His ministry was the beginning also of the 70th week; (3) that His entire mission lay within the compass of that last week; and (4) that in that week we must needs look for the accomplishment of the six predictions of Daniel 9:24.

We have not thus far referred to the latter part of Daniel 9:25. It merely tells that the street and wall (of the city) were to be built again "even in troublous times." The period of "seven weeks", mentioned in the verse, was no doubt the measure of those troublous times. This will serve to explain why the entire period of 70 weeks was divided into three parts—seven weeks, sixty-two weeks, and one week. In the first portion (7 weeks), the rebuilding of the city and temple took place, and God's last messages to Israel were given through Haggai, Zechariah, and Malachi. Then follows a long stretch of 62 weeks, which period was uneventful, so far as this prophecy is concerned. Chapter 11, however, (as we shall show later on) foretells the principal events of this period, which brings us "unto the Messiah," and then comes the last and most momentous "weeks," which appropriately stands by itself, for in it occurred the most stupendous events of all time.

The Prince

The fact that the angel Gabriel, in speaking of the Messiah, gave Him the title "Prince" (Daniel 9:25) suggests an inquiry, which, when pursued, is found to yield fruitful results.

Two of the great visions which Daniel records give an outline of the history of human government,, from the time of the vision to the very end of world government in the hands of men; and in both of these visions it, is shown that the last of the world kingdoms will be followed, and the whole system of human rule will be displaced, by the Kingdom of God. The vision of Chapter 2 shows this kingdom as a stone, carving itself out of the mountain without the agency of hands (this being a special feature of the vision), smiting the great, image (which represents human rule in its entirety) upon its feet, demolishing the whole image, and finally becoming itself a mountain which fills the whole earth. Daniel, in expounding the vision, said that this stone represented "a kingdom" which "the God of heaven" would set up, and which should "stand forever" (Daniel 2:44). Plainly the Lord Jesus had this Scripture in mind when, in warning the Scribes and Pharisees that the Kingdom of God was to be taken from them (for the promise of the Kingdom, along with all other promises, had been given to the Jews), He spoke of "the Stone which the builders refused," and declared that whosoever should fall upon it (then, at His first advent) should be broken; but on whomsoever it should fall (at His second coming in power) it should grind him to powder (Matthew 21:42–44).

The companion vision (Daniel 7) reveals further details concerning this Kingdom of God. Particularly does it show that it was to be conferred in heaven upon One like the Son of man, to whom was to be given "dominion, glory, and a kingdom, that all people, nations and languages should serve Him: His dominion is an everlasting dominion and His Kingdom that which shall not be destroyed" (Daniel 7:13–14).

In view of these two preceding visions which speak so definitely of a kingdom, it might he expected that the angel in announcing in the vision of Chapter 9, the coming of the Anointed One, who, of Course, is the One Who is to receive the kingdom, would have referred to Him as "Messiah the King." And indeed, if His coming to which the Seventy Weeks was the determined measure of time had been with a view to setting up a kingdom which would forthwith displace the earth rule of man, then the title "King" would be the appropriate one to use. But, in view of the actual purpose for which Christ was to come at that Lintel and of the work He was then to accomplish, there is a wonderful suitability in the title "Prince." And not only so, but this title serves as a connecting link with certain New Testament Scriptures, referred to below, in which His work for this age is set forth in a comprehensive way.

For the title "Prince" is given to the Lord Jesus Christ by the Holy Spirit, four times; whereas He was not once proclaimed by Heaven's authority as King, at His first coming. (He was referred to as the King by the Gentile Magi, by Nathaniel when he first. met Him, by the excited multitude at His last entry into Jerusalem, when their nationalistic expectations had been raised to a high pitch by the miracle of the raising of Lazarus, and by Pilate in derision. He was not so styled by John the Baptist, by Himself, or by His immediate disciples and apostles. These latter called Him "Master" and "Lord".)

The four New Testament passages to which we refer are these:

1. Acts 3:15: "And killed the Prince of life, Whom God hath raised from the dead."

2. Acts 5:31: "Him hath God exalted with His right and to be a Prince and a Savior, for to give repentance to Israel and forgiveness of sins."

3. Heb. 2:10: "For it became Him, for Whom are all things, and by Whom are all things in bringing many sons unto glory, to make the Captain (Prince) of their salvation perfect through sufferings."

4. Heb. 12:2: "Looking unto Jesus, the Author (Prince) and Finisher of faith, Who, for the joy that was set before Him, endured the cross, despising the shame, and is set down at the right, hand of the throne of God."

Taken together, these four scriptures present a wonderful view of the work of the Anointed One at His

first advent. To begin with it should be noticed that in each passage His sufferings are made prominent. Peter says to the Jews at Jerusalem, "Ye denied the Holy One and The Just, and desired a murderer to be granted unto you; and killed the Prince of life." Again, in Acts 5:30, he said: "The God of our fathers raised up Jesus, Whom ye slew and hanged on a tree, Him hath God exalted with His right hand to be a Prince and a Saviour." In the third scripture we read that it became God, in bringing many sons unto glory, to make the Prince of their salvation perfect through sufferings. And finally, we read that as the Prince of faith, the One to Whom we must trustfully look while running the race set before us, He endured the Cross, despising the shame. It is needless that we should point out how perfect is the agreement in all this with the one thing foretold of Messiah the Prince in Daniel 9:25–26) namely that He should be cut off and have nothing. All these Scriptures then agree in their testimony that this Anointed "Prince" was, for the accomplishment of His mission, to suffer and to die.

Again, viewing these scriptures together, we see in them God's fourfold objective in sending forth His Son in the likeness of man, and in anointing Him with the Holy Ghost and with power. It was (1) that He might be the Prince of life, thus to meet the deepest need of His perishing people, for he came "that they might have life"; (2) That He might also be the Prince and Savior empowered to grant repentance and forgiveness of sins; (3) that He might be the Prince or Leader of the salvation of God's many sons, to bring them all safe home to glory; and (4) that He might also be the Leader as well as the Finisher of that faith whereby God's people are to run (and without which none can possibly run) with endurance the race which is set before them, This fourfold object of the purpose of Christ's mission at His first advent seems to present a comprehensive setting forth of His work.

In these Scriptures then we view Him as the Prince of life exalted by God's right hand; as the Prince and Savior, granting repentance and pardon, and giving the Holy Spirit "to them that obey Him" (for He will accept only willing obedience); as the Prince of the complete and final salvation of God's "many sons" whom by death, He has delivered from him who has the power of death, that is the devil (verses 14–15); and lastly as the Prince and Completer of a faith which triumphs through all difficulties, and sustains us to the end of the race.

To summarize: The first passage has to do with the birth of the children of the kingdom; the second with their pardon and justification; the third with their protection and safety while on their journey to the glory; and the fourth with the perfecting of their faith for the endurance of all the trials of the way. Taken altogether they give us the character of that kingdom which we have received through grace, and which is described in Hebrews 12:28 as "a kingdom which cannot be moved."

CHAPTER 5

Messiah "Cut Off"—The "Hour"

"And after threescore and two weeks shall Messiah be cut off, and have nothing" (Daniel 9:26, margin.)

The first clause of verse 26 focuses our attention upon the greatest of all events. It tells us definitely that Christ was to be "cut off, and have nothing" (the marginal reading, "and have nothing" is undoubtedly correct). He was to have no people, no throne, no place even, on earth. But to the Israelites the words "cut off and have nothing" would convey the meaning of dying without posterity, without a "generation," with none to perpetuate his name. This was regarded by them as the greatest of all calamities; and there was a special provision of the law whereby, in case a man should die, leaving no seed, his brother or near kinsman should "raise up the name of the dead" (Deuteronomy 25:5-6; Ruth 4:10). But here is the astonishing statement that the long promised and ardently looked for Messiah was to be completely "cut off"!

There is, in these words, a striking agreement with the prophecy of Isaiah, which contains the following: "And who shall declare His generation? For He was cut off out of the land of the living" (Isaiah 53:8). There could seemingly be no "generation" for one who was "cut off." Yet with that marvellous prophecy runs the apparently contradictory promise, "He shall see His seed" (verse 10).

Considering now the statement, "And after three score and two weeks shall Messiah be cut off," the unity of the prophecy is seen in this, that the words, "after three score and two weeks," bring us to the last of the "Seventy Weeks," that is, to the period referred to in verse 24; and the words, "Messiah shall be cut off," declare the means whereby the six predictions of that verse were to be fulfilled. Every part of this prophecy is thus firmly bound to every other part. It all has to do with the coming of Christ and what He was to suffer at the hands of His people; and it includes also a foretelling of the judgments that were to befall them for putting Him to death.

We would, therefore, fix our attention for a little while upon this special period of time, this three years and a half from the anointing of the Lord at His baptism to His crucifixion. That period is frequently referred to in the Gospels as the "time" or "this time," meaning the time of the Messiah. Thus, when our Lord said, "The time is fulfilled" (Mark 1:15), He doubtless had reference to the time revealed to Daniel, the time when Christ was to be made manifest to Israel. Again, in Luke 12:56, where he asked, "How is it that ye do not discern the time?" and in Luke 19:44, where he said, "Because thou knewest not the time of thy visitation," we may properly conclude that He had in mind the same "set time," which had been definitely marked off in the unchangeable counsels of God and which He had communicated to Daniel, the man who was greatly beloved. The last mentioned passage (Luke 19:41–44) is very closely related to the prophecy of the seventy weeks, for it is itself a prophecy by Christ of the same destruction of Jerusalem which is foretold in the prophecy of the seventy weeks.

Surely there was no "time" like that, when God's blessed Son, in lowly human form, went about doing good and healing all that were oppressed of the devil. Many prophets and kings had desired to see those things, and the angels desire to look into them. We should therefore be greatly impressed by the fad that God had, hundreds of years before, foretold that "time," had given the measure of it, and had declared how it should end.

But more than this, the Lord made frequent reference also to a particular "hour," calling it "My hour." The "time" was that of His personal ministry in Israel, according to this prophecy; and the "hour" was that of His being "cut off," according to the same prophecy.

We would call to mind some of those passages, which must ever awaken love and praise in the hearts of those for whose sake he endured the agonies of that awful and mysterious "hour." Thus, when certain Greeks desired to see Him, their interest being prompted by the great commotion caused by the raising of Lazarus, and when crowds were thronging to see Him and Lazarus also (John 12:9), He referred to the approaching "hour" when He, being lifted up from the earth, should draw "all men," Greeks as well as Jews, unto Him, and said, "The hour is come that the Son of man should be glorified"; and again, "Now is My soul troubled; and what shall I say? Father save me from this hour? But for this cause came I unto this hour" (John 12:20–27). Also in John 17:1 we read His words, "Father, the hour is come." And a little later that same evening He prayed in the garden, asking "that if it were possible the hour might pass from Him" (Mark 14:35). It is plain that, in these passages, He was speaking of the hour when He should be made a sacrifice for sin upon the Cross—the hour when Messiah should "be cut off and have nothing."

The Judgment. "The Prince That Shall Come".

The verse we are now considering (Daniel 9:26) foretells not only the crowning sin of Israel in putting their Messiah to death, but also the great and terrible judgment that was to follow the perpetration of that unspeakable deed. There is a direct logical connection between the two events, which will account for the fact that the chronological order is not strictly followed.

There are differences of opinion among competent scholars as to the proper translation of the latter part of verse 26. In the text of the AV it reads:

> "And the people of the prince that shall come shall destroy the city and the sanctuary; and the end thereof shall be with a flood, and unto the end of the war desolations are determined."

The RV makes clearer the meaning of the last clause. It reads: "and unto the end shall be war; desolations are determined."

Notwithstanding, however, the differences of translation, it is not difficult to gather the meaning of the passage. Indeed, so far as we are aware, all expositors agree that it foretells the exterminating judgment of God, which in due time was executed by the Roman armies under Titus, by whom the city was overwhelmed as "with a flood" (a figure often used for an invading army), and the city and the land were given over to the age long "desolations," which had been "determined" in the counsels of God. Doubtless the Lord had this very passage in mind when, speaking of the then approaching siege and destruction of Jerusalem by the Romans, He said: "For these be the days of vengeance, that all things that are written may be fulfilled" (Luke 21:22). The "things that are written" were the things foretold in this verse of the prophecy (Daniel 9:26), which were "fulfilled" at that time. The Lord's words recorded in Matthew 23:32–36, and Luke 19:43–44, also refer to the calamities foretold in Daniel 9:26, its will be clearly seen by turning to those passages.

The following then is the meaning we derive from the text of the AV and RV: That the people of a "prince" (i.e., a leader or commander), who was to come with arms against Judea and Jerusalem, would utterly destroy both the city and the temple; that the destruction thereof should be as if a flood had swept everything away; that to the end there should be war; and that "desolations" for the land and city were definitely "determined."

Thus the entire prophecy of the Seventy Weeks embraces in its scope the rebuilding of the city and the temple, and the final destruction of both. It covers the stretch of time from the restoration of the people to their land and city in the first year of Cyrus, down to their dispersion by the Romans among all the nations of the world.

In this connection we would again call the reader's attention to the striking agreement between this part of the prophecy and the word of God to Isaiah (Chap. 6:9–13).

Who is "The Prince That Shall Come"?

At this point we are confronted with a question which very seriously affects the interpretation of the prophecy. Taking the words according to their apparent and obvious meaning (which should always be done except where there is a compelling reason to the contrary) it would seem quite clear that "the prince," whose people were to destroy the city and the sanctuary, was Titus, the son of the then emperor Vespasian, he (Titus) being the "prince" or "leader" who was in actual command of those armies at the time. In fact we are bold to say that the words of the prophecy, which are the words of God sent directly from heaven to Daniel, do not reasonably admit of any other interpretation. Nor, so far as we are aware, was any other meaning ever put upon them until within recent years, and then only by those belonging to a particular "school" of interpretation. According to the "school" referred to, the words "the prince that shall come" do not mean the prince who did come, and whose armies fulfilled this prophecy by destroying the city and the temple, but they mean some other "prince," who in fact has not yet come, and who (of course) could have nothing whatever to do with the subject of the passage, to wit, the destruction of the city and the temple.

According to the view we are now considering, the passage is taken to mean that there is a "prince" who is to "come" at some unknown time yet future, which prince will be of the same nationality as the people (the Roman armies) by whom the city and the Sanctuary were to be destroyed. It is further assumed, and taught with much confidence, that this "coming prince" will be in league with Antichrist, if indeed he be not Antichrist himself. This is a very radical idea, one which changes the entire meaning of this basic prophecy, and affects the interpretation of all prophecy. It transfers the main incidents of the prophecy of the Seventy Weeks from Christ to Antichrist, and removes them bodily from the distant past to the uncertain future, thus separating them far from all connection with the period of seventy weeks to which God assigns them. This manner of dealing with Scripture is, so far as our experience goes, without parallel or precedent in the field of exegesis. Is it sound and sober interpretation of Scripture, or is it playing pranks with prophecy?

For, with all due and proper respect for those who hold this view, we are bound to say that it does the greatest possible violence to words which are not at all obscure or of uncertain meaning. There is no conceivable reason why any prince (i.e., commander) should be mentioned in this passage except the one whose armies were to accomplish the destruction of the city and temple, that being the subject of the passage. The words are appropriate to convey one meaning and one only. It is simply unthinkable that the destroying agency would be identified by reference to some prince who was not to come upon the scene for several thousand years, or that the Romans of the first century could be called his "people." Nor would anyone who possessed the slightest understanding of the use of language employ the words of the text in order to convey the information that the people, by whom the city was to be destroyed, would be of the same nationality as some "prince" who was to "come" (without saying whence, or whither, or for what) at some remote and unspecified time. And finally, even if it were supposable that such an utterly foreign subject as a prince, who was to come many centuries after the event prophesied, would be lugged into such a passage, then it would have been made to say not "the people of the prince that shall come shall destroy the city," but that a prince of the people who destroyed the city shall come.

Furthermore, we know that the armies of prince Titus did destroy the city and temple, and that to this day the seven-branched candlestick, which was carried in his triumphal procession, is sculptured on the arch which was erected at Rome in his honor. But we know nothing of any Roman prince who is to "come" (come where?) in the future. The term "Roman" pertains to nothing now except the papacy.

And besides all this, if any "prince" should hereafter "come" (it matters not whence or whither) it could not property be said that the people who destroyed Jerusalem in AD 70 were his people. The plain and simple words of the prophecy are "the people of the prince who shall come." Those words can only mean the man who was the prince or leader of the people at the time they destroyed the city and temple. Those Roman legions and auxiliaries were the people of prince Titus. But in no sense are they the people of some prince who may arise several thousand years later. The French armies which invaded Russia were the people of Napoleon their commander; but in no proper sense were they the people of General Foch. They were all dead long before he was born.

This prophecy has nothing whatever to do with any future Roman prince; nor is there, so far as we are aware, any ground for saying that a Roman prince will arise to play a part in the time of the end of this age. During the centuries that have now elapsed such changes have taken place that no potentate of the approaching end times could be described as the prince of the people by whom Jerusalem was destroyed.

The prophecy of the Seventy Weeks is manifestly an account, given beforehand, of the second period of the national existence of the Jewish people. They were to last as a nation only long enough to fulfill the Scriptures, and to accomplish the supreme purpose of God, in bringing forth the Messiah, and. putting Him to death. The time allotted for this was 490 years. This being accomplished, God had no further use for Israel. His dealings thenceforth were to be with another people, that "holy nation" (1 Peter 2:9), composed of all who believe the gospel, and who "receive" the One Who was rejected by "His own" (John 1:11–13).

Yet the predicted judgment did not immediately follow; for Christ prayed for His murderers in His dying hour, "Father, forgive them; for they know not what they do" (Luke 23:34). In answer to that prayer the full probationary period of forty years (AD 30 to AD 70) was added to their national existence, during which time repentance and remission of sins was preached to them in the Name of the crucified and risen One, and tens of thousands of Jews were saved.

The perfect accuracy of Scripture is seen in this, that while it was definitely stated that the six things of Daniel 9:24 were to be accomplished within the determined period of seventy weeks, and while the destruction of the rebuilt city and temple was also predicted, that event is not among the things which were to happen within the seventy weeks.

In this connection it is important to observe that, while the predicted events of verse 24 were to happen within the measured period of seventy weeks, and the events of verse 27 were to happen in the midst of the last week of the seventy, the time of the predicted judgments is not specified. Thus the prophecy left room for the exercise of mercy even to that evil generation.

CHAPTER 6

The Seventieth Week

"And he shall confirm the covenant with many for one week, and in the midst of the week he shall cause the sacrifice and the oblation to cease" (Daniel 9:27)

We come now to the last verse of the prophecy, which verse is of surpassing interest and importance. It has to do specifically with the seventieth week of the prophecy. The expiration of 69 weeks brought us "unto Christ," but not to His crucifixion, nor to that which is the great subject of all prophecy, "the sufferings of the Christ" (1 Peter 1:11). Particularly it should be kept in mind that the six things of Daniel 9:24 depended for their accomplishing upon His atoning death, His resurrection, and His ascension into heaven. All these events were "after the threescore and two weeks."

When Moses and Elijah appeared with Christ in glory on the Mount of Transfiguration, they "spake of His exodus which He should accomplish at Jerusalem" (Luke 9:31). His "exodus" or "way out" of this world was the consummation of the purposes of God, the climax of all prophecy, the supreme event of all the ages. Thereby he accomplished eternal redemption, opened a fountain for sin and for uncleanness, scaled the everlasting covenant, and set aside forever the sacrifices appointed by the law.

The first part of Daniel 9:27, quoted at the head of this chapter, is quite clear except for the words "for one week," which will be explained later on. The meaning of the clause (apart from those three words) is, we believe, easily discerned in the light of the New Testament scriptures. "To confirm" the new covenant (Jeremiah 31:31– 34; Hebrews 8:6–13; 10:1–18), that is, to make it sure, was the great purpose for which the Son of God came into the world in the body of flesh prepared for Him (Hebrews 10:5). Moreover, it was by His death as a sacrifice for sin that He displaced and abolished the sacrifices of the law, thus causing them "to cease." God had had "no pleasure" in these because they "could never take away sins," whereas "it pleased the Lord to bruise Him", making "His soul an offering for sin" (Isaiah 53:10).

If we take the pronoun "He" as relating to "the Messiah" mentioned in the preceding verse, then we find in the New Testament scriptures a perfect fulfillment of the passage, and a fulfillment, moreover, which is set forth in the most conspicuous way. That pronoun must, in our opinion, be taken as referring to Christ, because (a) the prophecy is all about Christ, and this is the climax of it; (b) Titus did not make any covenant with the Jews; (e) there is not a word in Scripture about any future "prince" making a covenant with them. Other reasons in support of this conclusion will appear later on. But the foregoing are sufficient.

There are three points in the passage we are now studying, and each of them is completely fulfilled in the inspired accounts of the work of the Lord Jesus Christ given in the New Testament. Those three points are: (1) confirming the covenant with many; (2) what happened in the midst of the week; (3) causing the sacrifice and the oblation to cease. We will briefly examine these three points in order.

1. *Confirming the covenant with many.* We ignore for the present the words "for one week," which words would seem to limit the duration of the "covenant" to the short period of seven years. It

will suffice for now to say that there is no preposition "for" in the text, and that the words "one week" do not refer to the duration of the covenant, but to the time when it was confirmed; for that covenant was confirmed by the shedding of the blood of Christ (Hebrews 9:14-20) in "the one week," the last of the seventy which had been "determined." This will be clearly shown later on.

As to the fulfillment of this important feature of the prophecy we have a clear announcement from the Lord's own lips. For when, in the institution of His memorial supper, He gave the cup to His disciples, he uttered these significant words, "This is My blood of the new covenant, shed for many for the remission of sins" (Matthew 26:28). In these words we find four things which agree with the prophecy: ONE—"the One" who was to confirm the covenant, Christ; TWO—"the covenant" itself; THREE—that which "confirmed" the covenant, the blood of Christ; FOUR—those who receive the benefits of the covenant, the "many." The identification is complete; for the words correspond perfectly with those of the prophecy, "He shall confirm the covenant with many." There could not be a more perfect agreement.

It is to be noted in this connection that the prominent feature of the new covenant is the forgiveness of sins (Jeremiah 31:34; Hebrews 10:1-18). Hence the significance of the Lord's words, "for the remission of sins." His mission in coming into the world was to "save His people from their sins" (Matthew 1:21). That is the prominent feature of His gospel (Luke 24:47; Acts 10:43).

It is further to be noted that, although the promise of the New Covenant was made to the entire "house of Israel and house of Judah," not all of them entered into its benefits. Those who rejected Christ were "destroyed from among the people" (Acts 3:23). They were, as branches, "broken off" (Romans 11:17). We see then the accuracy of Scripture in the words of the prophecy "with many," and those of the Lord Jesus "shed for many."

This use of the word "many" is found in other like scriptures. Thus, in a similar prophecy it is written: "My righteous Servant shall justify many" (Isaiah 53:11). Again, "And many of the children of Israel shall he turn to the Lord their God", (1:11, 16). This was said by the same heavenly messenger, Gabriel, when he announced to Zachariah the birth of his son. And yet again—this time from the lips of Simeon—"This Child is set for the fall and rising again of many in Israel" (Luke 2:34). And yet once more, in the words of the Lord Jesus, "For the Son of man came not to be ministered unto, but to minister, and to give His life a ransom for many" (Matthew 20:28). In each of these scriptures the word "many" applies to those who receive by faith the benefits of the New Covenant which Christ made sure by the shedding of His blood upon the Cross.

2. *In the midst of the week.* These words are important in helping to identify the fulfillment of the prophecy. Considering the supreme importance of the death of Christ, upon which depended not only the six predictions of verse 24, but all the purposes of God; and considering also that the prophecy gives the time when the Lord's ministry as "the Messiah" was to begin, we should expect to find in it a statement when His ministry was to end by His being "cut off." This information is given in the words "in the midst of the week", that is the seventieth week. The expiration of 69 weeks brought us "unto the Messiah." Only "one week" of the seventy remained; and in the midst of that last week He was crucified.

We have here (as already indicated) a valuable means of checking up our conclusions and testing their correctness. For, as has been often pointed out since very early times, the Gospel of John contains information by which it appears that the ministry of Christ lasted three and a half years. In fact Eusebius, a Christian writer of the fourth century, is quoted as saying: "It is recorded in history that the whole time of our Savior's teaching and working miracles was three years and a half, which is half a week. This, John the evangelist will represent (i.e. will make known) to those who critically attend to his Gospel.

Thus the length of our Lord's ministry, as disclosed by the Gospel of John (half a week), strikingly confirms the prophecy, which gives 69 weeks unto the beginning of the Lord's ministry, and fixes the ending thereof "in the midst of the week" following.

3. *He shall cause the sacrifice and oblation to cease.* No one will dispute that, when Christ suffered and died on the Cross, thus offering "one sacrifice for sins forever," he then and there caused the sacrifice, and oblations of the law to cease as a divine appointment. Even when in full vigor they were but the shadows of that perfect and all-sufficient sacrifice which he, as the Lamb foreordained before the foundation of the world, which was to offer in due time. Hence they were completely displaced when Christ, through the eternal Spirit, offered Himself without spot to God.

Neither can there be any question that the removal of those sacrifices (which could never take away sins) was a great thing in the eyes of God, a thing so great and well-pleasing to Him, to warrant its having a prominent place in this grand Messianic prophecy. In proof of this important point we direct the attention of our readers to Hebrews, chapters 8, 9 and 10. In those chapters the Spirit of God puts before us in great detail, and with solemn emphasis, the setting aside of the Old Covenant, with all that related to it, the "worldly sanctuary," the priesthood, the "ordinances of divine service," and particularly those many sacrifices (by which a remembrance of sins was made every year); and he puts before us also the confirming of the New Covenant, with its heavenly sanctuary, its spiritual priesthood, its sacrifices of praise and thanksgiving, all based upon the atonement of Christ. The great subject of this part of Hebrews, as of the prophecy of the Seventy Weeks, is the Cross.

Chapter 10 of Hebrews dwells largely upon the sacrifices which were "offered by the law," emphasizing the imperfection and insufficiency thereof to purge the conscience of the offerers, and declaring that, for that reason, God had no pleasure in therein. It was because of this ("wherefore") that the Son of God said, "Lo, I come (in the volume of the Book it is written of Me) to do Thy will, O God" (verse 7). This relates the passage directly to the prophecy of the Seventy Weeks, which has for its subject the coming of Christ into the world and the purpose for which He came. How full of significance then, and how conclusive for the object of our present study, are the words which follow!

> "Above when He said, Sacrifice and offering and burnt offerings and offering for sin Thou wouldst not, neither hadst pleasure therein; which are offered by the law; then said He, Lo, I come to do Thy will, O God. He taketh away the first, that He may establish the second" (Hebrews 10:8-9).

This is the climax of the whole matter. "He taketh away" those sacrifices and oblations wherein God had no pleasure! What perfect agreement with the words of the prophecy, "He shall cause the sacrifice and oblation to cease"! And when we find, both in the prophecy (Daniel 9:27) and in Hebrews 10, that this setting aside of the sacrifices of the law is connected directly with the confirming of the New Covenant, we are compelled to conclude that the passage in Hebrews is the inspired record of the fulfilment of this Prophecy.

We ask careful attention to the fact that in Hebrews 10:12 it is expressly stated that Christ took away the sacrifices of the law when He offered Himself as the "one sacrifice for sins forever," ere he "sat down on the right hand of God." Those sacrifices, therefore, ceased to exist in God's contemplation from the moment Christ died. From that moment God regards no longer the sacrifices of the law. It is impossible, therefore, that the words "he shall cause the sacrifice and oblation to cease" could refer to any event subsequent to the crucifixion of Christ. To this we purpose to return. But at this point we would simply raise the question, where shall we look for a fulfillment of the prophecy, if we reject that recorded in Hebrews 10:9?

The Seventieth Week

"For One Week"

We come now to the words "for one week" (Daniel 9:27), which have been the means of leading astray sonic
who have undertaken to explain this prophecy.

Manifestly those words are utterly inconsistent with the view that the covenant spoken of is the New Covenant, since that is "everlasting" (Hebrews 13:20). But it is hardly conceivable that any covenant—particularly one of such importance as to have a prominent place in this prophecy—would be confirmed for such a brief term as seven years Even if we suppose, as some do (though with no proof whatever to support them), that the prophecy refers to some agreement which the supposed "prince" of the future will supposedly make with "many" Jews, permitting them to resume the long abolished sacrifices of the law, can we conceive that such a covenant would be limited to the insignificant term of seven years?

In view of the difficulty presented by the words "for one week," we consulted a Hebrew scholar, asking him if there were any preposition "for" in the original text, or anything to imply it. His reply was that there is no "for" in the text, nor anything to imply it. This information removed the chief difficulty; but it left still unsettled the meaning to be given to the words "one week." That further information, however, was supplied by the same Hebrew scholar (formerly a Jewish Rabbis but now a servant of the Lord Jesus Christ), who gave us the English rendering of the Septuagint Version of Daniel 9:27. This Septuagint Version is a translation of the Hebrew scriptures into Greek, made nearly three hundred years before the birth of Christ. It has a claim on our acceptance as an authoritative version, because our Lord and His apostles frequently quoted from it.

Particularly do we ask attention to the fact that when our Lord, in His prophecy on Mount Olivet, quoted from the latter part of Daniel 9:27, He used the words of the Septuagint version, namely, "the abomination of desolation" (Matthew 24:15). Therefore We have a special Warrant for following the sense of the Septuagint. We give the English translation of the entire verse as it appears in the Septuagint.

> "And one week shall establish the covenant with many; and in the midst of the week my sacrifice and drink offering shall be taken away; and upon the temple shall be the abomination of desolation; and at the end of the time (the age) an end shall be put to the desolation."

From this wording the meaning of the first clause is easily grasped. It is a common form of speech to say for example, "the year 1776 established the independence of the American colonies"; "the year 1918 restored Alsace and Lorraine to France," etc., which is a figurative way of saying that such or such an event took place at the time specified. This form of expression is used when it is desired to call special attention to the year, or other period, in which a certain event occurred. So here, the previous verses having accounted for 69 of the total of 70 weeks, it was most appropriate to emphasize that last week; and especially so for the reason that the last week was not only to fulfill the six predictions of verse 24) but it was to be the climax of all the ages.

The sense of the passage then is this: That the one remaining week would witness the confirming of the covenant (which could only mean the promised New Covenant) with the many; and that, in the midst of that last week, Christ would cause the entire system of sacrifices appointed by the law to cease, by the offering of himself in the all-sufficient sacrifice for sins.

This gives to the last week of the seventy the importance it should have, and which the prophecy as a whole demands, seeing that all the predictions of verse 24 depend upon the events of that last week. On the other hand, to make this last Week refer to a paltry bargain between Antichrist (or a supposed Roman prince) and some apostate Jews of the future, for the renewal (and that for a space of only seven years) of those sacrifices which God has long ago abolished forever, is to intrude into this great scripture a matter of trifling importance, utterly foreign to the subject in hand. and to bring the entire prophecy to an absurdly lame and impotent conclusion.

"My Sacrifices and Drink Offering"

In further elucidation of the sense of verse 27 we would call special attention to the words of the Septuagint Version, "my sacrifice and drink offering shall be taken away." Before the death of Christ the sacrifices of the law were God's. But he Would never call His the sacrifices which apostate Jews might institute under agreement with Antichrist. This we deem to be conclusive.

Subsequently to the first appearance of these papers we have had access to Dr. Wm. M. Taylor's excellent book entitled, Daniel The Beloved, in which the above rendering of verse 27 is confirmed. Dr. Taylor gives Dr. Cowle's version of that verse, as follows: "One seven shall make the covenant effective to many. The middle of the seven shall make sacrifice and offerings to cease," etc.

We quote also from Dr. Taylor's comments, which afford confirmation of the conclusions we had already reached:

> "It is well known by those acquainted with chronology that Christ was born four years earlier than the first of the era which we call by His name. Therefore, at the year 26 AD our Lord would be really thirty years of age; and we know (Luke 3:23) that His baptism, or public manifestation to the people, took place when He 'began to be about thirty years of age'.
>
> "Further, at the end of half a seven of years, or in the middle of the heptad, Messiah, according to this prediction, was to cause the sacrifice and offerings to cease. Now, if we suppose this to refer to the fact that Christ's death, being a real and proper sacrifice for sin, virtually abolished all those under the law, which were only typical, we have here a date harmonizing with that of the Crucifixion. It is as near as possible demonstrable from the Gospel by John that our

Savior's public ministry lasted three years and it half (see Robinson's Harmony of the Gospels, Appendix); and this is corroborated by the parable of the barren fig tree (Luke 13:69) which seems to indicate that three years of special privilege to the Jews had run their course, and that a fourth, or a portion of a fourth, was to be given them. Here again, therefore, we have a coincidence of date between the prediction and the history.

"The exposition we have given of this section of Daniel's prediction, find of the manner of its fulfillment is fitted to stir the heart even of the most indifferent. For myself, I feel awed by the sense of the nearness of God, which comes over me when I read these verses and when I remember how they have been confirmed by the events of which Calvary was the scene. God is in this history of a truth. But let us not forget that it differs from ordinary history only that here we are permitted to read out of the Book of Divine purpose and prescience; whereas in other cases that record is hidden from our eyes. God is in, all history as really and as much as he was in this. How solemn, yet how reassuring also is the thought!"

In view of all this, we would ask, how can any sober minded expositor of the Scriptures set aside the perfect and heart satisfying fulfillment of this wonderful prophecy, so clearly to be seen in "the events of which Calvary was the scene," and propose instead a contrived fulfilment, in a supposed covenant (whereof the Scriptures say not a word) between Antichrist and the Jewish people of the last days, relating to the imagined revival of the long abolished sacrifices of the law?

Therefore we conclude that the modern interpretation which takes Christ and the Cross out of the last verse of the prophecy, where it reaches its climax, and puts Antichrist and his imaginary doings into it, does violence to the Scripture and serious wrong to the people of God.

CHAPTER 7

Are the Seventy Weeks Consecutive?

The idea which we have discussed in our last chapter, namely that Daniel 9:27 refers not to Christ but to Antichrist is usually coupled with, another, also of a very radical sort, namely, that the 70th week of Gabriel's prophecy does not come where we would naturally expect to find it, that is, immediately after the 69th week, but that it is detached from the other 69, is separated from them by many centuries, is yet in the future, and will be found at the very end of this present age. The extent to which these ideas have found acceptance in our day makes it a matter of importance to inquire very carefully into the reasons that have been given in support thereof.

We do not know just when or how these ideas sprang up. That is not, of course, a reason for rejecting them; for God is pleased from time to time to give new light from His Word. But it is a reason for subjecting them to a rigid scrutiny. This we have sought to do, and the result is we have come to the conclusion that, not only are they destitute of support in the Word of God, but they are directly contrary thereto. This we shall endeavor to make clear.

As regards the idea that verse 27 (Daniel 9) refers to Antichrist, little more need be said. If the scriptures which we have cited in a preceding chapter establish that the verse was fulfilled by the Lord Jesus Christ when He died for our sins, His death having occurred "in the midst of the week" (which began with His anointing), then there is no need to show negatively that the passage (does not await a fulfilment by Antichrist, or other end-time potentate. Nevertheless the negative arguments are of value by way of corroboration.

We point out, therefore, that in order to make the "he" of Daniel 9:27 refer to Antichrist, it is necessary to make "the prince that shall come" of verse 26 to mean a future prince. We think we have already shown that this is absolutely inadmissible. But even if we make the unwarranted assumption that a future "prince" is referred to, still it is a question whether the pronoun "he" of verse 27 refers to him or to Christ. At this point all our previous evidences and arguments would come in to show that the pronoun must in any case be taken as referring to "the Messiah". The fulfillment of the prophecy by Christ proves that the "He" refers to Him.

But beside all this, there are insuperable obstacles in the way of the acceptance of the view we are discussing. For we are bound to reject any and every interpretation which is not supported by the Scriptures. And how is it in this case? There is not one word of proof in support of any one of the following propositions, each and all of which must be proved ere the view in dispute can be considered established: (1) that a future Roman prince will make a covenant with many Jews; (2) that the supposed covenant will be for a term of one week; (3) that it will have for its purpose to permit the Jews to resume their ancient and long abolished temple sacrifices; (4) that the supposed prince will break the supposed covenant in the midst of the week, and thus "cause the sacrifice and oblation to cease." We repeat that we are bound to reject the interpretation referred to unless each and all these four propositions (which are involved in it) are established by evidence from the Word of God; and the fact is that there is not one word of proof for any one of them.

Those who advance this interpretation commonly refer in support of it to Matt. 24:15; 2 Thess. 2:3–9; and Rev. 13:3–15.

But, without discussing those scriptures, it is quite sufficient for our purpose to say that none of them makes the remotest allusion to any covenant between Antichrist (or any other personage) and the Jews. The interpretation we are discussing has no basis whatever in the Scriptures. It is entirely a work of the imagination, resting upon nothing but unprovable assumptions.

We come now to the view, held and taught by many modern expositors of good repute, that the week which came next after the 69th week from the starting point, and which was in fact the 70th actual week, as time is ordinarily reckoned, is not to be taken as the 70th week of the prophecy; but that the prophetic period is to be regarded as having been interrupted at the end of the 69th week, "the clock of prophecy having stopped." They hold that some period of seven years yet in the indefinite future is to be taken (when it comes) and added to the 69 weeks now past to make up the complete number of 70. Or, as it is sometimes expressed, this entire age of over 1900 years, comes in as a "parenthesis" between the 69th and the 70th week of the prophetic period. We deem this view to be erroneous, and believe we can show clearly that it is not supported by, but is contrary to, the testimony of Scripture. We maintain that the 70th week of the prophecy occurred just where we would expect to find the 70th number of any series, and that is next after the 69th; or in other words that the 70th actual or historical week was also the 70th prophetic week.

The idea that the 70th week of the prophecy is detached from its companions and is relegated to the distant future, is a necessary corollary of the idea already referred to, namely, that the "he" of verse 27 (Daniel 9) refers, not to Christ, but to a future Antichrist. Manifestly those two ideas stand or fall together; for if verse 27 relates to Christ, then the last week. followed immediately after the 69th; but if it relates to Antichrist, or a coming Roman prince, then it is yet future.

Therefore, all the facts and reasons we have given in proof that verse 27 speaks of Christ, and all the facts and reasons given to show that the prince that is to come of verse 26 was Titus, avail equally to prove that the 70th week joined directly on to the 69th. And conversely, all the facts and reasons we are now about to set forth in proof that the 70th week was indeed one of the "seventy," and not a detached and remote period, avail equally to prove that verse 27 refers to Christ.

We would point out to begin with that the words "Seventy weeks are determined," etc., are words of clear and certain meaning. They are just the words which would be used by one who wished to be understood as saying that, within the measure of 70 weeks, the six things specified in Daniel 9:24 would happen. If the speaker meant something very different, even that the specified things would not occur for more than two thousand years, then manifestly the words used by him could serve only to mislead those who trusted in them.

Therefore again, as in the case of the clause, "the people of the prince that shall come," we appeal first of all to the words themselves, which are the best evidence of their own meaning.

Never since the world began has a described and "determined" measure of time, expressed in the way always used for that purpose (that is, by stating the number of time units making up the complete measure) been treated according to the view we are now discussing. Never has a specified number of time units, making up a described stretch of time, been taken to mean anything but continuous or consecutive time units. The Bible usage in this regard will be shown presently. If, therefore, the period of the "seventy weeks" be an exception to a rule so universal and so necessary, we should at least require Of those who maintain that view such clear and convincing proof as to leave no room for doubt.

But what do we find? There is no proof of any sort in support of the idea referred to; but, on the contrary, the 70th week of the prophecy is tied to the other 69 by at least seven unbreakable bands. Six are found in verse 24, and a seventh in verse 27. This will be shown later on.

We ask careful attention to the following points:

1. Where periods of time are given beforehand in the prophecies of the Bible they always mean that the time units composing the period named are continuous? This must be so, else the prediction would serve only to deceive those who believed it. We have no other way of describing and limiting a period of time than by stating the number of time units (hours, days, months, or years) contained therein. It is therefore a necessary law of language that the time units be understood as being connected together without a break.

As a most pertinent example of this, let us consider the period of seventy years, with which the period of seventy weeks of years is so closely connected. God had foretold to Jeremiah that "after seventy years be accomplished at Babylon, I will visit you, and perform My good word toward you, in causing you to return to this place" (Jeremiah 29:10). From this word Daniel "understood the number of Years whereof the word of the Lord came to Jeremiah the prophet"; and thereupon he set his face to seek the fulfillment of that promise. Have not we exactly the same reason to understand that the "seventy weeks" of years mean what they appear to mean, that Daniel had for understanding that the words "seventy years" were to be taken in accordance with their plain and obvious meaning?

Surely the two instances are exactly alike. Can we even imagine such a thing as that God, in giving that promise to Jeremiah, intended that the seventieth year of the predicted period that in which the captivity of Israel was to be returned was to be separated from the other sixty-nine, and postponed for say five hundred years? Would not Daniel, in that case, have been miserably deceived through simply believing the Word of God? For obviously, everything depended upon that seventieth year, without which the period would not be one of "seventy years." Take away the seventieth year, and a plain simple statement becomes utterly devoid of meaning. Have we then any more right or reason to imagine that the last week of the seventy that in which the six great things, of Daniel 9:24 were to be accomplished is to be separated from the other sixty-nine, and postponed for a score of centuries? We submit to every candid mind that the two cases are exactly parallel, and that the same principle of interpretation must be applied to the seventy weeks of years, as to the seventy years. And the more so are we bound to apply the same principle of interpretation to both because there is manifestly an intended parallel between the seventy years which ended with the decree of Cyrus, and the seven times seventy years which began at that great event. For just as the ending of the captivity of Judah in the seventieth year was necessary "that the word of the Lord might be fulfilled," so likewise the accomplishment of the six things predicted in Daniel 9:24 must take place in the seventieth week of years, else the prophecy would utterly fail, and the word of the Lord would be falsified. That those six things did take place, one and all, in the seventieth consecutive week from the starting point of the prophetic period, is a fact which cannot be disputed. To this we will come later on.

Furthermore, in every other case in Scripture where God has foretold the measure of time within which a specified thing was to happen, the time measure so indicated was intended to be taken in its plain and ordinary sense. We give some examples:

1.) The 430 years sojourning of Abraham's posterity, whereof God had spoken to him (Genesis 15:13; Exodus 12:40; Galatians 3:17) were accomplished to a day (Exodus 12:41–42).

2.) The seven years of plenty and seven years of famine, which Joseph foretold, were fulfilled according to the plain meaning of the words (Genesis 45:6).

3.) The forty years wanderings of the Israelites in the wilderness, which God appointed as a punishment for their unbelief (Numbers 14:34), were forty consecutive years.

But let us take a stronger illustration. Our Lord, in foretelling His own death, declared again and again that "the third day," or "in three days", or "after three days", He would rise again. Those expressions all mean one and the same thing, and would never be taken in any sense but one. Suppose, however, that some ingenious person should now come forward with the idea that Christ did not rise from the dead on the third consecutive day after His death, but that His resurrection is yet future; and suppose he should endeavor to make the words of Christ agree with this view by saying that the third day, on which He was to rise, did not follow immediately after the other two, but there was an unmentioned "parenthesis" of about two thousand years in between, would he not have for his view as much foundation in the words of Scripture as those who would insert a "parenthesis" of two thousand years between the 69th and 70th week of Gabriel's prophecy?

In reply to this argument one might say: "But we have other proof that the third consecutive day was meant, in that Christ actually arose on the third consecutive day." That fact does indeed help to show the meaning of the words "three days," though it does not impart the meaning to them; and likewise in the case we are considering, the meaning of the words "seventy weeks" is further established by the fact that the six things which were to take place within that period actually happened in the seventieth consecutive week from the starting point.

We are bold, therefore, to lay it down as an absolute rule, admitting of no exceptions, that when a definite measure of time or space is specified by the number of units composing it, within which a certain event is to happen or a certain thing is to be found, the units of time or space which make up that measure are to be understood as running continuously and successively. "Seventy years" would invariably mean seventy continuous years; "seventy weeks" would mean seventy continuous weeks; "seventy miles" would mean seventy continuous miles.

If, for example, one journeying along a road were informed that, within seventy miles from a given point he would come upon certain specified things, as a hill, a tower, a stream, a mill, and the like, there is manifestly but one sense in which he could understand the statement. Suppose in such a case that he should proceed on his way for 69 miles without meeting any of the specified things, would he not confidently expect to find them in the one remaining mile of the 70? Suppose, however, he should traverse that mile without coming upon any of those things, would he not have a right to say he had been grossly and intentionally deceived? And would it set the matter right for the one who made the deceptive statement to say that the 70th mile he had in mind did not join on the 69th, but was two thousand miles further on?

We say the deception in such case would, be intentional; for if one uses an expression which has a definite and well-settled meaning, but gives to it in his own mind a very different meaning, which he keeps to himself, he can have had no other purpose than to mislead those who might act upon his words.

2. We have thus far appealed only to the plain and obvious meaning of the words "seventy weeks are determined upon thy people and upon thy holy city to finish the transgression," etc. But there is much more in this prophecy to bind the last week of the Seventy firmly to the other sixty-nine. The 69 weeks brought us "unto the Messiah," but not to His death, by which Israel "finished the transgression." In order that there should be not the slightest uncertainty as to this, the prophecy says, "And after the three score and two weeks shall Messiah be cut off." Thus the 69 weeks are nothing, except years which must elapse a blank space of time— whereas the 70th week is everything to the purpose of fulfilling the

six predictions of verse 24. If then, we know when the Messiah was cut off, we know when the six things of verse 24 were accomplished. And we do know, both by the words of the prophecy, and also by the information given in the Gospel according to John, that Christ was crucified within the "week" (seven years) following His anointing and manifestation to Israel. We know, in other words, that he was "cut off" in the seventieth week counting in the ordinary way from the given starting point. And this would be true regardless of what decree be taken as that starting point. This double witness, that of the prophecy itself and that of the Gospel records, puts the matter beyond all doubt. By means thereof we know to a certainty that none of the six great things foretold in verse 24 happened within the sixty-nine weeks, but that each and all of them came to pass within the week which came next thereafter, that is to say in the seventieth consecutive week from the starting point. Nothing could be better established upon clear scriptural evidence than this.

This matter, however, is important enough to warrant our dwelling a while longer upon it. In view of the facts stated above no one will or can deny that the crucifixion occurred in the 70th week from the starting point of the prophecy. The proof of this is absolute. It only remains then to point out that the crucifixion of Christ accomplished the predictions of verse 24. That also is, we should suppose, a fact which is not reasonably open to dispute. An attempt, however, has been made to escape the force of the evidence of verse 24 by saying that it refers to the time when Israel as a nation will enter into the benefits of the death and resurrection of Christ. But the words of verse 24 will not bear such an interpretation. They plainly declare that, within the measure of 70 weeks of the history of Daniel's people and city, certain things would take place. The verse says not a word about the time when the Jewish nation should enter into the benefit of the atonement. It speaks definitely of the time of the happening of the specified events, quite regardless of whether the Israelites as a nation Should ever enter into the benefits thereof. A new lease of existence was about to be given to the nation and city, and Daniel was informed, to his great distress, that 70 weeks of that renewed existence to people and city were allotted for them "to finish the transgression" etc.

Take for instance the words "to make reconciliation (or atonement) for iniquity." There can be no uncertainty as to the meaning of this. To deny that reconciliation (or atonement) was fully and finally completed when Christ died and rose again would be to deny the very foundation of Christianity. Moreover, the true Israel—the believing part of Daniel's people—did enter immediately into the benefits of the atonement. Beyond all question, then, the 70th week of the prophecy was that in which Christ died and rose and ascended into heaven.

3. The case is, however, still further strengthened by the corroborating evidence of Daniel 9:27. We have found a perfect fulfillment of this verse (confirming the covenant with many, and causing the ancient system of offerings to cease) in the atoning death of the Lord Jesus Christ; and we have shown that this was a work supremely great and glorious in the eyes of God. But more than this, the things predicted in verse 27 were the very means whereby those predicted in verse 24 were to be accomplished.

Thus the first and last parts of the prophecy are bound firmly together. It is impossible to detach the 70th week from the other 69 without destroying the prophecy as a whole. For if the 70th consecutive week from the starting point was not the 70th of the prophetic period, then none of the six predicted things came to pass within that period. In that view they all happened in an unmentioned gap between the 69 (which brought us "unto the Messiah") and the 70th which is yet future. Thus, according to this view, the prophecy has been completely falsified.

4. God has given a test whereby His people are to prove the

sayings of one who claims to be a prophet of the Lord. For it is written that, if the things predicted by the prophet "follow not nor come to pass, that is the thing which the Lord hath not spoken, but the prophet hath spoken it presumptuously" (Deuteronomy 18:21; see also John 14:29). Tested by this rule, the prophecy of the seventy weeks must be interpreted according to its plain and ordinary sense, else those who looked for the fulfillment of it in its time would have been fully justified. in rejecting it as the thing which the Lord had not spoken.

Why the Seventy Weeks Are Divided Into Three Parts

The fact that the last week is mentioned separately is often referred to as if it afforded ground for postponing it to a future era. But that circumstance affords no reason whatever for inserting a period of time, long or short, between the 69th and 70th weeks. The message of the angel also makes separate mention of the first "seven weeks" from the rest. But no one seems to have seen in that circumstance a reason for inserting a few millenniums between those two parts of the seventy weeks. Why then apply a different rule to the last week, the most important of all the seventy, and without which the period would have no significance?

Likewise the Lord Jesus mentioned "the third day" (after His death) separately from the other two. But does that afford any reason for inserting say a century or two between the second day and the third?

Surely, the transcendent importance of the events of that "third day," and of those of the final "week" of the seventy, affords reason enough for their separate mention.

The entire period is laid out in this way: The first portion consisted of seven sevens of "troublous times," within which the rebuilding of the temple and of the city, with its street and wall, were to be accomplished; then follow sixty-two sevens to the manifestation of Christ to Israel, that is to the time when Jesus of Nazareth was "anointed with the Holy Ghost and with power," and was publicly proclaimed to all the people of Israel by John the Baptist; and then comes the seventieth and last week, "in the midst" of which "Messiah was cut off," thus accomplishing God's great purpose in redemption, and fulfilling all the things predicted in verse 24.

The middle period of sixty-two weeks, within which no prophetic events were to occur, coincides with that silent stretch of years between Malachi and John the Baptist between "the word of the Lord to Israel by Malachi" and the day when "the word of God came unto John the son of Zachariah in the wilderness" (Luke 3:2) a period during which there was no voice front God to His people, and no happenings in which His hand is seen working in their affairs.

It is sometimes attempted to justify the detaching and postponing of the seventieth week of Daniel by reference to the fact that when, in the synagogue at Nazareth, the Lord read from Isaiah 61, He stopped in the very midst of a passage (the next words being, "and the day of vengeance"), and said, "This day is this scripture fulfilled in your ears," thus implying that the part He did not read was yet future (Luke 4:16–21). But it needs no great discernment to see that there is a wide difference between the two cases. For, in the first place, Isaiah had not said that the matters foretold by him were to happen within a certain measure of time. He said nothing at all as to that; whereas the time when the specified events were to take place is the very essence of the prophecy of the seventy weeks. But what is equally important, we have the word of the Lord Jesus declaring (or at least implying) that only so much of Isaiah's prophecy as He had read in their ears was fulfilled at that time. But we have no word or hint from Him, or from any source to which we should give heed, to the effect that the seventieth week of Daniel is yet in the future.

The Overspreading of Abominations (Daniel 9:27)

We come now to the last part of Daniel 9:27, which, as given in our AV, reads thus: "And for the overspreading of abominations he shall make it desolate, even until the consummation, and that determined, shall be poured upon the desolate" (margin, desolator).

These words are admittedly obscure. Nevertheless, even without help from other translations, it is at least clear that the main prediction here is that the city and temple were to be made a desolation, and that the desolation was to be for a protracted period "even until the consummation" (or end). Moreover it is also implied that at the end there should be restoration for the city: and that, at the time of the end, that which had been "determined" was to be "poured upon the desolator." This last prediction points to the outpouring of God's wrath upon the destroying agencies, as foretold in detail in the Book of Revelation (see Revelation 11:18, etc.).

This portion of the prophecy was repeated in substance, and in much plainer language, by the Lord Jesus in His Olivet discourse, as reported in Luke 21. He there speaks of "the days of vengeance" (which corresponds to the words "he shall make it desolate"), and He further declares that "Jerusalem shall be trodden under foot of the Gentiles, until the times of the Gentiles be fulfilled" (Luke 21:22, 24); which corresponds with the words, "even until the consummation" (or end).

We would also call attention to a parallel between verses 26–27 (of Daniel 9). The first part of verse 26 foretells that after the threescore and two weeks Messiah shall be cut off; and the first part of verse 27 contains the parallel prediction; "And He shall confirm the covenant with many", "and in the midst of the week He shall cause the sacrifice and oblation to cease". The second part of each verse speaks of the desolations of the city and sanctuary. This parallel affords further confirmation of the correctness of our reading of the prophecy.

The words "for the overspreading of abominations" are very obscure, and many suggestions as to their meaning have been offered. We shall not discuss these, for the reason that the Septuagint translation gives a clear rendering, and our Lord's adoption of it puts the authoritative stamp of His approval upon it. According to that version "the abomination of desolation" was to be upon (or to come against) the temple, that is, for its destruction. In other words there was to come an agency or force (which God terms an "abomination", which was to make the place a "desolation".

The Lord Jesus Christ used the same expression when, in warning His disciples of the approaching destruction of Jerusalem by the armies of Titus, He said: "When ye therefore shall see the abomination of desolation, spoken of by Daniel the prophet, stand in the holy place (whoso readeth, let him understand), then let them which be in Judea flee into the mountain", etc,

This reference by our Lord to the last verse of the Seventy Weeks' prophecy is a connecting link between that scripture and His own prophecy on Mount Olivet. The great value of this connecting link will appear later on.

The word rendered "abomination" means, according to the Hebrew and Greek lexicons, anything that is peculiarly loathsome or detestable. Hence it is sometimes used of an idol. But this is a secondary meaning, and it does not appear to be used in that sense in the New Testament. In Luke 16:15 it is applied to the covetousness of the Pharisees; in Titus 1:16 it is applied to those who deny God in their works; in Revelation 21:8 and 27 it is also applied to persons who do wickedly. Hence there is nothing either in Daniel 9:27 or in Matthew 24:15 to warrant the idea that those prophecies speak of idol worship being set up in some Jewish temple. Moreover Christ had disowned the temple at Jerusalem (Matthew 23:38) calling it "your house"; and henceforth it is not recognized as the House of

God. Much less will recognition be given to a temple such as may be put up by the apostate Zionists. On the other hand, the Word of God makes it quite plain, as we hope to show later on, that the "abomination, which was to make the city and sanctuary a desolation", was the army of Titus, "the people of the prince that shall come".

We have now completed our examination, clause by clause, of the wonderful prophecy of the Seventy Weeks. We have found—and without going beyond the Scriptures for our proofs a clear and satisfactory meaning for every statement, a meaning which is consistent with the scope and design of the prophecy as a whole. That prophecy has to do with the greatest of all subjects, the coming of Christ to Israel, and His rejection and crucifixion by Israel, with the marvelous consequences of His sacrifice for sins, and His victory over death and the grave.

We have based nothing upon conjecture or surmise, and have not found it necessary to appeal to systems of chronology , which are admittedly defective and uncertain nor to rely upon any human authorities.

Moreover, the evidence produced in support of our conclusions is of such a simple sort that "the common people" can easily understand it and appreciate the force thereof.

And finally, inasmuch as the proofs advanced herein are all taken from the Scriptures and the passages are cited, the reader has it in his power to bring all our conclusions to the test of Scripture, and this it is his responsibility to do. On the other hand (and we attach much importance to this) the current. interpretations, which fix the starting point of the Seventy Weeks at a date later than the decree of Cyrus, are each and all based upon some chronological scheme, built up from heathen traditions, obscure historical records, guesses at eclipses, and astronomical calculations, which the ordinary reader has no means whatever for verifying.

The Decree of Cyrus Again

In concluding this part of our study we would again call attention to that great historical landmark, the decree of King Cyrus, which stands, by God's express appointment, between two prophetic eras, and marks the ending of the one and the beginning of the other. The first era was the seventy years of "desolation," whereby the people were punished for their "transgression" against the law and the prophets. The other was seventy times seven years, within which they were "to finish the transgression" by the rejection of the gospel of the Kingdom, and by crucifying Him who came bringing the good tidings and publishing peace (Isaiah 52:7; Acts 10:36).

It was indeed an extraordinary decree. For first it was plainly foretold by Isaiah, by whom also the name of the monarch who was to make it was given; second, when the time was come for "the going forth" thereof, that monarch became the sole ruler of the world; and third, God Himself stirred up the spirit of Cyrus to make the decree, and to send it forth by proclamation throughout all his dominions.

It should be noted in this connection that inasmuch as God had said that the Seventy Weeks were to begin from "the going forth" of the commandment to restore and to build Jerusalem, the inspired record is careful to call our attention to the fact that Cyrus not only gave the word or commandment, but also "made a proclamation throughout all his kingdom" (Ezra 1:1).

These facts all bear witness to the exceptional importance of this epoch-making decree; and they also afford strong assurance that in it we have the true starting point for the prophetic period of seventy weeks. It was indeed a new start like a resurrection from the dead for Jerusalem and the people of Israel. It was the rebirth of the nation.

Nothing in all the history of the chosen people, with the one exception of the Exodus from Egypt, is made so much of in the

Old Testament as the return from Babylon. It was foretold by the prophets, sung by the psalmists, recorded by the historians. It stands out with such prominence upon the page of inspiration that it is a, wonder how any students of Scripture should have failed to grasp its significance, and should have gone groping about for some other decree to serve as a starting point for that divinely given measuring line which was to reach "unto Messiah the Prince."

The Remainder of the Seventieth Week

At this point in our exposition it appears desirable to notice a question which has arisen in the minds of some in regard to the fraction of the seventieth week remaining after the death, resurrection and ascension of Christ, whereby the predictions of verse 24 (of Daniel 9), as well as those of the first half of verse 27, were fulfilled. To some it seems that our exposition leaves three and a half years not accounted for if, however, we give attention to the terms of the prophecy we will clearly see that it affords no warrant for such a question. Those who ask it have evidently failed to take into consideration the fact that, in this prophecy, the unit of the time measure is a heptad, not a year. If we think of the Seventieth "Week" as a period of seven years, then it would indeed appear as if there were three years and over which were not accounted for by the exposition. But if, on the other hand, we take the. prophecy as it is given, that is to say, in heptads, not years, then it will be clearly seen that all the seventy heptads are accounted for. For our exposition simply follows the terms of the prophecy, which are quite plain, and which locate certain events "in the midst of" the last heptad, but do not locate any events at the end thereof. If, therefore, any part of the determined period is unaccounted for, it is the prophecy itself, and not this writer's exposition thereof, that is chargeable. But the fact is that the prophecy accounts first for sixty-nine heptads (which reached "unto the Messiah") and then it accounts specifically for the one remaining heptad, and for the whole of it, by telling what was to happen in the midst thereof. Thus the prophecy (and the exposition which simply follows it) leaves no part of the prophetic period unaccounted for.

Those who raise the above question must further assume that some predicted event was to mark the very end of the last "week" of the determined period. But a glance at the prophecy itself will suffice to show that such assumption is contrary to its terms. For by the express terms of the prophecy the climax of the things predicted in it that is to say, the death, resurrection and ascension of Christ—was to take place, not at the end of the last week, but "in the midst of the week" (verse 27).

According to verse 24, which gives the substance of the prophecy in condensed form, six specified things were to happen within a measured period of seventy heptads, starting, as appears by verse 25, from the going forth of the decree to restore and to build Jerusalem), which things required for their accomplishment that Christ should die, should rise again, and should ascend into heaven. From the fact that seventy heptads are mentioned it would be reasonable to infer that the full number (seventy) would be necessary to the complete fulfillment of the prophecy; and this inference is confirmed and made a certainty by what immediately follows; for the next verse disposes of sixty-nine weeks, which reach only "unto the Messiah", leaving all the six predicted things yet to take place. Hence they must needs take place in the seventieth heptad.

But there is nothing so far to indicate in what part of the remaining week those things were to be accomplished. Therefore, had they happened at the beginning thereof, the prophecy thus far would have been perfectly fulfilled, leaving no part of the seventy weeks unaccounted for. For it must be remembered that we have not to do with years but with heptads. But the last verse of the prophecy is more specific. It contains the definite statement that the great events which were to fulfill the predictions of verse 24 would happen "in the midst of" the last heptad. And, in agreement with this, it appears clearly by the Gospel of John that the crucifixion of our Lord took place in the midst of the heptad which began with the baptism of Christ and His manifestation to Israel (John 1:31), which began, in other words, at the end of the sixty-nine heptads which reached unto the Messiah. Thus the entire period specified in the prophecy is fully accounted for.

It is pertinent in this connection to point out that the Scriptures habitually disregard fractional remainders of a time unit, whether it be a day, a week, a month, or a year. Thus, if it were foretold that a thing (such as the return out of Babylon) would happen in a certain year, its occurrence in the first month of that year would be a perfect fulfillment of the prediction, and the remaining eleven months would be simply disregarded as being without significance for the purpose of the prophecy.

Or to take another example, our Lord declared to His disciples concerning His approaching death and resurrection that "in three days", and "after three days", He would rise again. If, therefore, He arose the very first hour of the third day, His prediction was fulfilled, the remaining hours of that day being without significance so far as the prediction is concerned. They do not have to be accounted for.

For one can readily see that if a prophecy should call for the happening of a certain event on a specified day, and the thing were to happen about noon of that day, the prophecy would be perfectly fulfilled, and there would be no question at all as to what becomes of the remaining half day. Precisely so it is with the Seventy Weeks, for it obviously makes no difference that the time unit is in this instance a "week" instead of a day. But the prophecy we are studying is more definite than the supposed illustration, in that it declares specifically that the things foretold would occur in the midst of the last week.

Several able expositors, including Dr. Pusey and Dr. Taylor, to whose works we have already referred, offer the suggestion that the fraction of a "week," which was unexpired at the date of the Crucifixion, measured the time (ending with the martyrdom of Stephen) during which the gospel was preached exclusively to the Jews. But inasmuch as the date of Stephen's death is not known with certainty we can accept the above only as a possibility. In our opinion the prophecy does not call for a specific event to mark the end of the last week, though such there may have been, and quite possibly the death of Stephen was that event.

God's Prophetic Time Measure

Because of the great importance of the subject of God's prophetic time measure, and of all that depends upon it, we return to it again, for the purpose of giving a concise statement of our conclusions in regard thereto, and of the reasons on which they are based.

The message of Gabriel, found in Daniel 9:24–27, differs from all other prophecies in several particulars, and chiefly in that it contains a measuring line of "determined" length, whereby the years were to be measured from a given event (one of the great landmarks in Jewish history) down to the coming of the Messiah and the accomplishment of His work of redemption. The full length of that line was seventy "heptads," i. e., sevens (or "weeks") of years, making a total length of 490 years. The declared purpose of the prophecy (verse 24) was to foretell the exact time of the occurrence of certain things which are of supreme importance to mankind.

The prophecy reveals, moreover, that the last heptad, or "week", of the seventy was to be the most important era of all time, for that in that "week" the Messiah was to be cut off and have nothing (which act of wickedness by the Jews would "finish the transgression" and bring judgment upon them); and for that in it also the new covenant "with many" was to be confirmed in His blood (Matthew 26:28), the numerous sacrifices and oblations of the law were to be displaced by the "one sacrifice" of Christ (Hebrews 10:9), an end was to be made of sins, reconciliation (or atonement) was to be made for iniquity, everlasting righteousness was to be brought in, and the most holy (place) was to be anointed. One has only to read with proper care the plain words of this great prophecy to see that it comes to its climax in the "week" in which the death and resurrection of Christ and the coming of the Holy Spirit were to take place, that is to say, in the last, week of the seventy; and hence that to remove that week from its place in the series, and to "postpone" it to a time far in the future, simply makes havoc of the entire prophecy.

Furthermore, in the light of this sure word of prophecy it is easy to see that, when the Lord Jesus began preaching in Galilee, saying "The time is fulfilled, and the kingdom of God is at hand; repent ye, and believe the good news" (Mark 1:14–15), He was referring to "the time" measured out or "determined" in this prophecy, and that He was calling upon the people of Israel to "repent" and "believe", as the condition of receiving the new birth (John 3:3, 5) and thereby entering into the salvation of the kingdom of God.

True it is that most of the people, and nearly all their leaders, refused to repent and believe the good news; and the reason was that the Messiah they were expecting was to be a temporal prince and a conquering hero, and the kingdom they looked for was to be the restoring of earthly dominion to Israel, and the setting up again of the throne of David at Jerusalem.

It is impossible, however, that, when the Lord said, "The time is fulfilled, and the kingdom of God is at hand", He could have been speaking of the restoration of the kingdom of Israel; for "the time" of that event (assuming, which we do not admit, that it is ever to occur) has not been revealed to anyone, not even to the Son of God Himself (Matthew 24:36). This is proved conclusively by the Lord's reply to the question put to Him by His disciples after

His resurrection) "Lord, wilt Thou at this time restore again the kingdom to Israel?" His reply being, "It is not for you to know the times or the seasons, which the Father has put in His own power" (Acts 1:6–7). But it is quite the other way in respect to the kingdom of God, which is "righteousness, and peace, and joy in the Holy Ghost" (Romans 14:17), or in other words, the day of salvation and the acceptable year of the Lord; for that is an era whose "time" was fixed in the counsels of God, and definitely foretold in the prophecy of the seventy weeks, besides being announced by John the Baptist and the Lord Himself. Or, to state the matter in different terms, the "time" of the first coming of Christ was definitely "determined" and foretold, and therefore it is written that "when the fullness of the time was come, God sent forth His Son, to redeem them that were under the law" (Galatians 4:4–5); but the "time" of His second coming is kept secret in the unrevealed counsels of the Father.

It should be specially noted in this connection that one of the most important uses of this prophecy is as a witness against the Jews; for it proves conclusively that Jesus of Nazareth, Who came at the predicted time, and Who accomplished the predicted things—i.e., making atonement for iniquity, bringing in everlasting righteousness, confirming the new covenant, taking away the sacrifices of the law, etc. is the true Messiah. For now that the "determined seventy weeks", within which the Messiah was to come, and to be "cut off" are long past, it is absolutely impossible that one can come and fulfill the prophecy. Hence the time element is of vital importance.

But this use of the prophecy is completely frustrated by the current idea that God's measuring line is an elastic one, and that it was intended—not to measure seventy weeks of years, as all simple-minded persons have understood, but—to be stretched out to a length of thousands of years, and that the things predicted in verses 24 and 27 are not even yet fulfilled. Inasmuch as the evident

Are The Seventy Weeks Consecutive?

purpose of the prophecy was to limit the "time" within which those vital things upon which the salvation of men depends, were to be accomplished, it follows that, to postpone the seventieth week to the distant future, makes shipwreck of the entire prophecy.

The alteration of God's measuring line whereof we are speaking has been effected by the strange expedient of inserting many centuries of time (more than nineteen hundred years thus far) between the sixty-ninth and the seventieth week. And the result is that, instead of a definite and "determined" measuring line of 490 years, we have one which already is over 2,400 years in length, and is growing longer every day.

Nothing can be more evident than that the usefulness of a measuring line depends firstly, upon its accuracy, and secondly, upon the user's knowledge of its length. Hence to tamper with and alter the dimensions of a measure or gauge of time or space, or to change the location of any of the markings thereon, is to destroy its usefulness. In the case of the measuring line of Daniel 9:24–27 there are two intermediate markings. One is at the end of seven heptads, which indicates the finishing of the street and wall of the city, and also apparently the ending of Old Testament prophecy in the days of Malachi; the other is at the end of the 69th heptad, which reached "unto the Messiah, the Prince." This subdivision of the entire period of seventy weeks has the (evidently designed) effect of setting apart in a special way the final week; and the obvious reason for this is to concentrate attention upon that particular era of time within the brief limits whereof were to occur the most stupendous events of all the ages, namely, the crucifixion and resurrection of the Divine Redeemer, and the coming of the Holy Ghost. Thus the climax of the prophecy falls within the last week; and it follows that to remove that week out of its proper place is to make havoc of the Scripture. And this is not reasonably open to dispute by any who believe that Jesus of Nazareth is the promised Messiah; for it is certain that, if the Messiah did come at the end of 69 weeks, as foretold in verse 251 then He was "cut off" within the text ensuing week of years, and that in that next ensuing week (the seventieth of actual historic time) He fulfilled all the predictions of verses 21 and 27.

But, not only has God's measuring line been altered as already stated, but it has been changed from a line of determined length to one of indeterminate length. (It would really seem as if the word "determined" had been inserted in the angel's message as a caution and warning against this very mutilation). For, according to the idea we are discussing, the number of years to be inserted between the sixty-ninth and seventieth week is still an unknown quantity. The last week, when thus detached from its 69 companions, does not belong to any known series whatever. This, in our opinion, not only destroys the usefulness of the prophecy, but turns it into an absurdity. For a measure of time or space, even when tampered with, is still a measure of fixed quantity, though deceitful because inaccurate. But a measure which has no limits at all, one which continues to enlarge its dimensions, which, from an original length of 490 years, has already been stretched to 2400, and is still elongating itself, is not a measuring line at all. It is an absurdity.

Finally, it is clear beyond all dispute that the exposition we are discussing detaches the predicted events of verses 24 and 27 entirely from the prophetic seventy weeks, of which they constitute the very soul and essence, and leaves them to happen whenever they may. Indeed, it severs the predictions of verse 27 from Christ altogether, and transfers them to some future Antichrist, though of that feature of the case we need not speak at present. It follows that, just as the Jews, having closed their eyes to the coming of Messiah the Prince at the predicted time, and to the complete fulfillment of this and other prophecies in His day (Acts 13:27) by His being "cut off," are vaguely looking for a fulfilment of their expectations at some indefinite time in the future, even so the expositors referred to , having closed their eyes to the complete fulfilment of verses 24 and 27 in the seventieth actual week from the given starting point, are looking vaguely and vainly for some other fulfilment, at an indefinite future time, in the imaginary doings of some Antichrist, who they say (but without a word of Scripture to support them) will make a bargain with "many" Jews about renewing their temple sacrifices, and will break that supposed bargain after three and a half years. The only difference is that, whereas the Jews have thrown the prophecy overboard completely, the expositors referred to are trying to show respect for it, and to make it agree with their interpretation, by the expedient of carrying the last week of the seventy all down the centuries of our era, purposing to find a place for it on the chart of time when their imaginary fulfilment shall come to pass—if ever.

CHAPTER 8

Daniel's Last Vision

We come now to a prophecy (Daniel 10–12) which is closely related to that of the Seventy Weeks; and forasmuch as this climax of Daniel's visions throws much light upon those which preceded it, and forasmuch also as it is seldom studied as it should be, we propose to examine it with all possible care. It will be found to contain, particularly in the latter part, matters of much importance because of their bearing upon the subject of prophecy in general.

Before entering upon this interesting part of our study, it would be well to notice the relation, one to another, of the four visions which occupy the last six chapters of the Book of Daniel.

The vision of the four beasts of Chapter 7 is the most comprehensive of all. It fills the whole period of time from the rise of the Babylonian empire, figured (as commonly shown in Babylonian sculptures which exist until the present) as a lion having eagles' wings, through that of Medo-Persia, then that of Greece, to and including the entire period of the Roman empire down to the very end thereof, when human government as a whole is to be displaced by the Kingdom of God under the sovereignty of the Son of man. In this vision there are references to "the saints of the Most High," who are persecuted under the fourth beast, but the Jewish nation is not seen at all.

The vision of Chapter 8, that of the ram and the he goat, is much more limited in scope, being confined to the period of the Medo-Persian and Greek empires. This is definitely stated in the explanation given by Gabriel (Daniel 8:20–25) so that we must needs find the fulfillment of all the details of this prophecy during the Persian and Macedonian eras. It fits into and fills out the broad outline of the preceding vision.

The vision of Chapter 9 is yet more definite and specific. It too fits into the broad outline of Chapter 7, but it has to do mainly with the affairs of Daniel's people and city down to the destruction of the latter and the scattering of the former. The connection between this vision and the last one of the entire series is very close. In fact the additional revelations contained in chapters 10, 11 and 12 were given to Daniel in response to his earnest prayer (Daniel 10:12), in order to enlighten him as to matters which were to befall his people during the period of the seventy weeks which had then just begun (for the supplemental vision was "in the third year of Cyrus, King of Persia", (Daniel 10:1). A new era of national life for Israel had now begun; and this second term of Jewish history, starting with the return from Babylon in the first year of Cyrus (BC 457)[2] is called "the latter days", to distinguish it from the first era of Israel's national existence, which is called "the former days". This will be more fully explained later on. The prophecy of the Seventy Weeks had filled Daniel's soul with grief; for while it foretold the coming of the Messiah, and gave the time thereof, instead of showing that His advent would mean deliverance and prosperity for Daniel's people, it declared that Messiah would be cut off, and that a terrible judgment was to follow. So Daniel mourned and chastened himself for three full weeks, while he set his heart to understand the matter. In response to this desire an angelic being of wondrous beauty and glory was sent to him, who spoke to him, saying: *"O Daniel, a man greatly beloved, understand the words that I speak unto thee, and stand upright; for unto thee am I now sent."*

By this it clearly appears that this fresh communication from heaven was for the express purpose of enabling Daniel to understand matters concerning his people which had not been disclosed by the prophecy of the Seventy Weeks.

Furthermore, upon carefully examining this new communication to Daniel (which occupies chapters 11 and 12) it is found to be a complete account, in the form of a continuous historical narrative, of the second period of Jewish national existence, from the reign of Cyrus (when the vision was given) to the destruction of Jerusalem by the Roman armies under Titus. And not only so but and this is a matter of the deepest interest the fulfillment of every statement in this long prophetic narrative is found to be recorded in histories of indisputable authenticity, which have come down to our day. We, therefore, regard this part of our study (Daniel 10, 11 and 12) as of exceptional importance and interest. For that reason we would ask special attention to it, and particularly to the exposition of the latter part of Chapter 11 and first part of Chapter 12.

Daniel 11

Daniel 11 makes difficult reading for those who are unacquainted with the history of the times to which the prophecy recorded therein relates. The latter part of the chapter has proved difficult also for expositors, among whom there is a wide difference of opinion as to the persons and events referred to. Down to the end of verse 30 there is practical agreement among expositors as to the meaning of the prophecy, and the events by which its several predictions were fulfilled. We are not aware of any sound and competent teacher who does not see, in verses 1–30, the main outlines of Persian history, the rise of Alexander of Macedon, the division of his empire between his four generals, the incessant wars between the Seleucids (kings of Syria, "the north") and the Ptolemies (kings of Egypt, "the south"), and the career of Antiochus Epiphanes that odious persecutor of the Jews, spoken of as the "vile person" (verse 21). Indeed, so closely does the history of those times correspond with the prophecy, that Porphyry and other infidels have cited that correspondence as proof that the prophecy of Daniel must have been written after the reign of Antiochus Epiphanes.

But there has been a disagreement as to the application of verses 31–35, and as to who is meant by "the people that do know their God," who "understand" and "instruct many." Some of the older commentators, as Bishop Newton, leap over some centuries at this point, and locate the fulfilment in the times of the gospel, making "the people who do know their God," etc. to be the apostles and preachers of our era. But this is quite inadmissible, according to the plain terms of the prophecy itself, as we shall point out. And indeed the great body of competent expositors finds the fulfillment of these verses (31–35) in the doings of that remarkable family of Asmoneans, generally called the Maccabees, who arose for the deliverance of the Jews in the reign of Antiochus, and who faithfully served their people as rulers and priests for 130 years. We shall presently show, by authentic histories of those times, that this part of the prophecy was fulfilled with literal exactitude.

Verse 35 brings us to within half a century of the nativity of Christ, up to which date the prophetic narrative refers, in regular order, to all the main points of Jewish history, passing over nothing of importance. This creates a strong presumption that the prophecy, in its remaining portion, continues to follow the course of Jewish history without any break. For it is impossible to conceive of any reason why the narrative should follow the course of events for the greater part of the period of "the latter days," and then, when the most important events of the period were reached, should abruptly break off and fly away to the remote future, passing over a score of centuries at a single bound.

The strongest magnifying glass fails to reveal the slightest sign of such a remarkable "break." On the contrary, the several clauses of the prophecy at this point (see verses 35–36) are directly connected together by the particle "and." If, therefore, the reader, in passing from verse 34 to verse 35 (or, as some say, from verse 35 to verse 36) is carried in the twinkling of an eye across a period of more than two thousand years, there is not a thing in the text to apprize him thereof, or even to suggest such an extraordinary thing. Where those who assert it obtain their information is a deep mystery to us.

We recall again that the one clothed in linen had declared to Daniel that he had come to make him understand what was to befall Daniel's people "in the latter days" (Daniel 10:14). The prophecy makes it perfectly clear that the period here designated as "the latter days" is that second term of Jewish history which began at the restoration from Babylon (two years before this vision was given to Daniel in the third year of Cyrus, (Daniel 10:1) and ended with the destruction of Jerusalem, and the scattering of the people by Titus, in AD 70.

There is little room for doubt as to the meaning of the term "the latter days;" for the angel, after having declared that the purpose of his coming was to inform Daniel of the things which were to happen to his people "in the latter days," began from that very time to tell of the successors of Cyrus on the throne of Persia, of the rise of Alexander the Great, and of events in the reigns of his successors for hundreds of years, next ensuing. This proves conclusively that "the latter days" was this second term of Jewish history following the restoration from Babylon, and makes it impossible to assign any other meaning to it. Moreover, the Scripture contrasts this period with the first period of their history, which it calls "the former days" (Zechariah 8:11), just as it distinguishes the prophets of that first period as "the former prophets" (Zechariah 1:4; 7:7; 7:12).

It would be strange indeed if an account of "the latter days" of the Jewish people, whether the account were historic or prophetic, were to give with detail the chief events thereof from the very beginning down to about 30 years before the birth of Christ, and then suddenly to break off and fly away to a far distant future, ignoring all those greatest events, and without giving the slightest indication of any interruption in the orderly and continuous flow of the narrative.

Of evidence in support of the idea of such a "break" there is absolutely none. The idea rests upon no other basis than that many modern commentators, being unaware of the historical fulfillment of the latter part of this prophecy (notwithstanding that its fulfillment is marvelously complete and exact, as we hope to show) and ignoring the limitations of the prophecy itself, have surmised and contrived a fulfilment which (they say) will take place at the end of this present gospel dispensation. We expect, in the course of our study of this chapter, to show plainly, not only that there is no evidence whatever for the supposed "break" at verse 35 or 36, but that the idea is altogether inadmissible.

The "Thing" Revealed to Daniel

The three visions given to Daniel, all within the space of a few years, (1) that of Chapter 8, the Ram and the He Goat, (2) that of Chapter 9, the Seventy Weeks, and (3) that of Chapter 10–12, "That which is noted in the Scripture of Truth" (Daniel 10:21), all relate to events which were to take place in the new term of Jewish national existence, which began with the going forth of the decree to restore and to build Jerusalem in the first year of Cyrus.

1. As to the first vision, the ram with two horns is declared to be "the kings (or kingdom) of Media and Persia"; and the he goat is declared to be "the king (kingdom) of Greece"; and "the great horn is the first king", i.e., Alexander the Great (Daniel 8:20–21). This vision astonished Daniel, and made him sick with distress, but he did not understand it (Daniel 8:27).

2. A few years later, that is, in the first year of Darius (Daniel 9:1), Daniel became aware of God's purpose, as foretold by Jeremiah, to

bring the captivity of Israel to an end after seventy years. This led him to seek the Lord earnestly by prayer, with fasting and ashes, thereby speaking, and praying, and confessing his own sin and the sin of his people, and making supplication for the people, the city, and the sanctuary of God. The response from heaven to this prayer was the coming of Gabriel to Daniel with the prophecy of the Seventy Weeks. This prophecy also has to do with the era of the Persian, Greek and Roman empires, down to and including the coming and crucifixion of Christ.

    3. The effect of this second vision was to cause still greater distress to Daniel; for although the promised restoration from the captivity of Babylon had come, and the seventy years' desolations of Jerusalem were now ended, here was the prediction that Messiah was to come at a specified time, but instead of being victorious, and setting His people on high over the nations, He was to be "cut off," the city and sanctuary were to be destroyed "as with a flood," and desolations of unmeasured length were determined. Hence we find Daniel, in the third year of Cyrus, mourning three full weeks, during which time he ate no pleasant food, neither did flesh nor wine come into his mouth (Daniel 10:1–3).

    Again there comes to this devoted man of God a response from heaven in the person of a celestial being, from whose words we learn that the object of Daniel's fasting and praying was that he might be given understanding of the previous visions. For the angel said, "Thy words were heard, and I am come for (because of) thy words…Now I am come to make thee understand what shall befall thy people in the latter days" (Daniel 10:11–14). So this long and detailed prophecy, recorded in Chapter 11, was given for the express purpose of making Daniel understand what he had not been able to understand concerning what was to befall his people during the additional term of seventy weeks of national life which had been granted to them.

Thus the great subject of the prophecy is declared to be the history of the people of Israel, for whom Daniel had been interceding. By keeping this fact in view we shall carry along with us a clear light whereby we may be able to explore the terms of this prophecy.

The importance of the "thing" which the angel came to make clear to Daniel is indicated by the pains taken by the former to encourage and strengthen the man greatly beloved, who now was in advanced years, weakened by fasting, and overcome with sorrow (Daniel 9:18–19).

We shall now proceed to show the fulfillment of the details of this prophecy. It is not difficult to do this with the help of reliable histories particularly I and II Maccabees, and Josephus. These are not, of course, inspired writings, but they are authentic and trustworthy histories, which have, in the providence of God, come down to us from ancient times, that by their records the faith of His own people might be encouraged, and that those who reject His Word might be without excuse.

The Persian Era

The first four verses of Daniel 11 foretell events which are familiar matters of history. This shows that the prophecy was to have a very literal fulfillment; and it shows also that the fulfillment was to begin from that very time. For verse 2 declares that four more Persian kings were to arise (after Cyrus). It further foretells that the fourth king would be immensely rich, and that he would stir up all his realm against Greece. This was the famous Xerxes, who, after long preparations in every part of his realm, invaded Greece with a huge army and navy, but was ignominiously defeated by land and sea, thus preparing the way for the downfall of the Persian empire (see Anstey's Bible Chronology, p. 239).

Alexander the Great

Verses 3–4 predict the rise of a mighty king who should rule with great dominion, and accomplish his will. His kingdom, however, was to be broken and divided into four parts, but not to his own posterity. This was literally accomplished in the career of Alexander the Great, who, after his conquest of Persia and of the world, died without children, and whose vast dominions were divided between his four generals. These did not rule "according to his dominion," for their kingdom was again and again "plucked up, even for others beside themselves."

Alexander's Successors

After the partition of Alexander's dominions, the Jewish people came into contact with only two of the four kingdoms which succeeded him the Seleucids, the kings of Syria ("the king of the north") and the Ptolemies, rulers of Egypt ("the king of the south"). These waged incessant warfare against each other, and the Jews suffered in turn from each.

Verses 5–19, inclusive, of Daniel 11 describe the wars and intrigues between the king of the north (Syria) and king of the south (Egypt). (Daniel 11:5-19) At first the kings of Egypt prevailed. The prophecy foretold this; for it says, "And the king of the south shall be strong, and one of his princes; and he shall be strong above him, and have dominion; his dominion shall be a great dominion" (verse 5).

Verse 6 says: "And in the end of years they shall join themselves together" that is, the king of the north and king of the south shall form a league "for the king's daughter of the south shall come to the king of the north to make an agreement; but she shall not retain the power of the arm; neither shall he stand, nor his arm. But she shall be given up, and they that brought her, and he that begat her, and he that strengthened her in these times."

Answering to this very definite prophecy we have historical records of an alliance between the two rival kingdoms, when Ptolemy Philadelphus gave his daughter Berenice in marriage to Antiochus Theos of Syria, upon condition that he should put away his wife, Laodice. But, as foretold in the prophecy, this league did not last; for Ptolemy died soon after, and then Antiochus put away Berenice, and took back his former wife, who subsequently requited him by procuring his murder, and also the murder of Berenice.

The brother of the latter, Ptolemy Euergetes (referred to in the prophecy as "one out of her roots"), undertook to avenge her death by an invasion of Syria, in which he was successful. This appears to be what is foretold in verses 7–9, which tell of one who should "enter into the fortress of the king of the north," and who should "prevail," and should "also carry captives into Egypt, their gods with their princes, and with their precious vessels of silver and of gold."

Antiochus the Great

Later on, however, under Antiochus the Great, the Syrians became the more powerful. That monarch prosecuted the war against Egypt with vigor, and at first with some success, as indicated in verse 10. But, as verse 11 foretold, the king of Egypt was moved with fury against him, and defeated him with great loss. Yet, though he "cast down many ten thousands" he was not permanently "strengthened thereby" (verse 12). For, about fourteen years later, Antiochus renewed the war, fulfilling the words: "For the king of the north shall return, and shall set forth a multitude greater than the former." In this expedition he was aided by reprobate Jews, spoken of in the prophecy as "robbers of thy people" (verses 13–14). For this aid rendered by the Jews Antiochus was, for a time, very favorable to them. When he entered Palestine he was received by them with great demonstrations of joy; and so as foretold, "he stood in the glorious land" (verse 16); but in the end this proved to be a calamity for the Jews, for he fulfilled the words, "And he shall stand in the glorious land, which by his hand shall be consumed."

Further, in the attempt to accomplish his designs against Egypt, Antiochus gave his daughter Cleopatra in marriage to Ptolemy Epiphanes. But this did not work to his advantage, for she sided with her husband, instead of her father. Reference to this political incident may be seen in the words, "And he shall give him the daughter of women, corrupting her; but she shall not stand on his side, neither be for him" (verse 17). Then he turned to make war against the Romans, but was defeated by Scipio Africanus; after which he returned to his own land, and was slain by his people, who were aroused to fury by the burdensome taxes exacted by him to defray the expenses of his unsuccessful war and the tribute laid upon him by the Romans. It is easily seen that these incidents, which brought the career of Antiochus the Great to a close, respond to the predictions of verse 19.

The Raiser of Taxes

In the foregoing paragraphs we have simply condensed the historical information which has been gathered with painstaking care by able expositors, such as Prideaux ("Connection of the Old and New Testaments"), Pusey ("Lectures on Daniel"), Anstey ("Romance of Bible Chronology") and Taylor ("Daniel the Beloved").

There is some uncertainty as to who is meant by "a raiser of taxes" (or, as the margin reads, "one that causeth an exacter to pass over") mentioned in verse 20. Taylor applies this verse to the son of Antiochus, who succeeded him, and who had to raise enormous sums in taxes in order to pay the annual tribute to the Romans, and we may accept this as correct (since we seem to be following here the succession of events in Syria); but a close correspondence to verse 20 is also found in the career of one Jason who "stood up" in Palestine at that time, obtained the high priesthood by bribery, and lost it shortly thereafter (II Maccabees, ch. 4).

Antiochus Epiphanes—the "Vile Person"

Verse 21 foretells the rising up of a "vile person." Nearly all expositors of repute are agreed that this "vile person" (an expression signifying one greatly abhorred and detested) was Antiochus Epiphanes successor to Antiochus the Great as king of Syria. This odious person occupies a very large place in the prophecy; for verses 21–35 are taken up with the foretelling of his abominable actions toward the Jews. In I Maccabees 1:10 he is described as "a wicked root." His deeds of cruelty and sacrilege far surpassed anything the Jews had suffered under previous rulers. Many pages in Maccabees and Josephus are devoted to the history of this tyrannical king, and his ill treatment of the Jews.

In the prophecy (Daniel 11:21, 23) it was foretold that, "he shall come in peaceably, and obtain the kingdom by flatteries.., and after the league made with him he shall work deceitfully." This was fulfilled quite literally, for Josephus relates that the king (Antiochus), having determined to make war on the king of Egypt, "came up to Jerusalem, and, pretending peace, got possession of the city by treachery" (Bk. II, 5, 4). The Cambridge edition of the Bible cites II Maccabees 4:7, 10, 23–31 in connection with the foregoing verses.

Again, according to the prophecy (Daniel 11:24), this "vile person", after entering peaceably upon the fattest (i.e., the richest) places of the province, would do "that which his fathers had not done, nor his fathers' fathers; he shall scatter among them the prey, and spoil, and riches," etc. In agreement with this is the fact that none of the predecessors of Antiochus had ever interfered in the slightest degree with the worship, laws, or religious observances of the Jews; nor had they ever violated the temple in any way. Thus, in plundering and profaning the temple, and in his acts of cruelty and sacrilege (to which we will refer below), Antiochus Epiphanes did "that which his fathers had not done, nor his fathers' fathers."

Verse 25 of the prophecy foretells this ruler's military expedition against Egypt (II Mac. 5:1). The histories give a full account of this campaign. In fact the Cambridge edition of the Bible, and some others, have in the margin a note on this verse which reads, "Fulfilled BC 170."

Verses 28–30 tell of his return in a second expedition against Egypt, and of its failure: "For the ships of Chittim shall come against him. Therefore he shall be grieved (disappointed or made despondent) and return and have indignation against the holy covenant," etc. (Daniel 11:28–30) The record of this unsuccessful expedition against Egypt, and of the fury of Antiochus which he proceeded to vent upon the Jews, is given in Maccabees and Josephus. Anstey thus condenses their account:

> "BC 168. Popillius met Antiochus Epiphanes four miles from Alexandria, drew a circle round him in the sand, and forced him to cease his war in Egypt. Whereupon Antiochus began his savage persecution of the Jews, which led to the rise of Mattathias and the Maccabees."

In the Cambridge Bible verse 28 has a note, "Fulfilled BC 169"; and verse 30 a note, "Fulfilled BC 168". At verse 31 it cites I Mac. 1:59; II Mac. 6:2. At verse 32 it cites I Mac. 1:62, II Mac. 6:19, 7:1. At verse 34 it cites I Mac. 3:17; 4:8; II Mac. 2:21. And at verse 35 it cites I Mac. 6:12.

This brings us to the climax of the wicked deeds of Antiochus, which the prophecy foretells distinctly, and which the histories record with great detail. We refer to his gross impiety and sacrilege in respect to the temple, the sacrifices, and the religious customs of the Jews. Verse 30 speaks of his coming to an understanding "with them that forsake the holy covenant." For many of the Jews apostatized at that time, forsaking God, and turning against all their religious customs. Thus in I Maccabees 1:41–43, 52 we read:

> "Moreover, King Antiochus wrote to his whole kingdom, that all should be one people, and everyone should leave his laws. So all the heathen agreed according to the commandment of the king. Yea, many also of the Israelites consented to his religion, and sacrificed unto idols, and profaned the Sabbath....Then many of the people were gathered unto them, to wit, every one that forsook the law; and so they committed evils in the land."

The fulfillment again is most exact. Verse 31 of Daniel 11 foretold that "Arms shall stand on his part", or more literally, "arms from him shall stand." This was fulfilled by Antiochus' sending an army into Judea (I Mac. 1:29 et seq.).

They also "polluted" at this time the sanctuary of strength and caused the daily sacrifice to be taken away; for it is recorded in I Maccabees 1:44 et seq. that Antiochus sent letters commanding them to follow strange laws, and forbidding "burnt offering and sacrifice, and drink offerings in the temple; and that they should profane the Sabbath and festival days; and pollute the sanctuary of the holy people."

We quote here from Dr. Taylor's well written account of the deeds of this atrocious character:

> "When he was informed of the satisfaction with which the news of his reported death was received by the Jews, and especially of the attempt made by the rightful high priest to regain his position, he chose to believe that the entire Jewish nation had revolted; and, marching with all haste, he laid siege to Jerusalem and took it, slaying in three days more than forty thousand persons, and taking as many more captives to be sold as slaves. Not content with this, he forced his way into the Temple, entered the very Holy of Holies itself, and caused a great sow to be offered in sacrifice upon the altar of burnt offering, while broth, made from the same unclean flesh, was sprinkled by his order over the sacred precincts for the purpose of defiling them. On his departure he took with him the altar of incense, the golden candlestick, the table of shew bread, and other sacred vessels, to the value of eighteen hundred talents of gold...Two years after the commission of these enormities, returning from another invasion of Egypt, where he had been checkmated by the Romans, he vented his disappointment upon the Jews, and detailed his army, twenty two thousand men, under Apollonius, with orders to destroy Jerusalem. On his arrival at the holy city Apollonius conducted himself peaceably, concealing his purpose till the Sabbath; but on that day, when the people were

assembled in their synagogues, he let loose his soldiers upon them, and commanded them to slay all the men, but to take captive all the women and children. These orders were only too faithfully obeyed, so that the streets were filled with blood...Thus the sad description in the seventy ninth Psalm was verified, 'O God, the heathen are come into Thine inheritance; Thy holy temple have they defiled; they have laid Jerusalem on heaps. The dead bodies of Thy servants have they given to be meat unto the fowls of heaven, the flesh of Thy saints unto the beasts of the earth. Their blood have they shed like water round about Jerusalem; and there was none to bury them. We are become a reproach to our neighbors, a scorn and derision to them that are round about us."

The words "and shall place the abomination which maketh desolate" (Daniel 11:31) call for special examination, because of their recurrence in (Daniel 12:11), and of their use by the Lord Jesus Christ, in (Matthew 24; Mark 13). We have already shown, and expect to refer to the matter again, that the expression "the abomination which maketh desolate" means an armed heathen force. Such a force was placed by Antiochus in the city of David (I Mac. 1:34–35).

Verse 32 of the prophecy speaks of two classes of Jews, (1) "such as do wickedly against the covenant;" and (2) those "that do know their God." Of the former it is said that they shall be corrupted "by flatteries;" and of the latter that they "shall be strong, and do exploits."

Concerning the first class it is recorded in I Mac. 1:11 et seq. that "In those days there went out of Israel wicked men who persuaded many, saying: Let us go and make a covenant with the heathen, that are round about us...Then certain of the people were so forward herein that they went to the king, who gave them license to do after the ordinances of the heathen." Many Jews, including even Jason, the brother of Onias the high priest, were corrupted and won over to Antiochus by flattery and self-interest (II Mac. 4:7–14).

The Uprising of the Maccabees

The second class of persons spoken of in verse 32 of Daniel 11, "those that do know their God," is easily and completely identified in Mattathias, the godly and patriotic priest, and his five sons, who led a successful revolt against Antiochus, and in those of his family who ruled Israel as governors and priests for 130 years. These were indeed made "strong" through "knowing their God," and performed "exploits" of greatest valor particularly Judas, who was surnamed Maccabeus, that is the Hammer of God. This nickname of Judas has been applied to the whole family, but they are properly the Asmonean Princes.

There is no need to speak of the heroic "exploits" of Judas and his brothers, Jonathan and Simon, who succeeded him, for they are well known. But the terms of verses 33–35 call for some explanation. (Daniel 11:33–35)

Verse 33 reads: "And they that understand among the people shall instruct many." Upon good authority we can say that the tense of the Hebrew verb used calls for the rendering "they that cause to understand." Likewise in Chapter 12:3 the literal rendering would be "they that cause to be wise." These terms aptly designate those who have the Word of God and who teach others therein those who impart to others the knowledge of the ways of God, and who cause them to be "wise unto salvation."

This description, therefore, applies particularly to Mattathias and his family, who not only were priests by their birthright, and thus the divinely ordained teachers of Israel, but were true priests, faithfully performing their duty to God and to His people.

Further verse 33 says: "Yet they shall fall by the sword, and by flame, by captivity and by spoil (many) days." This was most literally fulfilled in the history of the Asmoneans. Judas himself, and a great part of his army, were slain by the sword (I Mac. 9:17–18). Jonathan also was slain with a thousand men (I Mac. 12:48). The chief tax collector set Jerusalem on fire (I Mac. 1:31; see also II Mac. 7). Forty thousand captives were carried away by Antiochus (II Mac. 5:14).

Verse 34 says: "Now when they fall they shall be holpen by a little help" (or better, by the help of a few); "but many shall cleave to them by flatteries."

To be "helped" in Scripture means to be helped effectually; and what is here pointed out is that the Maccabees should accomplish their great victories with the "help" of a small number; and this was wonderfully fulfilled in that Judas, time and again, defeated, with very small forces, large armies of Syrians, Idumeans, and others (I Mac. 2:28; 3:9–11) etc. But later on, many did cleave to them by flatteries, professing friendship to them, etc. (I Mac. 10). Thus Alexander Bala, successor to Antiochus Epiphanes, made with Jonathan a league of mutual assistance and friendship (I Mac. 10:65).

Daniel 11:35 foretells that some of them of understanding, or that cause to be wise that is to say the teachers of God's people shall fall, to try them, and to purge them, and to make them white, unto the time of the end. The family of Mattathias continued for several generations to serve the people of Israel in the capacity of priests and teachers (I Mac. 10:21; 14:35; 10:24; and Josephus Ant. XIII 8, 1). Of these "some" fell by violent deaths and by captivity (I Mac. 6:46; 9:18; 9:36, 42; 12:41–48; Ant. XIV 4, 5; XIV 13, 10; XV 6, 2). And this continued to the very "end" of the Asmonean era; for the last of the family, Aristobulus, who held for a short time the high priesthood, was murdered at the command of Herod (Ant. XV 3, 3).

The words "unto the end" would most naturally be taken to mean the end of the Asmonean era, which had a very definite beginning and an equally definite end; for it is in connection with the history of that family that the term is used. But if it be taken that verse 35 describes a state of things which was to continue to the time of the end (the final era) of this period of Jewish national existence, it would be true in that sense also. For to this final era verse 35 brings us.

CHAPTER 9

The King

We come now to a remarkable personality, one who fills a large and prominent place in the prophecy, and who is introduced in these words:

> "And the king shall do according to his will; and he shall exalt himself, and magnify himself above every god, and shall speak marvelous things against the God of gods and shall prosper until the indignation be accomplished" (Daniel 11:36).

Here we reach that part of the prophecy in regard to which there is the greatest difference of opinion among expositors; and yet, if we be not greatly mistaken (as to which our readers must judge) it is an easy matter, in the light of history, both sacred and profane, to identify that "king" whose character and doings are set forth in such striking words in our prophecy. Because, however, of the disagreement referred to, it behooves us, at this point, to exercise special diligence and care in examining and applying the proofs; and we ask the reader, on his part, to give close attention to the exposition of these verses; for one's understanding of the word of prophecy as a whole will depend very largely upon the view he may take of them.

We will first point out some of the current explanations of this part of the prophetic narrative of Daniel 11.

According to one view (that presented by Smith's Bible Dictionary and other reputable authorities such as Taylor) this portion of the prophecy (Daniel 11:36 to end) has still to do with Antiochus Epiphanes, and that tyrant is "the king" of verse 36. That view of the passage is necessitated by the general scheme of interpretation adopted in the work referred to, which makes the first coming of Christ and the Kingdom He then established, to be the "stone," which strikes the great image of Gentile dominion upon its feet (Daniel 2:34–35). Now, inasmuch as it is a matter of Bible fact, as well as of familiar history, that Christ did not come into destructive collision with the Roman empire, but rather strengthened it, this scheme of interpretation is compelled to ignore the Roman empire, and to make up the four world powers by counting Media as one and Persia as another. This makes Greece the fourth, instead of the third, and compels the idea that the entire Chapter 11 has to do with the Greek era.

But this whole scheme is shattered by contact with the undisputed facts. For first, Scripture declares plainly that Media and Persia formed one kingdom, not two. Even during the short time that "Darius the Mede" (Daniel 11:1) was on the throne it speaks expressly of "the laws of the Medes and Persians" (Daniel 5:26; 6:8), which shows that, from the very first, the two constituted one government. The Scripture also says plainly, "The ram which thou sawest, having two horns, are the kings of Media and Persia, and the rough goat is the king of Greece" (Daniel 8:20–21). The meaning of this is unmistakable. It shows that the two "horns" (or powers) were united to form one kingdom; and that it was this united kingdom (and not that of Persia alone) which was overthrown by Alexander the Great.

Secondly, it was the power of Rome, not that of Christ's Kingdom, which brought the Greek dominion to an end. This happened at the battle of Actium, a quarter of a century before Christ was born.

Therefore, the view stated above must be dismissed as directly contrary, to the plainest facts. It may be added, moreover, that there are certain definite statements made concerning this "king" which cannot possibly be made to apply to Antiochus, as for instance that he should "prosper until the indignation be accomplished." We therefore concur with the large number of expositors who hold that this part of the prophecy cannot be taken as applying to Antiochus Epiphanes.

The "Break" Theory

According to another view (one that is widely held at the present day) there is a complete break in the prophecy at the end of verse 34 (or as some say at the end of verse 35), all the rest of the Chapter being assigned to the days of Antichrist, which were then in the far distant future. The supposition, however, that an abrupt break occurs at this point, and an unmentioned interval of many years, where the text has the form of a continuous historical narrative, is a very radical one; and it certainly ought not to be accepted without convincing proof. The strongest magnifying glass would fail to reveal the slightest indication of any such "break," but on the contrary every item of the subject matter of verses 34–36 is connected with the one which precedes it by the conjunction "and." On the other hand we find strong reasons for the view that the prophecy is just what it appears to be, namely, an outline, in continuous historical form, of the main events of "the latter days," that is to say, the second term of Jewish national existence. The view we hold requires that the last three of the four prophesied world powers should come into view within the period of this chapter. At the time it begins the Babylonian empire was already a thing of the past. Hence the continuance of the prophecy should bring us successively to the eras of Persia, Greece, and Rome. That it conducts us to the era of Persia and then to that of Greece is agreed to by all. Why then imagine that, when we come to the Roman era, which is far the most important of all, the prophecy (without giving the faintest intimation of such a thing) takes a sudden leap of many centuries into the future? The only reason why that strange idea has been entertained by any is that they have not known of any historical personage who answers to what is stated in these verses. Yet there is such a personage, and he stands forth very conspicuously in both Bible history and secular history, as we shall now proceed to show. But first we ask our readers to bear in mind that the presumption is strongly against there being any "break" in the prophecy, as is assumed by those who hold the theory we are now considering. This presumption stands upon the following grounds:

1. The form in which the prophecy is given, that of a straightforward narrative, in continuous historical order, omitting no happening of any importance, precludes the idea of there being any break, such as is supposed.

2. The prophecy has expressly for its subject the events of "the latter days" of Jewish history, and the text itself shows this to be the designation of the second term of national life for Israel, which began under Cyrus. This forbids the cutting off of the last (and most important) part of the prophecy and the application of it to a remote age.

3. After verses 36–39, which speak of the character and doings of "the king," we find the words, "And at the time of the end shall the king of the south push at (or with) him; and the king of the north shall come," etc. (Daniel 11:40). This and succeeding verses (where mention is made of Edom, Moab, and the children of Ammon peoples which have now long ago ceased to exist) afford clear proof that the prophecy is still occupied with the era of the wars between Syria and Egypt, which continued till the battle of Actium, BC 30. Fourth. Finally a conclusive reason for the view we are now presenting is found in the words of the angel recorded in (Daniel 12:7). It will be observed that the prophecy continues without interruption to Chapter 12:4, where it reaches its end. But then Daniel

asked a question concerning "the end of these wonders" which the angel had been foretelling. To this question the angel gives a reply which makes it perfectly certain that the prophecy extends to the dispersion of the Jews at the time of the destruction of Jerusalem by Titus, and no further. For he said, "And when He (God) shall have accomplished to scatter the power of the holy people, all these things shall be finished." We do not see how it can be contended, in the face of these clear words, that the prophecy has to do with events subsequent to the scattering of the national power of the Jewish people; and it is not open to dispute that that took place in AD 70. We shall refer to this at greater length later on.

We have seen that verses 32–35 have to do (as is generally agreed) with the Asmoneans or Maccabees, verse 35 telling what was to befall them to the time of the end. What, therefore, we would be led to expect next is a reference to that order of things in Israel which followed immediately after the era of the Asmonean princes. And that is exactly what we do find. For there is no need (and no ground) either for the attempt to make the next succeeding verses apply to Antiochus Epiphanes, or to make a sudden and gigantic leap into the far distant future, in order to find a person whose career might conceivably answer to this part of the prophecy. For history, both sacred and profane, sets before us a most notable character, one who appears upon the scene and occupies the center of the stage in Israel just at "the end" of the Asmonean era, and one who answers to every item of the prophetic description. We have reference to that strange, despotic, ungovernable and unspeakably cruel personage, whom the evangelists designate emphatically as—

"Herod the King"

that remarkable character, who was a usurper upon the throne of David when Christ, the true King, was born. The proof which enables us to identify "the king" of Daniel 11:36–39 with Herod the

Great and his dynasty, is so convincing that we feel warranted in saying that the prophecy could not possibly mean anyone else.

It would be strange indeed if, in an outline which gives prominence to Xerxes, Alexander, the Seleucids, the Ptolemies, Antiochus Epiphanes, and the Maccabees, there were no mention of that remarkable personage who exerted upon Jewish affairs and destinies an influence greater than they all, and who sat upon the throne of Israel when Christ was born.

The words, "the king," should suffice, in the light of the context, without further description, to identify Herod to those who thoughtfully read their Bibles; for Herod alone is called by that title in the Gospels, and he alone had the rank and authority of "king" in Israel in the days after the captivity, "the latter days." The text does not speak of a king, but of the king, the emphatic Hebrew article being used. This is in marked contrast with the terms of verse 40, where the original speaks of "a king of the north," and "a king of the south."

A glance at the context is enough to show that "the king" of verse 36 cannot mean either of the kings of verse 27. Moreover, these are never spoken of as "the king," but always, both before and after verse 36, as "the king of the north," or "the king of the south," as the case may be. Nor does the Scripture speak of any "king" who is to arise at the time of the end of this present age, and who answers at all to the description of the prophecy. The "man of sin," described in (2 Thessalonians 2:3–10), is supposed by some to be "the king" of Daniel 11:36. But he is not called a king, nor described as having kingly rank, but rather as one claiming divine worship in the temple of God, and backing up his pretensions by means of miracles and lying wonders. The "king" of Daniel 11:36 is a very different personage, and achieves his ends in a very different way, as will be clearly seen by all who diligently compare the two passages.

What has caused able commentators to go astray at this point, and in some instances to seek far afield for the interpretation of this passage, is the fact that they were unable to find anyone among the successors of Antiochus who answers at all to the description of "the king." But they have overlooked two things which, had they heeded them, would have kept them from being so misled. Those things are, first, that the prophecy has not for its subject the kingdoms of Syria or Egypt, but the people of Israel, and hence the expression, "the king," without other qualification, would mean one who was king over Daniel's people; and second, that the verses immediately preceding (31–35) relate wholly to the affairs of the Jews under the Asmonean princes, and hence the terms of the prophecy itself lead us to look at this point for the beginning of a new order of things in Israel. And that is just what history certifies to us; for, precisely at this juncture of affairs, the Asmonean dynasty was brought to an end by violence and bloodshed, and it was replaced by that of a "king," who answers perfectly to the description of the last part of the prophecy.

Moreover, and to this we would specially invite attention, it is said of this king that "he shall prosper until the indignation be accomplished" (or until wrath be completed), in fulfillment of which is the fact that the dynasty of Herod retained, through all the political upheavals of the times, its favour with Rome, and flourished in authority in Palestine, until the destruction of Jerusalem, which is the "wrath," or "indignation," or "tribulation," to which these prophecies of Daniel so frequently refer as "the end" of Jewish nationality. For it was "Herod the king" who sought to compass the death of Christ soon after His birth, and whose successors of his own family put to death John the Baptist (this was done by Herod Antipas) and James the brother of John (by Herod Agrippa I, who also imprisoned Peter, intending to deliver him to the Jews) and finally sent Paul in chains to Rome (which was done by Herod Agrippa II, the last of the dynasty, the man who is best known to the world as he who was "almost persuaded").

"According to His Will"

The first thing said of this king is that he should "do according to his will." This is usually taken to mean that he would be of an exceptionally self-willed disposition, one of the sort who act without restraint, and without regard to the rights or the feelings of others. This may indeed be in part the meaning of the words; but much more than this is implied. Self-willed people are so very numerous that, if that were all that were meant, the words could not serve for purposes of identification. But not many are so placed, and have such power in their hands that they are able to "do," that is, to achieve or accomplish what they "will" or plan to do; and this is what is meant. For the expression is used in this same prophecy of two other notable personages. The first of these is Alexander the Great, of whom it is said that he "shall rule with great dominion, and do according to his will" (Daniel 11:3). The other (Daniel 11:16) has been identified as Antiochus the Great. Of him also it is said, "he shall do according to his own will;" and history shows that this monarch, too, was very successful, during the first part of his reign, in carrying out his various designs.

This is what distinguished Herod the Great in a remarkable degree. For history records nothing of this nature more notable than Herod's success in rising up from a lowly origin to the rank and authority of king, in securing for himself despotic power and retaining it through all the political changes of the times, and in the way he used that power for the accomplishment of all his designs, however stupendous in magnitude (as the rebuilding of the temple) or atrocious in character (as condemning to death his own wife and children). For Herod contrived to secure the favor and confidence, first of Julius Caesar, then of Mark Anthony, and then of Octavius Caesar, though he had assisted Anthony and Cleopatra against him.

But, taking the expression in the other sense, we may say that it would be difficult to find in history one who so ruthlessly executed the designs of his own tyrannical and cruel heart, even upon those of his own flesh and blood, as Herod the king. His murder of his best loved wife, the beautiful Mariamne, who was a princess of the Asmonean family, is, in its special circumstances, without parallel in history. He put to death also three of his own sons (two of them by this favorite wife) because he suspected them of aspiring to his throne; and similar deeds of willfulness characterized his entire reign. Josephus gives many instances of this (see for example Ant. XII 9, 4).

Exalting and Magnifying Himself

Further it is said of this king that "he shall exalt himself and magnify himself above every god, and shall speak marvelous things against the God of gods." These words are descriptive of Herod. The words "above every god" may be taken to mean every ruler and authority in Israel, just as "God of gods" means the Supreme Authority above all authorities. Herod did successfully aspire to the lordship over every authority in the land, whether priests or rulers. He assumed to appoint whom he would to the office of high priest. He put his own brother-in-law, Aristobulus, Mariamne's brother, in that office, and shortly after had him murdered (Ant. XV 3, 5).

Herod also uttered great things against the God of gods. This, we believe, refers specially (though not exclusively) to his decree for the slaughter of the babes of Bethlehem, the express purpose of which was to get rid of Immanuel, God come in the flesh to be the Ruler of His people, and to be "Prince of the kings of the earth" (Revelation 1:5). Herod's way of making himself secure upon the throne was to put to death every suspected rival. For Herod, in common with the Jewish teachers in his day (and with some teachers in our own day who ought to know better) mistakenly supposed that the Christ of God was coming at that time to occupy the earthly throne upon which Herod was then seated. We shall have occasion to refer again to this prominent act in the career of Herod.

The Desire of Women

Verse 37 reads: "Neither shall he regard the God of his fathers, nor the desire of women, nor regard any god; for he shall magnify himself above all."

These words call for special comment. The first clause manifestly could not apply to any heathen king like Antiochus. For whether or not a heathen king should change his national gods is a matter of no importance whatever. But with a king of Israel it is a matter of supreme importance. Now Herod, though supposedly of Idumean (i.e. Edomite) origin, was virtually a Jew; for all the remaining Idumeans, who had come into Judea several centuries previous, had been amalgamated with the Jews. In addressing the people Herod habitually used the expression "our fathers" (Ant. Bk. XV Ch. 11, See. 1). So fully was Herod regarded as a Jew, that the Herodians even held him to be the Messiah. Therefore, in introducing the worship of Caesar, Herod conspicuously failed to "regard the God of his fathers." Moreover, in this connection, it should not be forgotten that Esau was Jacob's twin brother, and hence that the God of the fathers of the Edomites was the same as the God of the fathers of the Jews.

The words, "nor the desire of women," are very significant. There can scarcely be any doubt that they refer to Christ, and that Daniel would so understand them. For, of course, the "women" must be understood to be women of Israel; and the ardent "desire" of every one of them was that she might be the mother of Christ. The same word is found in (Haggai 2:7): "And the Desire of all nations shall come." Evidently then it is Christ who is referred to as "the desire of women"; and if so, then we have a striking fulfilment of these words in Herod's attempt to murder the infant Messiah. For the record given in (Matthew 2:1–16) makes it quite clear that Herod's deliberate purpose was to put to death the promised Messiah of Israel. It was for the accomplishment of that purpose that he inquired of the chief priests and scribes as to where Christ should be born. The slaughter of the babes of Bethlehem was an act of atrocity almost without parallel in history. It was, moreover, an event that had been foretold by Jeremiah in the words, "A voice was heard in Ramah, lamentation and bitter weeping, Rachel weeping for her children," etc. (Jeremiah 31:51, quoted in Matthew 2:17–18). Each one of those murdered infants was "the desire" of his own mother; and thus Herod fulfilled Daniel 11:37 in another sense.

The God of Forces

Verse 38 (Daniel 11:38) reads: "And in his estate," or for his establishment, "shall he honor the god of forces," or god of fortresses; "and (or even) a god whom his fathers knew not shall be honour, with gold and silver, and precious (or costly) stones, and with pleasant (or valuable) things."

Herod's career affords a most striking fulfillment of this verse. The expression, "god of forces, or fortresses," is so unusual that it furnishes a most satisfactory means of identification; for it applies to the Caesars as to none others in history, seeing that the Roman emperors claimed for themselves divine honors, and that it was by "forces," or "fortifications," that they extended and maintained their power, and enforced the worship they demanded. This honor Herod paid to them, and after the most extravagant fashion; and he did it, of course, in order to make himself secure, that is to say, "for his own establishment," as the text of verse 38 may be rendered. This honor paid by Herod, first to Julius Caesar, then to Anthony, and then to Anthony's conqueror, Augustus, was one of the most conspicuous features of Herod's policy. Josephus records how he sent delegations to Rome, and also to Anthony and Cleopatra in Egypt, bearing the most costly presents; also how he converted the ancient Strato's Tower into a magnificent seaport, and named it Caesarea, in honor of Caesar, and how later he rebuilt Samaria, and renamed it Sebaste (Sebastos being the equivalent of Augustus). He built many other fortified cities and named them in honor of Caesar.

The same subject is continued in Daniel 11:39, which reads: "Thus shall he do in the most strongholds with a strange god whom he shall acknowledge and increase with glory; and he shall cause them to rule over many, and shall divide the land for gain," or "parcel out the land for hire."

Here we have a reference to one of the most prominent acts of Herod's long reign, namely, his rebuilding of the temple, and his making the temple area a stronghold for Caesar. He made the temple the most famous building in the world for its dimensions, its magnificence, and particularly for the size of the stones whereof it was built, to which the disciples specially directed the Lord's attention (Mark 13:1), and which Josephus says were 25 cubits long, 12 broad, and 8 thick (Ant. XV II, 3). But, in rebuilding it, Herod took care to convert it into a fortress for his own purposes, this being the "most stronghold" of the land. As a part of this plan he constructed on the north side of the temple, and overlooking it, a strong citadel which he named the Tower of Antonia, after Mark Anthony. Josephus says:

> "But for the Tower itself, when Herod the king of the Jews had fortified it more firmly than before, in order to secure and guard the temple, he gratified Antonius who was his friend and the Roman ruler by calling it the Tower of Antonia" (Ant. XV. 11:4–7).

Further this historian says that the fortified places "were two, the one belonging to the city itself, the other belonging to the temple; and those that could get them into their hands had the whole nation under their power, for without the command of them it was not possible to offer their sacrifices" (Ant. XV. 11:7–8).

It was from the stairs leading to this famous Tower, up which the apostle Paul was being taken by the soldiers to save him from the violence of the people, that he stilled them by a gesture of his hand, and gained their attention by addressing them in the Hebrew tongue (Acts 21:34–40).

Again Josephus says of Herod that,

> "When Caesar had further bestowed upon him another additional country, he built there also a temple of white marble, hard by the fountains of Jordan;" and also "to say all at once, there was not any place in his kingdom fit for the purpose, that was permitted to be without somewhat that was for Caesar's honour; and when he had filled his own country with temples, he poured out like plentiful marks of his esteem into his province, and built many cities which he called Caesareas" (Wars I, 21:2).

In connection with the prediction of what this king would do in the chief strongholds "with a strange god," mention should be made of the many images, statues of Caesar, which Herod set up to be worshipped in various fortified places. He even went so far in his sacrilege as to place a huge golden eagle (the adored emblem of imperial Rome) at the very gate of the temple, thus giving rise to a tumult and insurrection among the people. In this way did he, in his estate (office), "honor the god of forces" (Caesar) whose statues he everywhere introduced as objects of worship. He fulfilled with literal exactness the words, "Thus shall he do in the most strongholds," (which expression would apply to the citadel of the temple, where he erected the Tower of Antonia) "with a strange god, whom he shall acknowledge, and increase with glory" (Daniel 11:39). The last clause finds a striking fulfillment in Herod's extravagant pains to glorify Caesar, which, as we have shown, went beyond all bounds.

The words "dividing the land for gain" (or parceling it out for hire) were fulfilled in the practice adopted by Herod of parceling out among persons favorable to himself, the land adjacent to places which it was important for him to control in case of emergency. Josephus speaks of this (Ant. XV 8, 5).

We thus find that every item foretold of "the king" was completely fulfilled in the career of Herod, and that the record of this fulfillment has come down to us in an authentic contemporary history, which is on all hands acknowledged to be trustworthy in an unusually high degree.

Other predictions concerning this "king" are given in verses 44–45. These also were fulfilled with literal exactness, as will be shown when we come to the exposition of those verses.

The Time of the End

In order to avoid confusion it is needful to observe that "the time of the end" may mean one period in one place, and a very different period in another. The meaning is controlled, and is also revealed, by the context. But this is quite frequently overlooked; and we have observed that even careful writers on prophecy have a disposition to take the words "the time of the end" as meaning the end of the gospel dispensation, even when the passage in which they occur does not relate to the present dispensation at all.

Particularly should it be noted that in the Book of Daniel there are two distinct sets of prophecies. The first set, found in chapters II, VII and 8, relate to the great Gentile world powers, and the prophecies of chapters II and VII carry us on to the end of the times of the Gentiles (Chapter 8 gives details of the Greek empire, thus filling in the outline given in the vision of Chapter 7). But the second series (chapters 9–12 inclusive) have to do with the history of Daniel's own people and his holy city. Hence the expression "time of the end," where it occurs in these later prophecies, means the last stage of the national existence of Daniel's people, that is to say, the era of the Herods.

The period of Jewish history occupied by Herod and his dynasty was therefore "the time of the end" in the sense required by the context; so we have a strong confirmation of the view we have been presenting in the fact that, just at this point in the prophecy, there

The King

is given us an outline of those great events (which occurred during the reign of Herod) whereby political supremacy in the world was given to the Caesars, and all was made ready for the coming of the Redeemer. This outline is found in (Daniel 11:40-43), and brings us to the subjugation of Egypt (the last of the great independent monarchies to fall under the spreading power of Rome) with the Libyans and Ethiopians. The records of history correspond so exactly to the predictions of this prophecy (as we shall presently point out) that there can be no question at all as to its fulfillment.

In reading this chapter it is to be remembered that the prophecy is not primarily concerned with Syria, Egypt, Rome or any other alien power, but that it refers to them only insofar as they come in contact with, and affect the destinies of, the Jews.

Caesar Augustus

Hence these verses (Daniel 11:40-43) have a parenthetical character. They read as follows:

> "And at the time of the end shall a king of the south push at him (or with him); and a king of the north shall come against him like a whirlwind with chariots and with horsemen, and with many ships; and he shall enter into the countries, and shall overflow, and pass over. He shall enter also into the glorious land; and many countries shall be overthrown; but these shall escape out of his hand, Edom, and Moab, and the chief of the children of Ammon. He shall stretch forth his hand also upon the countries, and the land of Egypt shall not escape, but he shall have power over the treasures of gold and silver, and over all the precious things of Egypt; and the Libyans and Ethiopians shall be at his steps."

The events foretold in this part of the prophecy took place "at the time of the end;" that is to say they were coincident with the last era of Jewish history, the era of the Herods. At that time a king of the south (Cleopatra, the last to occupy the throne of Egypt, aided by Mark Anthony) made a push with Herod, who was in league with them, against Syria, which had meanwhile become a Roman province. This was the beginning of the great Actian war.

As to the manner in which that war began, we have a very clear account in Plutarch's "Life of Mark Anthony," by which it appears that the fulfillment of the prophecy was marvelously exact, not only as regards the manner in which the war began, but also in respect to the sides on which the different parties were at first engaged in it, in regard also to the outcome, to the peculiar arms, "chariots and horsemen and many ships" by means of which the victories of Augustus were achieved, and finally, in regard also to the rapidity of his conquest, which was effected within the space of a single year.

"Daniel's Last Vision"

Our papers on Daniel 11, in which we identified Herod as "the king" of verse 36, and showed that verses 40–43 were fulfilled in the events whereby Egypt fell under the all conquering arms of Augustus Caesar, were completed ready for the printer in the early part of 1922. Prior to August of that year we were not aware that anyone had previously pointed out that the predictions concerning "the king" were fulfilled by Herod, or that the fulfillment of the last verses of the Chapter was to be found in the stirring and world changing events of his reign.

But in August of 1922 there came into our hands in a strange way (which seemed providential) an old book, now long out of print, in which, to our great surprise and gratification, we found our conclusions as to the above matters set forth, and supported by proofs more ample than we ourselves had collected. The book was written by James Farquharson, and was printed in Aberdeen, Scotland, in 1838. It bears the following quaint and lengthy title: Daniel's Last Vision and Prophecy, respecting which Commentators have greatly differed from each other, showing its fulfillment in events recorded in authentic history.

In our comments, which here follow, on verses 40–43, we are indebted to this volume for the quotations from Plutarch's Life of

Mark Anthony, which set the fulfillment of those verses in such a clear light.

Plutarch's Description of the Actian War

The first move in the Actian war was made by Anthony (at the urgency of Cleopatra), in which he was assisted by Herod. Says Plutarch:

> "Anthony, being informed of these things" (that is of certain disputes between Augustus and others in the Senate at Rome) "immediately sent Canidus to the seacoast with sixteen legions. In the meantime he went to Ephesus attended by Cleopatra. There he assembled his fleet, which consisted of 800 ships of burden, whereof Cleopatra furnished 200 besides 20,000 talents, and provisions for the army."

Anthony advanced to Athens, with constantly increasing forces, Augustus being wholly unprepared to meet him; for says the historian:

> "When Caesar was informed of the celerity and magnificence of Anthony's preparations, he was afraid of being forced into war that summer. This would have been most inconvenient for him, for he was in want of almost everything. ...The auxiliary kings who fought under his (Anthony's) banner were Bocchus of Africa," etc. a list being given: "Those who did not attend in person, but sent supplies were Polemo of Pontus, Malchus of Arabia, Herod of Judea, and Amyntas of Lycaonia and Galatia."

Thus a king of the south was the first to make a push in this war, and he pushed with Herod. As showing the accuracy of the prophecy it should be noted that, as Plutarch records, the Senate of Rome declared war with Cleopatra alone, ignoring Anthony, so that it was strictly between a king of the north, and a king of the south.

Mr. Farquharson points out that the predictions of the prophet were strictly fulfilled also in respect to the character of the forces engaged in the war. For, notwithstanding that each side assembled large numbers of infantry, and notwithstanding that such are the arms usually relied upon to decide a war, yet in this case the infantry were not engaged at all, the issue being decided (as the prophecy indicates) by chariots and horsemen, and many ships.

A strange feature of the affair is that, although Anthony's footmen outnumbered those of Augustus, and although his generals urged him to bring the matter to an issue in a land battle, nevertheless (to quote again from Plutarch):

> "Such a slave was he to the will of a woman that, to gratify her, though much superior on land, he put his whole confidence in the navy; notwithstanding that the ships had not half their complement of men."

This brought on the great naval fight of Actium, which ended in a complete victory for Augustus; and thus did a king of the north come upon a king of the south, with the effect of a whirlwind, with many ships. A more literal and exact fulfillment of prophecy could not be found.

But that is not all. For Plutarch records that, after the disaster at Actium, Anthony's infantry deserted him, so that the infantry were not engaged during the entire war.

> "But," says Farquharson, "when Anthony arrived in Egypt, and endeavored to defend it, to fulfill the prediction of the Prophet that the king of the north would come with chariots and horsemen, as well as with many ships there were actions with cavalry." For Plutarch says, "When Caesar arrived he encamped near the hippodrome (at Alexandria); whereupon Antony made a brisk sally, routed the cavalry, drove them back into their trenches, and returned to the city with the complacency of a conqueror. It was the conduct of their fleets and cavalry that sealed the fate of Anthony and Cleopatra, and left them without resource in their last retreat."

"The Countries and the Glorious Land"

The course pursued by Augustus after his triumph over Anthony and Cleopatra follows most literally the predictions of the prophecy.

For he entered into the countries, and overflowed, and passed over them, possessing himself of regions of Africa, Upper Cilicia, Paphlagonia, Thrace, Pontus, Galatia, and other provinces from Illyria to Armenia. Moreover "he entered also into the glorious land," that is to say the land of Judea, which has already been designated (Daniel 11:16) "the glorious land." For Augustus chose to invade Egypt by way of Palestine, at which time Herod (who had already with great prudence and foresight made his submission to Augustus, and with such skilful diplomacy that it was accepted), rendered him much assistance. Josephus says:

> "Caesar went for Egypt through Syria when Herod received him with royal and rich entertainments; and then did he first of all ride along with Caesar, as he was reviewing his army about Ptolemais, and feasted him with all his friends, and then distributed among the rest of his army what was necessary to feast then withal" (Wars I, 20, 3).

Edom, Moab and Ammon

The reference in verse 41 to the countries of Edom, Moab and Ammon should be enough, without anything further, to show that we must seek the fulfillment of this part of the prophecy in Bible times. Those names had a geographical significance to Daniel, and to others of his day, who would understand by them the mingled peoples of the lands adjacent to Judea on the east and south. Now it is recorded in history that those countries did escape, in a remarkable manner, out of the hand of Augustus, in strong contrast with what the next verse says concerning Egypt, "And the land of Egypt shall not escape" (Daniel 11:42).

Augustus sent an expedition into the countries referred to under Aelius Gallus, in which he was joined by five hundred of Herod's guards (Josephus, Ant. XV 9, 3). Dean Prideaux, the well known commentator, refers to this expedition and its failure, citing Pliny, Strabo, and Dio Cassius (Prideaux' Connections. Vol. II, pp. 605 et seq.). The Universal History, in a note added to their account of the expedition, says: "The bad success that attended Aelius in this expedition deterred both him and others from any further attempts on that country" (Ancient Universal History. Vol. XIII, p. 498).

The Treasures of Egypt

The prophecy makes special reference to the vast treasures of Egypt, saying: "But he shall have power

over the treasures of gold and of silver, and over all the precious things of Egypt" (Daniel 11:43).

Here again are words which make it perfectly clear that the fulfillment of this prophecy must be sought in the days of Egypt's greatness and wealth, and is not to be found in the squalid and poverty stricken Egypt of later times, which, according to the sure word of prophecy, was to become "the basest of the kingdoms," and not to exalt itself any more (Ezekiel 29:15).

But in the days of Herod and Mark Anthony the treasures of Egypt were of fabulous value; and here again history furnishes us with such a marvelous fulfillment of this item of the prophecy that we can but think the records have been providentially cared for. Speaking of Cleopatra's vast and famous treasures of gold, silver and precious stones, and other rare and costly objects, Farquharson says that "the history of the fate of her treasures is very singular, and is worthy of a more detailed reference to it."

So he shows how this great treasure had been accumulated during the centuries of the Macedonian rulers of Egypt (the Ptolemies), being drawn from the great grain trade of the country, and from the very lucrative commerce of Alexandria "through which passed the gems, pearls, spices, and other rich produce and merchandise of India, which from earliest ages have been in high request in the western part of the world."

Continuing his account Farquharson says:

"Augustus Caesar was very desirous of securing the treasures of the sovereign of this wealthy city; but there was, on two occasions, the utmost hazard that they should elude his grasp. For after Cleopatra fled from the battle of Actium Plutarch says, 'she formed the design of drawing her galleys over the isthmus into the Red Sea, and purposed, with all her wealth and forces, to seek some remote country.'"

That design was abandoned; but

"When Caesar afterwards, approaching from Judea, took Pelusium and entered Egypt, the same author says, 'Cleopatra had erected near the temple of Isis some monuments of extraordinary size and magnificence. To these she removed her treasure, her gold, silver, emeralds, pearls, ebony, ivory, and cinnamon. ...Caesar was under some apprehensions about this immense wealth, lest, upon some sudden emergency, she should set fire to the whole. For this reason he was continually sending messengers to her with assurances of generous and honorable treatment, while in the meantime he hastened to the city with his army.' ...Her person and the treasures in the monument were afterwards secured by a stratagem, as related by Plutarch; and thus a king of the north had power over the treasures of gold and silver, and over all the precious things of Egypt."

The Libyans and Ethiopians

The prophecy also says concerning this victorious king, "and the Libyans and Ethiopians shall be at his steps" (Daniel 11:43). Commenting on these words Farquharson says:

"The conquest of Egypt and maritime Libya laid inner Libya and Ethiopia open to the steps, that is, as we may interpret the term, to the inroads of Augustus Caesar, and his officers, of which advantage was soon after taken by them."

And this author proceeds to show the conquest of the countries named in the prophecy, by Cornelius Balbus, which was considered so great an achievement that Balbus, though not a native Roman, was, contrary to all precedent, allowed a triumph. Thus, while Augustus did not himself subdue those countries, they were "at his steps," as the prophecy says, at the time he left Africa and returned to Rome.

Thus ancient history, which has been preserved to our day, shows to us a series of events of the highest importance in shaping the course of human affairs, which events correspond with marvelous exactitude, and in just the right sequence, to the several details of the prophecy, the entire series having taken place at precisely the era we should look for them to occur, if we take the prophecy to be what it appears to be, namely, a continuous prophetic narrative. If then this be not a fulfillment, there is nothing that can be with certainty recognized as a fulfillment of inspired prophecy.

Tidings From East and North

We come now to the last two verses of Chapter 11, which read thus:

> "But tidings out of the east and out of the north shall trouble him; therefore he shall go forth with great fury to destroy, and utterly to make away many. And he shall plant the tabernacles of his palace between the seas in the glorious holy mountain; yet he shall come to his end and none shall help him" (Daniel 11:44–45).

It is not at first glance apparent who is the antecedent of the pronoun "he" in these verses. But upon close attention to the text it will be seen that we have here a return to the main subject of this part of the prophecy, "the king" of verse 36, the course of the prophecy having been diverted in verses 40–43 to the subject of the conquests of Augustus Caesar. Very often, in reading the Hebrew prophets, we have to look a considerable distance backwards to find the antecedent of a pronoun. As an instance of this, Farquharson cites Bishop Horsley as saying, in commenting upon Isaiah 18, "To those to whom the prophetic style in the original is not familiar, but to those only, I think, it will appear strange that a pronoun should refer to an antecedent at so great a distance." And Farquharson adds: "And the correctness of this view of the whole passage is confirmed by the literal manner in which the predictions in this 44th verse, and in the remaining verse of the Chapter, were fulfilled by Herod."

Indeed we do not see how any fulfillment could be more complete and literal than that which is given us in Matthew's Gospel of the words "But tidings out of the east shall trouble him." For it is written that "When Jesus was born in Bethlehem of Judea, in the days of Herod the king, behold there came wise men FROM THE EAST to Jerusalem, saying, Where is He that is born king of the Jews? for we have seen His star IN THE EAST, and are come to worship Him. When Herod heard these things he was TROUBLED, and all Jerusalem with him" (Matthew 2:1-3). So here we have the exact thing prophesied, namely, "tidings out of the east" which "troubled him."

Nothing was so well calculated to "trouble" Herod as reports that someone was aspiring to his throne. In this case it is among the most familiar of all facts that Herod, being set at nought by the wise men, from whom he sought to learn the identity of the new born babe, "was EXCEEDING WROTH, and SENT FORTH, and slew all the children that were in Bethlehem, and in all the coasts thereof, from two years old and under" (Matthew 2:16). Thus we have almost verbal agreement with the words of the prophecy, "he shall Go FORTH, with GREAT FURY, to destroy and utterly to make away MANY."

At about the same time, that is, in the last years of Herod's life, "tidings out of the north" also came to "trouble" that self-tormenting monarch. For Antipater, his oldest son (a despicable character), then at Rome (which had now become the center of what is indefinitely called in this prophecy "the north") conspired to have letters written to his father giving information that two other of his sons, whom he purposed to make his successors, had calumniated their father to Caesar. This caused Herod again to break forth with intense "fury" against his own sons, and their supposed abettors, as related by Josephus at great length (Ant. XVII 4-7; Wars 1:30-33).

In regard to these extraordinary events, Farquharson quotes a passage (which we give below) from the Universal Ancient History, saying he does so the more readily because the authors of the passage had no thought at all of recording a fulfillment of prophecy. They say:

> "The reader may remember that we left Herod in the most distracted state that can well be imagined; his conscience stung with the most lively grief for the murder of his beloved and virtuous Mariamne and of her two worthy sons; his life and crown in imminent danger from the rebellious Antipater, and ungrateful Pheroras; his reign stained with rivers of innocent blood; his latter days embittered by the treacherous intrigues of a sister; his person and family hated by the whole Jewish nation; and last of all, his crown and all his glories on the eve of being obscured by the birth of a miraculous Child, who is proclaimed by heaven and earth to be the promised and long expected Messiah and Saviour of the world. To all these plagues we must add some fresh intelligences which came tumbling in upon that wretched monarch; and which by assuring him still more, not only of the treasonable designs of the unnatural Antipater, but also of the bitter complaints which his other two sons, then at the Roman court, vented against them both, rendered him more than ever completely miserable" (Universal History, Vol. X. pp. 492, 493).

Herod's "great fury" (to use the words of the prophecy) was not confined to the babes of Bethlehem, and to members of his own family. For, says Josephus, "it was also during paroxysms of fury, that, nearly about the same time, he burned alive Matthias and forty young men with him, who had pulled down the golden image of the Roman eagle, which he had placed over the gate of the temple" (Ant. XVII 7). Furthermore Josephus relates the following characteristic action of Herod:

> "He came again to Jericho, where he became so choleric, that it brought him to do all things like a madman; and though he was near death, yet he contrived the following wicked designs: He commanded that all the principal men of the entire Jewish nation

be called to him. Accordingly there were a great number that came, because...death was the penalty of such that should despise the epistles that were sent to call them. And now the king was in a wild rage against them all;...and when they were come, he ordered them all to be shut up in the hippodrome, and sent for his sister Salome and her husband Alexas, and spake thus to them: 'I shall die in a little time, so great are my pains; ...but what principally troubles me is this, that I shall die without being lamented, and without such a mourning as men usually expect at a king's death.'" Therefore, in order to insure that the nation should be plunged into mourning, he left an order that, immediately upon his own death, all those leaders of the Jews, whom he had confined in the hippodrome, should be slain. That order, however, was not carried out.

His Palace and His End

We have already pointed out that Herod placed his royal dwelling places "in the glorious holy mountain," he having two palaces in Jerusalem, one in the temple area, and the other in the upper city. So they were "between the seas," that is, the Mediterranean and the Dead Seas.

The last word of the prophecy concerning him is: "Yet he shall come to his end, and none shall help him." As to this we cannot do better than to quote Farquharson's comment:

> "This part of the prediction obviously implies that, in his last hours, the king would apply for deliverance or remedy, from some affliction or disease, but would receive none. And how literally was this fulfilled in the end of Herod the Great! History has preserved to us few such circumstantial accounts of the last days of remarkable men, as that which Josephus has transmitted to us of his; but we deem it too long for insertion here. It exhibits the most fearful picture to be found anywhere of the end of an impenitent sinner, who, having cast out of his heart all fear of God and all feeling of responsibility to Him, had equally lost all sense of duty to man; and after committing innumerable crimes and cruelties in which he spared not those connected with him by the dearest and tenderest ties, any more than others was at last seized in his old age with a

painful and loathsome disease; and suffering alike from that, and from the pangs of guilty fear, yet continued in a course of extreme wickedness to his last hour, seeking no remedy for his evil passions, but exhausting all the resources of the physician's skill to mitigate his bodily distemper and lengthen out his wretched life. We refer to Josephus for an account of the remedies and expedients to which he had recourse by the advice of his physicians; all of which failed to relieve or arrest the disease which cut him off while he was meditating new crimes of matchless cruelty."

Thus he came to his end, and none helped him. He died a prey to horrible diseases, and to horrible remorse, just five days after he had ordered the execution of his oldest son. We have deemed the matter of sufficient importance to give to the explanation of this part of the Chapter (verses 36–45) a minute and detailed examination. For we are convinced that the theory of a "break" after verse 34 (or 35), involving the transference bodily of all the rest of the prophecy (including the part contained in Chapter 12) to a future day, deranges all that part of the prophetic Word which it is important for us to "understand" at the present time. Conversely, our belief is that, with this important passage correctly settled, other things, which have been involved in the general obscurity occasioned by the "break" theory, will be cleared up. Indeed we shall not have to go very far to find practical proof of this.

And now that we have reviewed the evidences which point to Herod the Great as the "king" foretold in this passage, our wonder is that any careful students of prophecy could have missed so plain a mark. For the passage foretells that, at a definite point in Jewish history, namely, just at the close of the Asmonean era, there should arise (what had not been in Israel for nearly five hundred years) a "king;" and the character and doings of this king (which are of a most unusual sort) are predicted in strong and clear words. In perfect agreement with this, as fully recorded in the Bible and in profane history, is the fact that, precisely at the point indicated, there did arise one who became "king" over Daniel's people, which king had precisely the character, and did precisely the things which the prophecy had foretold of him.

Let it be noted that at verse 35 we reach the end of the Asmonean era, as nearly all commentators have clearly perceived. But the history of the renewed Jewish nation did not end there, and neither does the prophecy end there. What was next? In the history of the Jewish people the next and last stage was occupied by a king, whose character was one of the most detestable, and whose doings were among the most atrocious, of any that have been recorded in the annals of the human race, he being, moreover, the only "king" over the Jewish nation in all this long period of more than 500 years. In perfect agreement with this we find that the next section of the prophecy, which also is the last, is occupied with a description of the character and doings of one who is simply designated as "the king." Furthermore, upon comparing the records of history with the detailed statements of the prophecy, we find an answer in each and every particular. We would not know where to look for a more complete and literal fulfillment of prophecy.

Again we would point out that, considering the nature and purpose of this prophecy, as divinely announced in Daniel 10:14 and as manifested in Daniel 11:1–35, it is simply impossible that "Herod the king" should not have a place, and a prominent place, in it. And even so in fact we find him there, just at the right place, and described with such detail and accuracy as to make it an easier matter to identify him, when we have the facts of history before us, than to identify any of the other notable characters to whom the prophecy refers.

It would seem that, in regard to this exceedingly plain matter, some sound and able teachers have been misled through having accepted the idea of a "break" in the preceding prophecy of the Seventy Weeks, to which (as we have pointed out) that of Chapter

11–12 is a supplement. That made it easy to surmise a similar "break" in Chapter 11 when they came to a personage whom, through their not having in mind the records of sacred and profane history, they failed to identify. We are confident, however, that no unbiased persons, after considering what we have presented above, will doubt that "the king" whose portrait is given in this passage is Herod the Great.

CHAPTER 10

Michael the Great Prince—The Time of Trouble—Many Awakening—Many Running To and Fro—Knowledge Shall Increase—How Long Until the End?

The first four verses of Daniel 12 should not be disconnected from Chapter 11, for they are an integral part of the prophecy, there being no break at all at the place where the chapter division has been made. These concluding verses of the prophecy read as follows:

"And at that time shall Michael stand up, the great prince which standeth for the children of thy people, and there shall be a time of trouble such as never was since there was a nation even to that same time; and at that time thy people shall be delivered, every one that shall be found written in the book.

"And many of them that sleep in the dust of the earth shall awake, some to everlasting life, and some to shame and everlasting contempt. And they that be wise (lit. cause to be wise) shall shine as the brightness of the firmament; and they that turn many to righteousness as the stars for ever and ever. But thou, O Daniel, shut up the words and seal the book, even to the time of the end; many shall run to and fro, and knowledge shall be increased."

These are the last words of the long prophecy, and they bring it to an appropriate climax. They tell what will happen "at that time," emphasizing this by repetition. This expression connects the passage directly with verse 40 of the preceding Chapter, where the words "at the time of the end" occur. The same words are repeated in verse 4 of Chapter 12, just quoted. There is, therefore, no room to doubt that the events here foretold were to occur during the very last stage of "the latter days" of Jewish history. Moreover, the statement of verse 7, that when the power of the holy people should be scattered, then all these things should be finished, absolutely confines the fulfillment of the entire prophecy to the period anterior to the capture of Jerusalem by Titus. We specially ask attention to the great oath recorded in this verse, and trust that our readers will not miss the meaning of it.

Four things are specified in the passage last quoted. They are:

1. The standing up of Michael, the great prince who stands for the children of Daniel's people.

2. A time of trouble such as never was, at which time those found written in the book were to escape.

3. Many to awake from the dust of the earth, some to everlasting life, and some to shame and everlasting contempt, in which connection is given a great promise to those who cause to be wise, and who turn many to righteousness.

4. Many to run to and fro, and knowledge to be increased.

Michael the Prince

Many able and sound expositors hold that Michael is one of the names of the Lord Jesus Christ, and hence that this part of the prophecy was fulfilled by His first coming. But the reasons that have been advanced in support of this view do not seem to us sufficient to establish it. This prophecy makes several references to great angelic beings, which are deeply interesting. Thereby it appears that national destinies are in some way presided over, and shaped, by mighty angels; and that Michael is specially charged to care for the interests of the people of God.

Jude speaks of "Michael the archangel" as contending with the devil about the body of Moses (Jude 9); and in (Revelation 12:7), Michael is again seen in conflict with the devil. Paul mentions the archangel (without naming him) as having to do with the resurrection of the saints (1 Thessalonians 4:16).

In Daniel there are three references to Michael, all in this prophecy given by the angel who appeared to Daniel on the banks of the Tigris. The first reference is in (Daniel 10:13,) where the angel says that the prince of the kingdom of Persia had withstood him, but Michael, one of the chief princes, came to his aid. Again in the same Chapter (Daniel 10:20-21) are the words: "And now I will return to fight with the prince of Persia; and when I am gone forth, lo, the prince of Greece shall come...And there is none that holdeth with me in these things, but Michael your prince."

From these words it appears that the political destinies of the great heathen nations of earth are presided over by mighty beings, who are rebels against the authority of God, high potentates in the Kingdom of Satan. None of those angelic beings stands for God "in these things" i.e., the affairs of the world except Michael, the archangel. This is in accord with the words of the Lord Jesus who speaks of the devil as "the prince of this world" (John 14:30, etc.).

Commenting upon Daniel 10:20-21, Dr. Taylor says:

> "Then resuming his former theme, the heavenly revealer indicated that he had to return to fight again with the Persian evil angel, and that while he was going forth for (or continuing) that conflict, the prince of Greece would come, and a new battle would begin with him, in which the representative of God's people would be left to his own resources, with the single exception of the assistance of Michael.
>
> "This description of the conflicts in the spirit world between the rival angels foreshadows the opposition encountered by Zerubbabel, Ezra, Nehemiah and their compatriots during the reigns of the Persian kings Darius Hystaspes, Xerxes and Artaxerxes, and

also that which, at a later time, the descendants of the restorers of Jerusalem met with at the hands of the Syrian representatives of the Greek Empire. It prepares the way, therefore, for the literal statements which follow (Chapter 11) and from which we learn that, while the Persian kingdom lasted, the enmity of the World power to the people of God would be largely restrained, and the monarchs would be either positively favourable to them, or at least indisposed to harm them. But with the Grecian Empire, especially in one of the four divisions into which it was to be broken up, a different course would be pursued, and the descendants of Israel would be reduced by it, for a season, to the most terrible extremities."

There is no revelation of the precise part taken by Michael, the great prince, in the affairs of God's people in the critical days to which this part of the prophecy relates, that is to say, the beginning of New Testament times; for Michael is not mentioned by name in the Gospels or Acts. But it was a time of manifest angelic activity; and we may be sure that Michael had a leading part in the events which were connected with the coming of Christ into the World. Moreover, we read that "the angel of the Lord" appeared several times to Joseph; that "the angel of the Lord" came to the shepherds on Bethlehem's plain, announcing the birth of the Savior; that "the angel of the Lord" opened the prison doors, setting the apostles free (Acts 5:9), and again released Peter from the prison, into which he had been cast by Herod Agrippa I (Acts 12:7); that the same "angel of the Lord" smote that king upon his throne when, upon a great public occasion, he gave not glory to God (Acts 12:23); and the same angel came to Paul at the time of the great shipwreck with God's message of deliverance (Acts 27:23). If this "angel of the Lord" was Michael, then we have many instances of his "standing up," in behalf of the people of God "at that time." But especially at the great crisis of danger the siege of Jerusalem by the Roman armies, which was particularly and definitely revealed to Daniel would there be need of intervention by those celestial beings who "excel in strength," and no doubt Michael then "stood up" for the deliverance of Daniel's people, even on behalf of "as many as were found written in the book."

It should be stated, in this connection, that the expression "written in the book" had been known since the days of Moses (Exodus 32:32) as a figurative description of those whom the Lord acknowledges as His own.

A Time of Trouble Such As Never Was

The prediction of "a time of trouble such as never was since there was a nation even to that same time," is the last thing in the chain of national events revealed in this prophecy; and in perfect agreement with it is the well known fact that the Jewish nation came to its end with a time of tribulation, distress and sufferings, of a severity beyond anything that was ever heard since the world began. Of this period of unparalleled tribulation Josephus says, in the introduction of his Wars of the Jews:

> "It had come to pass that our city Jerusalem had arrived at a higher degree of felicity than any other city under the Roman government, and yet at last fell into the sorest of calamities again. Accordingly it appears to me that the misfortunes of all men from the beginning of the world, if they be compared to those of the Jews, are not so considerable as they were."

The sufferings of the Jews had this peculiar characteristic, namely, that they were mostly inflicted upon themselves by the warring factions within the city, concerning whom Joseph says in another place:

> "It is impossible to go distinctly over every instance of these men's iniquity. I shall, therefore, speak my mind here at once briefly: That neither did any other city ever suffer such miseries, nor did any age ever breed a generation more fruitful in wickedness than this was, from the beginning of the world" (Wars V. 10:5).

This "great tribulation" is commonly assigned to the future; and this view was held by the present writer himself until he made a personal study of the question. Our observations on this point, however, belong to the second division of our subject, the Lord's Prophecy on Mount Olivet (Matthew 24), so we will only say at present that so conclusive to our mind is the proof that the "great tribulation" of Matthew 24:21 was the then approaching siege of Jerusalem, that we are bound to believe that competent teachers who relegate it to the future have never examined and weighed the evidence.

Mr. Farquharson on this point says as follows:

> "Our Savior certainly referred to the tribulations attendant on the fearful destruction of Jerusalem and the dispersion of the Jewish people by the Roman arms under Titus; and when we understand Daniel's time of trouble as belonging to the same events, ...then the whole of his prophecy in Chapter 12 can be easily demonstrated to have received a signal and complete fulfilment in the Advent of Christ, in the deliverance wrought by Him, ...in the awakening of men from the death of sin, ...in the prophecy itself not being understood until explained by Christ (and then not understood by the unbelieving Jews, but understood by the Christian converts), in the continued impenitence and increasing wickedness of the unbelieving Jews, in the judgments at last sent upon them in the Roman war, in the duration of that war, and in the immediate abatement of the sufferings attending it upon Titus' getting unexpected possession of the last strongholds of Jerusalem."

In the last clause of the above quotation the author had in mind the words of Christ "and except those days should be shortened there should no flesh be saved" (Matthew 24:22), upon all of which deeply interesting matters we hope to comment in the second part of our work.

Many Awakening Out of the Dust

The words "and many that sleep in the dust of the earth shall awake," etc. are commonly taken as referring to the bodily resurrection of the dead, and this is one reason why the entire passage is frequently relegated to the future. But there is nothing said here about either death or resurrection. On the other hand, it can be abundantly shown that the words "sleep" and "awake" are common figurative expressions for the condition of those who are at first oblivious to the truth of God, but who are aroused by a message from Him out of that condition. Isaiah describes the people of Israel as being under the influence of "the spirit of deep sleep" (Isaiah 29:10); and again he says, "the people that walked in darkness have seen a great light; they that dwell in the land of the shadow of death, upon them hath the light shined" (Isaiah 9:2), which words are declared by the evangelist to have been fulfilled by the personal ministry of Christ in Israel (Matthew 4:14–16). Paul paraphrases another word of Isaiah (Isaiah 60:1) as having the meaning, "Awake thou that sleepest, and arise from the dead, and Christ shall give thee light" (Ephesians 5:14). And the Lord Himself declared that the era of this spiritual awakening had come, when He said, "The hour is coming, and now is, when the dead shall hear the voice of the Son of God, and they that hear shall live" (John 5:25). In both these last two passages the reference is to those who were spiritually dead, as all would agree.

The whole nation of Israel was "awakened" out of a sleep of centuries through the ministry of John the Baptist, followed by that of the Lord Himself, and lastly by that of the apostles and evangelists, who "preached the gospel unto them with the Holy Ghost sent down from heaven." It will be observed that the prophecy does not indicate that those who are "awakened" shall all be saved. On the contrary, it says that for some the awakening would be "to everlasting life," and for others "to shame and everlasting contempt." In agreement with this is the fact which the Gospels so clearly set forth that, although multitudes came to John's baptism, and "all men mused in their hearts concerning him," and while multitudes also followed Christ because of the miracles done by Him, and for the sake of the loaves and fishes, yet the outcome was that Israel was divided into two classes, those who "received Him," and those who "received Him not." Thus "there was a division because of Him." His own words distinguish the two classes: "He that believeth on Him is not condemned; but he that believeth not is condemned already, because he hath not believed on the Name of the only begotten Son of God" (John 3:18). The former class awoke to "everlasting life" (John 3:16), and the latter "to shame and everlasting contempt" (John 3:36).

To the same effect the apostle John writes: "Nevertheless, among the chief rulers also many believed on Him; but because of the Pharisees, they did not confess Him, lest they should be put out of the synagogue. For they loved the praise of men, more than the praise of God" (John 12:42–43). These, though awakened, refused to meet Christ's simple conditions of salvation by confessing Him (Matthew 10:32); therefore they awoke unto "shame," even as He Himself declared, when He said: "For whosoever shall be ashamed of Me, and of My words, of him shall the Son of man be ashamed, when He shall come in His own glory, and in His Father's, and of the holy angels" (Luke 9:26).

The next verse of the prophecy strongly confirms the view we are now presenting; for there we have mention of the reward of those who "cause to be wise," and who "turn many to righteousness." What class of persons could possibly be meant but those who spread the truth of the gospel? There are none others, and never will be others, who cause their fellows to be "wise" unto salvation, and "who turn many" from sin "to righteousness." Seeing, therefore, that we have the awakening foretold in verse 2 connected closely with a clear reference to those who preach the gospel of Christ, we have good reason to conclude that the passage had its fulfilment in that great and wonderful era of Jewish national existence, "the time of the end" thereof, during which Christ was announced and manifested, was rejected and crucified, was raised up and glorified, and finally was preached to the whole nation in the power of the Holy Ghost.

The nature of the reward promised to those "who cause to be wise" and "who turn many to righteousness" helps also to illustrate the meaning of the passage. These are to shine as the brightness of the firmament, and as the stars forever and ever. This reminds us that the people of God are to let their light shine before men, and that they are "the light of the world." In holding forth the word of life they "shine as lights in the world." Once they were darkness, but now are they "light in the Lord;" and their reward shall be to shine as the stars for ever and ever; for as "one star differeth from another star in glory, so also is the resurrection of the dead" (1 Corinthians 15:41–42).

Many Shall Run To and Fro

Various meanings have been assigned to the words "many shall run to and fro, and knowledge shall be increased." These words bring the prophecy to an end; and it is not difficult to see the resemblance they bear to the final words of the first Gospel, "Go ye, teach (or make disciples of) all nations." Another Gospel records their obedience to this command; for it is written that "They went forth, and preached everywhere, the Lord working with them" (Mark 16:20).

The word "run" in Daniel 12:4 is not the usual word for the action of running. Strong's Concordance says it means primarily to push, hence to travel or go about. What helps fix the meaning is that, in nearly all its occurrences in the Bible, it is joined, as here, with the words "to and fro," which signify a complete covering of the ground. Thus, the prophet said to King Asa, "The eyes of the Lord run to and fro throughout the whole earth" (2 Chronicles 16:9). Jeremiah says, "Run ye to and fro through the streets of Jerusalem, and see now, and know, and seek," etc. (Jeremiah 5:1); and again, "Lament, and run to and fro by the hedges" (Jeremiah 49:3). Amos says, "They shall run to and fro to seek the word of the Lord, and shall not find it" (Amos 8:12), this being just the reverse of the Word of the Lord seeking after them. Zechariah also has the expression, "They are the eyes of the Lord, which run to and fro through the whole earth" (Zechariah 4:10), signifying His discerning presence in every place.

By these scriptures, therefore, it appears that the words we are considering are most appropriate to describe that world wide activity in spreading the truth of the gospel which the Lord specially pressed upon His disciples, and to which the apostle Paul refers in the words, "How shall they believe in Him of whom they have not heard, and how shall they hear without a preacher? and how shall they preach except they be sent? as it is written, How beautiful are the feet of them that preach the gospel of peace, and bring glad tidings of good things" (Romans 10:14–5, quoting Isaiah 52:7). The gospel messenger is frequently figured as one who runs, because of the urgency of the tidings he bears (Habakkuk 2:2–3).

And what was the purpose, and what the result of this going forth of the disciples to every part of the world with the gospel? It was the increase of knowledge; and certainly, in such a prophecy, it is the knowledge of the true God that is spoken of (John 17:4; 1 Corinthians 15:34; Colossians 1:10). The world lay in the darkness of ignorance. Paul describes those times as "the times of this ignorance," wherein even the cultivated Athenians erected an altar to "the Unknown God" (Acts 17:23–30); and God Himself had said, even of the Jews, "My people are destroyed for lack of knowledge" (Hosea 4:6). Thus we see the direct relation of the two clauses, "Many shall run to and fro," and "knowledge shall be increased," and how both are clearly fulfilled in the activities of the first gospel preachers.

As to this Mr. Farquharson remarks:

> "The Divine 'knowledge,' which the apostles and first Christians ran to and fro to communicate to all nations, maintains, and ever

will maintain, a lofty and unapproachable superiority over all the knowledge that man can discover for himself...In this way then the prediction of Daniel was literally fulfilled. The day spring of true knowledge from on high waited upon the footsteps of the apostles of Christ, as they traversed the Gentile world, dispelling darkness, and doubt and fear, and diffusing light, and confidence and joy over every condition of human life."

Thus understood, the words "many shall run to and fro, and knowledge shall be increased," bring the prophecy to a most appropriate conclusion, and one that is strictly in keeping with its announced purpose, and with its purport as a whole; whereas, to make those words refer to the multiplication of rapidly moving conveyances, as rail road trains, automobiles, etc., and to the spread of "education" by means of schools, colleges, and books, is to introduce into the prophecy an element that is incongruous, almost to the point of absurdity.

How Long the End?

With Chapter 12:4, the long prophecy, which had proceeded without interruption, and without passing over any important event in the history of "the latter days" of the Jewish people, comes to an end. But a remarkable incident follows, and it affords help to the understanding of this part of the prophecy. At this point Daniel looked and beheld two others besides the one clothed in linen, which two were standing the one on the one side, and the other on the other side of the bank of the river (the Tigris). And thereupon one of these two put to the man who was clothed in linen a question, to which evidently it was desired that special attention be paid. Furthermore, the reply was given by the man in linen in the most solemn and impressive manner; for in replying he held up both hands to heaven, and sware by Him Who liveth for ever. This further goes to show that we have here a matter of exceptional importance. Let us then give special heed to it.

The question was, "How long the end of these wonders?" In quoting it thus we have omitted the words, "shall it be to," which the translators have supplied, and which materially change the sense. We have seen that the expression "the time of the end" means, not the actual termination, but the period of time at the very end, the last stage of the entire era of the renewed national life of Israel. Evidently it is the duration of that "time of trouble," spoken of in verse 1, and concerning which the Lord Himself when on earth was so deeply distressed and grieved, as we shall point out more particularly hereafter. It is the same period as that to which He was referring when He said, "these be the days of vengeance that all things that are written may be fulfilled" (Luke 21:22); and again, "And except those days be shortened there should no flesh be saved, but for the elects' sake those days shall be shortened" (Matthew 24:22). So it is concerning the duration of those days of unparalleled distress for Israel that the question was asked.

Let us then note carefully the reply of the one clothed in linen, which was in these words, "that it shall be for a time, times, and a half (or a part, margin); and when He shall have accomplished to scatter the power of the holy people, all these things shall be finished" (verse 7).

Here we have information, very clearly stated, which, if we give heed thereto, will make perfectly plain to us the time when this entire prophecy was to be fulfilled. For the celestial messenger, in answering the question, made known first what would be the duration of the closing period of "trouble such as never was," and second what was to be the end of the whole series of events, "all these things," predicted in the entire prophecy. The words are clear and precise. They tell us that the last act of all was to be the scattering of the power of the holy people, and that when God had accomplished that, then would "all these things be finished." To the same effect are the words of Christ, Who, in telling His disciples what the very end of those "days of vengeance" would be, said that "they shall be led away captive into all nations" (Luke 21:24).

This makes it certain that the entire prophecy spoken to Daniel by the one clothed in linen, including the time of trouble such as never was, and the awakening of many from the dust of the earth, was fulfilled at and prior to the destruction of Jerusalem, and the scattering of the power of the holy people by the Romans in AD 70. It also affords substantial help in understanding the Lord's discourse on Mount Olivet, to which we will shortly come.

A Time, Times and A Part

But before the scattering of the holy people a judgment which Moses had predicted (see Deuteronomy 28:49–68, and particularly the words, "And the Lord shall scatter thee among all people, from the one end of the earth even to the other," verse 64) a certain period of extreme distress, "the days of vengeance," was to run. This is given by the angel as "a time, times, and a part," which is understood by nearly all expositors to be three full years and a part (not necessarily the half) of a fourth. But no event was mentioned from which this era of three years and a fraction was to run. So Daniel says, "I heard, but I understood not;" and therefore he asks, "What shall be the end of these things?" (Daniel 12:6)

In replying to this question the one clothed in linen gave information additional to that asked for; but we will notice first what he said in direct reply to Daniel's question. This is found in Daniel 12:11–12) where we read: "And from the time that the daily sacrifice shall be taken away, and the abomination that maketh desolate set up, there shall be a thousand two hundred and ninety days. Blessed is he that waiteth (i.e., survives, or endures) and cometh to the thousand three hundred and five and thirty days."

It is to be noted that the two measures of time here given, 1290 days and 1335 days, both fall within the period of three years and a part, given in verse 7 as the full measure of the time of the end. This tends still further to confirm the view that by "a time, times, and a part" is meant three full rounds of the annual feasts of the Jews, and part of a fourth.

It will further be seen from this answer that Daniel's question had reference to the very last epoch of Jewish history; for it was in that very last stage of their national existence that the daily sacrifice was caused to cease, which was by them regarded (when it came to pass in the days of the siege of Jerusalem, as we shall presently show) the harbinger of some dire calamity.

The Taking Away of the Daily Sacrifice

We take the marginal reading (which is the more literal) as giving the sense, the words of the margin being "and to set up the abomination," etc. This reading would make the 1290 days the measure of time between the two specified events. But we have lately seen an interpretation, based on the text of the AV, which makes the taking away of the daily sacrifice, and the setting up of the abomination that maketh desolate, simultaneous events, both governed by the preposition "from." But this obviously leaves the verse without meaning; for it gives a measure of time from two specified events, without stating to what that measure brings us.

The "daily sacrifice" was the sacrifice of a lamb every morning and evening. This was to be kept up by the children of Israel throughout all their generations, and a special promise was given upon condition that this offering be continued (Exodus 29:38–45). (It should be observed that the causing of the sacrifice and oblation to cease, as foretold in Daniel 9:27, is a very different thing.)

Now, as a matter of historic fact, the daily sacrifice was taken away during the siege of Jerusalem; and this was counted by the Jews an event of such importance, and such a portent of approaching disaster, that Josephus has recorded the very date on which it occurred, saying:

"And now Titus gave orders to his soldiers that were with him to dig up the foundations of the tower of Antonia, and make a ready passage for his army to come up, while he himself had Josephus brought to him; for he had been informed that, on that very day, which was the seventeenth day of Panemus, the sacrifice called 'the daily sacrifice' had failed, and had not been offered to God for want of men to offer it; and that the people were grievously troubled at it" (Wars, VI. 2.1.).

The Roman army, which, by comparison of the Lord's words in (Matthew 24:15-16 Luke 21:20-21,) is clearly seen to be "the abomination which maketh desolate," encompassed Jerusalem before the failure of the daily sacrifice; whereas it might appear from the wording of the prophecy that those events occurred in the reverse order. But Mr. Farquharson shows that "there is nothing whatever in the verbs of the sentence to indicate which of the events should precede the other; the interval of time between them only is expressed."

The first approach of the Roman armies under Cestius is described by Josephus in his book of Wars, II 17, 10. This was in the month corresponding to our November, AD 66. The taking away of the daily sacrifice was in the month Panemus, corresponding to the Hebrew Tammuz, and our July, AD 70 (Hartwell Horne's Chronological Table). Thus the measure of time between the two events was three years, and part of a fourth.

But more than this: the measure 1290 days is exactly 43 great months (30 days each, according to the Hebrew method of reckoning), and inasmuch as their practice was to reckon by even weeks, months, and years the fulfillment of this part of the prophecy is seen in the fact that it is just 43 even months between the two events, ignoring the parts of the two months in which the events severally occurred.

In verse 12 those are pronounced "blessed," or happy, who survive a further period of 45 days, and thus come to the 1335 days. In correspondence with this is the recorded fact that, about a month and a half after the daily sacrifice failed, the siege was ended by Titus' getting sudden and unexpected possession of the upper city, the last stronghold of the besieged. This last action took place, according to Josephus, the seventh day of the Hebrew month Elul, answering to our September; so that the further duration of the siege after the failure of the daily sacrifice was approximately one month and a half (Wars, VI 8, 4, 5).

That those days were "shortened" (as the Lord had promised) by some Divine interference, is indicated by the abrupt and unexpected manner in which the last stronghold fell. Josephus tells how the "tyrants" (the dominant faction in the city):

> "Did now wholly deprive themselves of the security they had in their own power, and came down from those very towers of their own accord, wherein they could never have been taken by force. ... They left those towers of themselves; or rather they were ejected out of them by God Himself. ... The Romans, when they had gotten on the last wall without any bloodshed, could hardly believe what they found to be true" (ibid).

As regards the promised blessing of verse 12 (Daniel 12:12), it may be observed that Titus immediately extended clemency to the survivors and he set free those who had been bound by the tyrants (Wars, VI, 9, 1).

But we agree with Farquharson that blessing of a higher sort is here intended. For we would recall words of like import spoken by the Lord when, referring to the same period of unequaled distress, He said, "But he that shall endure unto the end, the same shall be saved" (Matthew 24:13). As to this Mr. Farquharson says:

> "Unquestionably this is His promise to the faithful and persevering and obedient in all ages of His Church; but, as being comprehended in His prediction of the destruction of Jerusalem, it has special reference to those who should endure under the trials peculiar to the last great war, in which that city was to be trodden

down. Those trials, He intimated, would be very severe. He said, 'There shall arise false Christs, and false prophets, and shall show great signs and wonders; insomuch that, if it were possible, they shall deceive the very elect.'"

But to those who should endure all those trials there was the assurance of special blessing.

In concluding our comments under this heading we would observe that, in Daniel's deep concern regarding this time of "the end," as to which he inquired with such anxiety, we see a further and a convincing reason for the view that the period in question was that of the unparalleled calamities which were to accompany the extinction of his nation and the destruction of the beloved city, as foretold also in the preceding prophecy of the Seventy Weeks. It is most unlikely that Daniel would have evinced such concern regarding the end of some far off Gentile dispensation characterized by the wide diffusion of secular knowledge, and by the many automobiles and other swiftly moving conveyances of this present time. Daniel had the spirit of the Lord Himself in showing acute sorrow because of the unequaled distresses which were to befall his people and their holy city and temple.

The Period of Three and A Half Years

In commenting upon the period of three and a half years, and upon the various theories to which it has given rise, Dr. Taylor says:

> "We cannot pass this note of number without remarking on the singular coincidences presented by its frequent occurrence both in history and prophecy. The drought in the days of Elijah lasted three years and six months. The little horn which appeared on the head of the fourth beast was to have the saints given into his hands 'until a time, and times, and the dividing of time.' The public ministry of the Messiah was to continue for half a week (or heptad) of years; that is, for three years and a half. His Gospel was to be preached to the Jews after His ascension for another half heptad before it was proclaimed

to the Gentiles. Then, in the Book of Revelation, it is said that the woman shall be nourished in the wilderness 'for a time and times and a half a time,' and that the holy city should be trodden under foot forty and two months, which are three and a half years.[3]

"Now all these are marvelous coincidences, and they point to the existence of some hidden harmony which has not yet been discovered. I might add that three and a half is the half of the number seven, which (found in the week) has been recognized as the symbol of completeness. The sacred lamp has seven branches; the seventh was the Sabbatic year; and at the end of seven sevens came the Jubilee. So also the seventy years of the captivity were made the basis of the seven seventies of years which were to run their course from the time when the edict to rebuild Jerusalem went forth until the appearance of the Messiah upon the earth. I do not know what to make of all this. I frankly acknowledge that it baffles me to find a reason for it. I merely state the fact, and leave you to ponder it for yourselves, that you may learn how much there is, not only in prophecy, but also in history, which lies beyond our ken …

"If any choose to regard all this as being not only applicable to Antiochus, but also through him, as typical of the New Testament Antichrist, and should take the days of the history of the one for years in the history of the other, I have only to say that I find nothing, either here or in the New Testament, to sanction such a procedure. For me, the interpretation which I have endeavored to give is sufficient. They who go further leave the domain of certainty for that of speculation, and the very number of their conflicting opinions is a warning to every expositor not to venture beyond his depth into these dark waters. For myself, I am content to stand upon the shore and wait, like him to whom were first addressed these reassuring words, 'Go thy way; for thou shalt rest, and stand in thy lot at the end of the days.'"

CHAPTER 11

"The Wise Shall Understand"
Have These Prophecies A Future Application?

We have reserved verses 9 and 10 until now, in order that we might deal with all the time measures together. So we come finally to the answer given to Daniel's question (Daniel 12:8), "What shall be the end of these things?" But it was not for Daniel to know this; for the reply was: "Go thy way, Daniel, for the words are closed and sealed up till the time of the end. Many shall be purified, and made white, and tried; but the wicked shall do wickedly; and none of the wicked shall understand; but the wise shall understand."

Here is one of those cases spoken of by Peter, where the prophet searched and inquired diligently what the Spirit of Christ did signify; and where it was not given him to know the things which were testified beforehand. For while Daniel was made to understand much of what was to transpire during the second period of Jewish history, there were matters connected with the final stage thereof which were to be sealed up until the time should be fulfilled, when Christ Himself should reveal them and then not to all, but only to "the wise."

In this view of the passage we can clearly see a wonderful fulfillment of it in the things which took place in the days of Christ, as recorded in the Gospels. For those inspired narratives present vividly the contrast between what our Lord repeatedly called a "wicked" generation, and the few who followed Him, and were made "wise" through His doctrine. This contrast appears clearly in those well known words recorded by Matthew: "I thank Thee, O Father, Lord of heaven and earth, because Thou hast hid these things from the wise and prudent and hast revealed them unto babes" (Matthew 11:25). Here the "babes" are they who were truly "wise;" and of them it is recorded that, after His resurrection, He "opened their understanding, that they might understand the Scriptures" (Luke 24:45). Moreover, it was to them that He gave those special revelations concerning the then approaching destruction of Jerusalem, which form the second part of our present study, and which throw light on the prophecies of the Book of Daniel.

Here we have, therefore, a conspicuous and inspired record of a particular era, the days of Christ, when it was given to the spiritually "wise" to "understand" these very matters concerning which Daniel inquired so eagerly; and this too was "the time of the end" of that very portion of Jewish history to which the prophecy relates. And not only so, but, at that very same time, there was another company expressly called by Christ Himself the "wicked" (Matthew 12:45, etc.) who continued to "do wickedly," even to the point of seizing their own Messiah, and with "wicked hands," putting Him to death. How could there be a more striking fulfillment of the words: "the wicked shall do wickedly, and none of the wicked shall understand"? Those words surely point to something very definite, and very important. It is certain that in such a prophecy the Spirit of God would not waste words by foretelling a matter of course thing, such as that wicked men in general will do wicked deeds in general. No, it was some particular and monumental act of wickedness that was in contemplation, and one, moreover, that would be perpetrated by a generation of men specially characterized by a lack of understanding of what was happening in their days. It was, in fact, the same deed of wickedness that is foretold in Daniel 9:24 as finishing the transgression. The fulfillment of this part of the prophecy calls for just such a deed as was described by Paul when he said of the Jews and their leaders that, "because they knew Him not, nor the voices of the prophets which are read every Sabbath day, they have fulfilled them in condemning Him" (Acts 13:27).

The ingenuity of expositors has been greatly taxed in the effort to make these words apply to the closing days of our own age. We are well aware of the natural propensity of the mind to seize upon such passages as this, and to seek a fulfillment in the last days of this present dispensation; yet it seems strange that the plain fulfillment, to which we are here calling attention, should be so generally overlooked. Every expositor of recent times, who has a scheme of interpretation of Daniel's prophecies to advocate, inevitably and blandly cites the words "the wise shall understand" as if they constituted a convincing proof of the correctness of his own scheme. For he takes "the time of the end" to mean the end of our own dispensation (as if it were the only era that had an "end") and then he further takes it for granted that he is one of "the wise" to whom it has been specially given to "understand" these previously hidden things. But we are persuaded that much which passes nowadays as an "understanding" of these matters, is but a misunderstanding after all; and that some who esteem themselves "wise" in regard thereto are quite otherwise.

Many purified and made white. We would also direct attention to the important words, "Many shall be purified, and made white, and tried," which stand in apposition to the words, "but the wicked shall do wickedly." It is easy to identify those who, in the last days of Jewish national life, were "purified and made white" through the blood of Christ, and who also were severely "tried" for the faith they professed. And again we say that such words, in such a prophecy, call for a special and definite fulfillment; for it virtually deprives them of all significance to interpret them in a way which would make them apply to any and every period. The fulfillment which these words call for is found in the early chapters of the Acts of the Apostles. There we read of "thousands" who were saved, of "many" of the priests who became obedient to the faith, of "multitudes both of men and women" who turned to the Lord. These were purified and made white; and then they were tried with a "fiery trial"; but to these (for they were the "wise") it was given to "understand" the things which were to befall their city and sanctuary at "the end."

But in contrast with this, history has preserved the most impressive evidence of the fact that none of the wicked (those who rejected Christ and His gospel, and who slew the messengers He sent to them) understood what was coming. On the contrary, up to the very day of the capture of the temple by the Romans, they were deceived by false prophets, and were fatuously looking for a miraculous intervention in their behalf. As to this we have the testimony of a most competent and impartial witness, Josephus, who says:

> "A false prophet was the occasion of the destruction of those people, who (the prophet) had made a public proclamation in the city that very day, that God commanded them to get up upon the temple, and that they should receive miraculous signs of their deliverance. Now there was a great number of false prophets suborned by the tyrants to impose upon the people, who announced this to them, that they should wait for deliverance from God" (Wars V. 11, 2 and VI. 5, 2).

But "the wise," those who were enlightened by the word of Christ and by the Spirit of God, did understand the prophecy and did secure their safety thereby; of which we purpose to speak in detail when we come to our Lord's prophecy on Mount Olivet.

Thus it will be seen that, not only do the terms of this prophecy confine us, in our search for the fulfillment of all its details, to the era of Jewish history anterior to the capture of Jerusalem by the Romans and the scattering of the holy people, but we are enabled, from the Scriptures themselves, and from authentic contemporary records, to find, in the stupendous events of that era, a complete and worthy fulfilment of every detail.

The last word in the prophecy, and in the Book, is a word of personal comfort to Daniel: "But go thou thy way till the end be; for thou shalt rest, and stand in thy lot at the end of the days."

The "lot" to an Israelite would mean his portion or inheritance. So to Daniel is given the assurance that all these calamities should not abridge his "rest" or his inheritance. Thus he was supported to hear and to record those wonders, by the comfort wherewith he was comforted of God.

Thus closes the Book of "Daniel the Prophet;" but the subject concerning which he prophesied, or rather concerning which a revelation was given him from heaven the destruction and desolations of Jerusalem under the judgment of God was taken up by the Lord Jesus Christ, and was made the theme of His own last prophecy. Therefore we may properly regard Daniel's prophecy as the introduction to Christ's Olivet discourse, and the latter as the completion of the prophecy of Daniel.

Have These Prophecies A Future Application?

In the foregoing pages we have sought to give the true interpretation of the last four chapters of Daniel. In so doing we have endeavored to show that "the latter days," wherein the last of those prophecies was expressly to be fulfilled, was that final period of Jewish history which stretched from the return from Babylon in the days of Cyrus, to the destruction of Jerusalem by Titus; and also to show that "the time of the end" spoken of in Daniel 12:4 was the very last stage of that period, including the days of Christ, and the time of gospel preaching which followed.

But the subject should not be left without some reference to the question whether these prophecies have any application at all to the present dispensation. We are deeply convinced that there is no warrant whatever for breaking off the last parts of these prophecies, and carrying the detached portions across the intervening centuries to the end of this gospel dispensation. This freakish system of interpretation has nothing in the Scripture to support it, so far as we can discover. But is it not a possibility nevertheless that the prophecies, or parts of them at least, may have a secondary and final fulfillment in the last days of our era?

This question cannot be dismissed as unworthy of serious consideration, seeing that many expositors of the highest ability have elaborated systems of interpretation wherein the time measures of Daniel are taken, on the scale of a day to a year, to measure from various epochs in the past to various critical events in this dispensation. Especially have those time measures been used to locate the second coming of Christ, and other events which pertain to the time of the end of this present age. Sometimes the periods are measured on the scale of a lunar year, sometimes on the scale of a solar year, sometimes on the scale of a calendar year (counting 360 days to a year). Mr. H. Grattan Guinness, in his well known books, The Approaching End of the Age, and Light for the Last Days, uses all three scales, and he seems to obtain remarkable results whichever scale he employs. Thus these figures appear to give, in many cases, the measures of time between important historical events of old, and corresponding events in our own era. All this suggests the possibility that the figures given in the Chapter 12 of Daniel may, when made to mean years instead of days, be found to measure accurately from some selected starting point to say the rise (or the fall) of the Papacy as a temporal power, or of Mohammedanism, or to the French Revolution, or to the outbreak of the World War, or to the taking of Jerusalem from the Turks.

Such studies are not without interest and value; but they do not, in our opinion, supply us with a basis upon which the date of any future event can be predicted; and most emphatically do we declare it as our judgment, that neither these figures nor any others have been given as a means whereby the date of the coming again of the Lord Jesus Christ can be calculated. To that judgment we are driven by His own definite statements in His Mount Olivet prophecy, which we are now about to examine. From those statements it will be clearly seen that, while on the one hand the Lord warned His disciples most explicitly concerning the exterminating judgments which were to fall upon the people, the city and the temple in that generation, and while He gave them an unmistakable sign whereby they might be warned of the approach thereof in time to escape, He took the greatest pains on the other hand to impress upon them that His own coming again would be at an unexpected season, and without any premonitory signs whatever.

Furthermore, it is obvious that, in order to measure long time intervals from a starting point in Old Testament days, it is necessary to have a correct chronology; and the practice of all who have made calculations of the sort referred to has been to assume some one or other of the existing chronological systems based upon the canon of Ptolemy, which Anstey has shown to be erroneous, or at least untrustworthy. And in this connection we would say that our confidence in all calculations of the sort referred to is much shaken by the fact that each scheme of interpretation yields equally remarkable results whether one system of chronology be chosen or another, and whether the "year" be taken as containing 365 days, or 360, or 354 (the last being the length of the lunar year). Now, inasmuch as it is manifestly impossible that all the different chronologies based on Ptolemy's canon should be equally correct, or that it is a matter of indifference whether the year, which is the time unit in all these calculations, be of one length, or another, we are unable to find in such systems of interpretation any basis solid enough to support settled conclusions. Therefore, as to the time of any of the as yet unfulfilled prophecies, we have no means for fixing, or even closely approximating, the year in which it will occur; and this statement applies in a special way to the coming again of the Lord Jesus Christ.

And finally we would say, after much consideration of the matter, and with the desire (which must be common to all) that we might have a divinely revealed measuring line and a starting point whereby future events could be accurately located on the chart of the years, yet we cannot see sufficient warrant for assuming that the "days" mentioned in these prophecies are really "years." We shall not take the time to examine the reasons usually given in support of that assumption, it being enough to say that we know of no proof that the word "day," in any time measure given in the Bible, means "year;" nor can we conceive of any reason why, if a year were meant, the word "day" should be used instead.

The case of the "seventy weeks" of Daniel 9:24 is not an instance of making the word "day" stand for a year; for the word means a heptad or seven, which might be one of days or years, and which the event proves in this case to be years.

CHAPTER 12

The Lord's Prophecy on Mount Olivet

We come now to that great utterance of the Lord Jesus Christ which connects directly with the prophecies recorded in the last four chapters of the Book of Daniel.

We have seen that sixty-nine weeks of the seventy mentioned by Gabriel in his message to Daniel reached "unto the Messiah," that is, unto what Edersheim calls "His first Messianic appearance," which was at His baptism; for then it was that He was anointed with the Holy Ghost, borne witness to by the Voice from heaven, and publicly proclaimed (or "made manifest to Israel") by John the Baptist (John 1:29–34).

That great event marked the beginning of the Seventieth Week of the prophecy, the "one week" which is separately mentioned in Daniel 9:27, the "fullness of the time" of (Galatians 4:4; cf. Mark 1:15). That "week" was, beyond all comparison, the most momentous period in all the course of time; for it was the great and wonderful era of Christ's own personal ministry among men, "the days of His flesh," when He glorified God upon the earth, and finished the work He had given Him to do. It was the brief period of earth's history whereof the apostle Peter spake when he told to a company of Gentiles "How God anointed Jesus of Nazareth with the Holy Ghost and with power; Who went about doing good, healing all that were oppressed of the devil, for God was with Him" (Acts 10:3). Never had there been a "time" like that.

Towards the midst of that "week," the Lord, after having preached the glad tidings of the Kingdom of God, after having worked the works of God and spoken the words the Father had given Him to speak, went to Jerusalem in order to fulfil all that was written of Him, by offering Himself as a sacrifice for the sins of His people. At that season, when Jerusalem was thronged with people for the observance of the Passover, the Lord uttered His "woes" upon the scribes and Pharisees, closing with these words, which have an important bearing upon our subject:

> "Wherefore ye be witnesses unto yourselves that ye are the children of them which killed the prophets. Fill ye up then the measure of your fathers. Ye serpents, ye generation of vipers, how can ye escape the damnation of hell? Wherefore behold, I send unto you prophets, and wise men, and Scribes; and some of them ye shall kill and crucify; and some of them ye shall scourge in your synagogues, and persecute them from city to city, that upon you may come all the righteous blood shed upon the earth, from the blood of righteous Abel unto the blood of Zachariah son of Barachias, whom ye slew between the temple and the altar. Verily I say unto you, All these things shall come upon this generation" (Matthew 23:31-36).

These words call for close attention, because of their bearing upon the prophecy (the Olivet discourse) which immediately follows, and also because of their bearing upon the prophecy of the Seventy Weeks, which we have been studying.

The Lord here speaks distinctly of a terrible retribution which was to come upon that generation; and He sums up the several items of the wickedness for which they were thus to be punished. He declared that, in putting Him to death they were about to prove themselves to be the children of those who killed the prophets; and they were also about to fill up the measure of their fathers. Nor would the wickedness of that "generation of vipers" stop there.

For when the messengers of Christ should come to them with the gospel of God's love and grace, they would scourge, persecute, kill and crucify them. Thus would they bring upon themselves a retribution of such terrible severity, that it would be as if they were visited for all the righteous blood that had ever been shed upon the earth. Most distinct and plain, and emphasized by His great "Amen" (Verily), are the Lord's words, "Verily I say unto you, All these things shall come upon this generation."

Here we have then a clear explanation of the words of (Daniel 9:24), "Seventy weeks are determined upon thy people and upon thy holy city, to finish the transgression"; and also of the words of (Daniel 12:10), "The wicked shall do wickedly, and none of the wicked shall understand."

Daniel's people were to be the agents, and his holy city the place, of the finishing of "the transgression;" and the seventieth week of the renewed national existence was to be the time when the transgression should be finished. We have also in these words of Christ, and in verses 38–39, which follow, a clear affirmation of that part of the prophecy of the Seventy Weeks which foretold the destruction of Jerusalem. We quote those heart melting words: "O Jerusalem, Jerusalem, thou that killest the prophets and stonest them which are sent unto thee, how often would I have gathered thy children together, even as a hen gathereth her chickens under her wings, and ye would not. Behold, your house is left unto you desolate. For I say unto you, Ye shall not see Me henceforth till ye shall say, Blessed is He that cometh in the Name of the Lord" (Matthew 23:38–39).

The Importance of the Destruction of Jerusalem

It is greatly to be regretted that those who, in our day, give themselves to the study and exposition of prophecy, seem not to be aware of the immense significance of the destruction of Jerusalem in AD 70, which was accompanied by the extinction of Jewish national existence, and the dispersion of the Jewish people among all the nations. The failure to recognize the significance of that event, and the vast amount of prophecy which it fulfilled, has been the cause of great confusion, for the necessary consequence of missing the past fulfillment of predicted events is to leave on our hands a mass of prophecies for which we must needs contrive fulfilment in the future. The harmful results are two fold; for first, we are thus deprived of the evidential value, and the support to the faith, of those remarkable fulfillment of prophecy which are so clearly presented to us in authentic contemporary histories; and second, our vision of things to come is greatly obscured and confused by the transference to the future of predicted events which, in fact, have already happened, and whereof complete records have been preserved for our information.

Obviously we cannot with profit enter upon the study of unfulfilled prophecy until we have settled our minds as to the predicted things which have already come to pass.

A striking instance of the dislocation of great historic events which happened in accordance with, and in fulfillment of, prophecy, lies before us in the case of that unparalleled affliction which is called in (Matthew 24:21) the "great tribulation such as was not since the beginning of the world," and which is doubtless the same as that spoken of in (Jeremiah 30:7) as "the time of Jacob's trouble," and in (Daniel 12:1) as "a time of trouble such as never was since there was a nation." From the clear indications given in the three prophecies just mentioned, and from the detailed records that have been preserved for us in trustworthy contemporary history, it should be an easy matter to identify the period thus referred to with the destruction of Jerusalem by Titus. The Lord's own predictions and warnings concerning that event, which was then close at hand, were most explicit. And not only so, but He plainly said that "all these things shall come upon this generation." Besides all that, He specified the very sins for which that generation was to be thus punished beyond anything known before, or that should be thereafter, thus making it a simple impossibility that the "tribulation" and "vengeance" which He predicted could fall upon any subsequent generation.

Yet, in the face of all this, we have today a widely held scheme of prophetic interpretation, which has for its very cornerstone the idea that, when God's time to remember His promised mercies to Israel shall at last have come, He will gather them into their ancient land again, only to pour upon them calamities and distresses far exceeding even the horrors which attended the destruction of Jerusalem in AD 70. This is, we are convinced, an error of such magnitude as to derange the whole program of unfulfilled prophecy. Hence our present purpose is to set forth with all possible fullness and care the available proofs, from Scripture and from secular history, whereby it will be clearly established that the "great tribulation" of Matthew 24:21 is now a matter of the distant past.

First then, we direct attention to the fact that, according to the words of Christ, spoken to the leaders of that generation of Jews (Matthew 23:32–39), the punishment, which was then about to fall upon the city and people, was to be of an exhaustive character. His words utterly forbid the idea of another and more severe national calamity reserved for a future day. Nobody (so far as we are aware) questions that the Lord's lament over Jerusalem, recorded in (Matthew 23:37; Luke 13:34), was wrung from His lips in view of her approaching devastation by the Romans. But if so, then clearly His words to His own disciples, which immediately follow (Matthew 24), and which include the reference to the "great tribulation," refer to the same matter.

But before taking up His discourse to His four disciples, on Mount Olivet, we would call attention to some additional passages of Scripture which tend to show what a tremendous event in the history of God's dealings with the Jews, and in the carrying out of

His purposes for the whole world, was the destruction of Jerusalem by the Romans.

We have referred already to our Lord's lamentation on leaving the city, as recorded by Matthew. From the Gospel by Luke we learn that, upon approaching Jerusalem on that last visit, He was so distressed in His heart at the realization of the awful calamities soon to overtake the beloved city, that He wept over it (Luke 19:41). Although His own Personal sufferings, His shame and agony, were much closer at hand; yet it was not for Himself, but for the city, that His heart was torn with grief, and His eyes flowed with tears. This is the record:

> "And when He was come near, He beheld the city and wept over it, saying, If thou hadst known, even thou, at least in this thy day, the things which belong unto thy peace! but now they are hid from thine eyes. For the days shall come upon thee, that thine enemies shall cast a trench about thee, and compass thee round (cf. Luke 21:20), and keep thee in on every side, and shall lay thee even with the ground, and thy children within thee; and they shall not leave in thee one stone upon another; because thou knewest not the time of thy visitation" (Luke 19:41–44).

Here is a wonderfully vivid, accurate and detailed prediction of what was about to befall the beloved city. But we cite the passage at this time for the special purpose of showing how great a matter, in the Lord's view, was the approaching destruction of Jerusalem great in its historical relation to the Jewish nation, great in the completeness of the overthrow, and great in the unspeakable sufferings that were to attend it.

Once more, when our Lord was being led forth to be crucified, and there followed Him a great company of people, and of women, who bewailed and lamented Him, He turned to them and said:

> "Daughters of Jerusalem, weep not for Me, but weep for yourselves, and for your children. For behold, the days are coming in the which they shall say, Blessed are the barren, and the wombs

that never bare, and the paps which never gave suck. Then shall they begin to say to the mountains, Fall upon us; and to the hills, Cover us. For if they do these things in a (the) green tree, what shall be done in the dry?" (Luke 23:28–31).

Thus we perceive that, even in that hour, the sufferings which were to come upon Jerusalem were more to the Lord Jesus than were His own.

Old Testament Prophecies Concerning Jerusalem

Let us also call to mind that in the Old Testament there are many pages of prophecy concerning the capture and desolation of Jerusalem by Nebuchadnezzar, showing that, in God's eyes, that was an event of much importance. It was, however, an affair of small magnitude in comparison with the destruction and desolation wrought by the Romans under Titus, whether we regard it from the point of view of the sufferings of the people, or of the numbers who were tortured and slain, or of the extent of the captivity which followed, or of the extinction of the nation, or of the "desolation" of the city, or of the sins for which these judgments were respectively the punishment. For the captivity in Babylon involved only a relatively small number of people; it lasted only seventy years; and the people were removed only a short distance from home. That foretold by Christ involved the complete extermination of national Israel, the scattering of the survivors to the very ends of the earth, and "desolations" of the land and city which have already lasted for nearly two thousand years.

The Lamentations of Jeremiah (especially chapters 4 and 5) show how distressing were the desolations of Jerusalem in those days, and how they grieved the heart of God, of Whom it is written, "In all their affliction, He was afflicted" (Isaiah 63:9); and of Whom it is also written that He "doth not afflict willingly nor grieve the children of men" (Lamentations 3:33). But the afflictions and desolations wrought by the Romans were incomparably greater.

Wrath to the Uttermost

But the greatness of the calamity which Christ foretold can best be understood by consideration of the gravity of the sin which brought it upon the city and people, in comparison with that for which God used Nebuchadnezzar as the instrument of His vengeance. Christ laid to the charge of the fathers that they had "killed the prophets," and stoned the messengers God had sent to them. This agrees with the record found in (2 Chronicles 36:14–17):

> "Moreover all the chief of the priests and the people transgressed very much after all the abominations of the heathen; and polluted the house of the Lord which He had hallowed in Jerusalem. And the Lord God of their fathers sent to them by His messengers, rising up betimes and sending; because He had compassion on His people and His dwelling place. But they mocked the messengers of God, and despised His words, and misused His prophets, until the wrath of the Lord arose against His people, till there was no remedy. Therefore He brought upon them the King of the Chaldees..."

But now (in Christ's day) they despised the words of God spoken by His Son; they mocked Him; and finally they betrayed Him and put Him to death. Who can measure the enormity of this crime? But there was even more. For not only did they reject Christ in Person, but they subsequently rejected, persecuted, killed, and crucified those whom the risen Lord sent to them with the offer of mercy in the Gospel. Christ included this in the iniquity He charged against them; and He said that thereby they would fill up the measure of their fathers.

The apostle Paul was one of those messengers who thus suffered at their hands. Speaking of this wickedness of the Jews he said:

> "Who both killed the Lord Jesus, and their own prophets, and have persecuted us; and they please not God, and are contrary to all men; forbidding us to speak to the Gentiles that they might be saved, TO FILL UP THEIR SINS ALWAYS FOR THE WRATH IS COME UPON THEM TO THE UTTERMOST" (1 Thessalonians 2:16).

Thus we are distinctly informed, both by the Lord Himself, and by His servant Paul, (1) that the sin and iniquity of that generation of Jews went far beyond the evil deeds of their fathers; and (2) that the "wrath" which was then about to be poured out upon them was to be "to the uttermost."

Such being the facts of the matter, we would ask, first, if there is to be a future generation of Jews upon which is to fall a yet greater tribulation, what is to be the occasion thereof? and what is to be the crime for which that future generation of Israelites is to be punished? What crime can they commit which would be in any way comparable to that of betraying and crucifying their Messiah?

Second, if indeed such a terrible punishment yet awaits "Israel's long afflicted race," how is it that every prophecy which speaks of God's future dealings with that people, holds out the prospects not of wrath to the uttermost, but of mercy? For we are not aware of any prophecy concerning the remainder of Israel, that gives any hint of such a thing as the greatest of all afflictions being yet in store for them, but rather blessing through believing the Gospel (cf. Romans 11:23).

For example, we have in Isaiah 51 a prophecy which plainly has its fulfillment in this present era of the gospel; for God there says: "My righteousness is near; My salvation is gone forth," and again, "My salvation shall be forever, and My righteousness shall not be abolished" (Isaiah 51:5–6); and He refers to "the people in whose heart is My law," saying to them, "Fear ye not the reproach of men, neither be ye afraid of their revilings" (Isaiah 51:7). Then comes this promise: "Therefore the redeemed of the Lord shall return and come with singing unto Zion; and everlasting joy shall be upon their head; they shall obtain gladness and joy; and sorrow and mourning shall flee away" (verse 11). My opinion is that this verse has its fulfillment in those who are now being saved through the gospel; but we cite it to show that the era to which this prophecy relates is not that which began with the return from Babylon. Hence what is written in the succeeding verses cannot refer to the capture of Jerusalem by Nebuchadnezzar, but must refer to that by Titus.

> "Awake, Awake! stand up, O Jerusalem, which hast drunk at the hand of the Lord the cup of His fury; thou hast drunken the dregs of the cup of trembling, and hast wrung them out...These two things are come unto thee: who shall be sorry for thee? desolation, and destruction, and the famine and the sword; by whom shall I comfort thee? Thy sons have fainted, they lie at the head of all the streets; as a wild bull in a net (are they taken); they are full of the fury of the Lord, the rebuke of thy God" (Isaiah 51:17-20).

Here is a strikingly accurate description of what took place at the capture of Jerusalem by Titus; and that must be the event referred to, because none would claim that there is yet another "desolation" and "destruction" in store for Jerusalem. This being so, there can be no uncertainty as to the meaning of what follows:

> "Therefore, hear now this, thou afflicted and drunken, but not with wine: Thus saith thy Lord, Jehovah, and thy God that pleadeth the cause of His people, Behold, I have taken out of thine hand the cup of trembling, even the dregs of the cup of My fury; THOU SHALT NO MORE DRINK IT AGAIN; but I will put it into the hand of them that afflict thee" (Isaiah 51:21-23).

From this it is dear that Jerusalem and the people of Israel will never suffer again as in the days of the siege by the armies of Titus.

Future Troubles for Mankind

We do not lose sight of the fact foretold by the last words of the prophecy we have just quoted, and by many other prophecies, that there are to be sore troubles for the world, distress of nations, wars, famines, pestilences and earthquakes; these being the final "birth pangs," of whose "beginning" the Lord spake in Matthew 24:8. No doubt there will be grievous tribulations and persecutions in the "latter days"; and we recall the predicted "woes" of the last three trumpets, the outpourings of the vials of wrath, and "the hour of trial" which is to "come upon all the world to try them that dwell upon the earth." But those yet future distresses (which were a new revelation given by the risen Christ to His servant John) were not what He spoke of to the disciples on Mount Olivet. What He then predicted was that "great tribulation," exceeding everything of the sort before or since, which was to come upon that generation of Jews, which most of those disciples would live to see, and concerning which they would need, and would thankfully avail themselves of, the warnings and instructions He then gave them.

The yet future troubles for mankind are distinctly mentioned by the Lord in this prophecy, and they are clearly distinguished from the "great tribulation"; for He tells what will happen "after the tribulation of those days" (Matthew 24:29), and then passes on to the subject of His second advent, in connection with which He says, "and then shall all the tribes of the earth mourn" (Matthew 24:30). The distinction is perfectly clear.

We do not understand that any comparison is to be made, or was intended by our Lord, between the distresses of the siege of Jerusalem and those which are yet to come upon "all them that dwell upon the earth." The two cases are too widely different for any comparison to be made. The fact is, and it fully verifies the words of Christ, that no city and no people have ever endured such terrible sufferings as those which attended the siege of Jerusalem by the Roman armies (whereof we shall speak more particularly later on); and we may well be thankful for His assurance that none of greater severity will ever befall a city and a people hereafter.

Further discussion of the troubles of the last days will be in order after we have examined our Lord's prophecy on Mount Olivet. We only wish at this point to guard against giving to any of our readers the impression that we are undertaking to show that there is no time of affliction and woe for the inhabitants of the earth at the end of this present age. We are not questioning at all that there will be "tribulation and wrath" during the closing days of this dispensation. Our contention is merely that our Lord, in His Olivet discourse, was not warning His disciples concerning the distresses of that far off period, but concerning those which were close at hand.

CHAPTER 13

Outline of the Olivet Prophecy

As the Lord was departing from the temple after His denunciation of the leaders of the people, certain of His disciples drew His attention to the massive stones of which the temple was built (some of these were 30 feet long); but while they were thus admiring its solidity and grandeur, He made what must have been to them the astounding statement that there should not be left of that huge pile of masonry one stone upon another that should not be thrown down (Matthew 24:1-2). This statement was the occasion of the Olivet prophecy. A little later, as He sat upon the Mount of Olives, which overlooked the city, four of His disciples (Peter, James, John and Andrew) asked Him privately for further information concerning the matters to which He had briefly referred (Mark 13:3). The words He had spoken to the Jews had indicated two things in a general way; first, that a severe judgment was to fall upon that generation of Jews; second, that He Himself was to come again visibly. This latter event was intimated in the words, "Ye shall not see Me henceforth, till ye shall say, Blessed is He that cometh in the name of the Lord" (Matthew 23:39). These words of the Lord will account for the form of the question put to Him by His disciples, which, as recorded by Matthew, reads thus: "Tell us when shall these things be, and what shall be the sign of Thy coming, and of the end of the world (age)?"

It is evident that in the minds of the disciples the destruction of Jerusalem ("these things") and the coming again of the Lord Jesus ("the sign of Thy coming, and of the end of the age") were closely connected together. They might well have inferred from what the Lord had said to the Jews that the two events would be contemporaneous. Hence, as reported by Mark and Luke, the question was, "When shall these things be, and what shall be the sign when these things shall be fulfilled?" The disciples were evidently taking it for granted that, when Jerusalem should be again attacked by alien armies, the Lord Himself would come "and fight against those nations," which idea would seem to find support in the prophecy of Zechariah (Zechariah 14:1-5). The disciples, therefore, were not in reality asking several different questions about several distinct and unrelated events, but were asking about what was, in their own minds, a series of connected events. That it was regarded by them as being all one matter, clearly appears by the form of the question as recorded by Mark and Luke.

It is important that we take note of this, for it explains why the Lord, in His reply, was so emphatic and so painstaking in warning the disciples not to expect His coming at the time of the siege of Jerusalem, and not to pay any heed to reports and false prophecies which were to be circulated at that time, to the effect that Christ was "here" or "there," "in the desert" or in some "secret chamber." It also explains why He was so careful to impress upon them that what He was foretelling would be the fulfilment not of prophecies such as Zechariah and (Joel 3:9-16,) which end well for Jerusalem but of the words of "DANIEL THE PROPHET," which end in utter and age long "desolations" for Jerusalem, to be attended by "a time of trouble" for the people, "such as never was since there was a nation even to that same time" (Daniel 12:1).

In fact it will be clearly seen, upon a careful reading of the entire discourse, that the Lord did not give, or purpose to give, any information whatever concerning His second advent, except that it would occur when not expected. All that He said definitely on that subject was that it would not be at the time of the then impending destruction of Jerusalem. It was manifestly of the utmost importance that His own disciples should not be misled by false reports and false Christs at that time, and should not be looking (as were the mass of the Jews) for a miraculous deliverance, but that they should heed the sign He gave them, and should make good their escape by "flight." To this end the Lord began His reply by saying, "Take heed that no man deceive you; for many shall come in My Name, saying, I am Christ, and shall deceive many" (Matthew 24:4-5). The particular deception against which He thus warned them was the false expectation that He would come and deliver the city. The fanatical Jews were sustained in their stubborn resistance to the Romans by the confident expectation of a miraculous deliverance, as in Hezekiah's day. Our Lord, therefore, took great pains that His own disciples should not share this deception. And He continued this sort of warning down to the end of verse 14, cautioning them also that they were not to take such things as wars, rumors of wars, famines, pestilence's, and earthquakes, as signs of His coming. Never were warnings more needed than these, or more generally disregarded. For all through the age the Lord's people have been prone to look upon wars, or other great commotions, as signs of the Lord's immediate coming.

We repeat then, that the Lord's purpose in this discourse was not at all to give His people signs of His coming again, but to warn that generation of the approaching destruction of Jerusalem, and to give to them a sure sign whereby they might, and whereby in fact His own people did, secure their safety by fleeing the land and city.

Viewing then the Lord's discourse as a whole we may clearly see in it the following purposes:

1. To warn His disciples against being led astray by false Christs and false prophets, a danger to which they were to be peculiarly exposed at the time of the Roman invasion of the land.

2. To warn them that wars, commotions, famines, pestilences and earthquakes were not at any time to be taken as indications

that His Second Advent was near. Manifestly it was the Lord's design that His people should be, from the very beginning, always in an attitude of expectancy of His coming' that they should not be looking for signs, but for Him (see Hebrews 9:26). As well stated by Edersheim: "All that was communicated to them was only to prepare them for that constant watchfulness, which has been to Christ's own people, at all times, 'the proper outcome of His teaching on the subject' i.e., the subject of His second coming."

3. To give them a sure sign, whereby they might know with certainty that the hour had come for them to flee from Jerusalem and Judea.

The first two purposes are purely negative, so far as those disciples, and others of that generation, were concerned. The third only is positive in character; and in it we find the main object of the prophecy.

The Great Tribulation. The Days of Vengeance.

What we desire chiefly to establish at this point is that when Christ spoke the words found in Matthew 24:21, "For then shall be great tribulation, such as was not since the beginning of the world to this time, no, nor ever shall be", He was warning the disciples of the approaching destruction of Jerusalem by the Romans, and was letting them know in advance (what the event abundantly confirmed) that the sufferings of the besieged people, and the horrors and atrocities of that awful time, would be without parallel in the history of the world, past or future. It was needful to impress this upon His people of that day, to the end that they should not delay their "flight" when the sign He gave them should appear. The prophecy was, as we have already seen, exceedingly practical. Its purpose was to save the lives of the Lord's own people at a time of extremist danger and distress. And we have only to glance at the three accounts of this utterance of the Lord to perceive that His warning concerning the great tribulation was given for the purpose that His own people might, through acting upon His words, escape from it. We shall call attention to this in detail; but in passing would just ask our readers to observe that the greatness of the tribulation was mentioned as the reason why the disciples were to pray that their "flight be not in the winter nor on the Sabbath day" (Matthew 24:20–21). Those words clearly confine the application of the prophecy to a time preceding the dispersion of the Jews.

Let it be understood then that we are not making any statements in regard to persecutions, tribulations and wrath, which are or may be yet in the future. That there will be such is certain. What we are asserting at this point is that the "great tribulation" whereof our Lord spoke to His disciples when He was on Mount Olivet, and which He called "the tribulation of those days" (Matthew 24:29), was the destruction of Jerusalem by the Romans in AD 70. And we would say that it is most needful, in order to the understanding of other prophecies, that this fact be grasped.

The proof is ample. Indeed the scriptures already cited make it plain that the wrath, which God was then about to pour out upon those who had both crucified His Son and had also rejected His mercy offered to them in the gospel, was "wrath to the uttermost," that all things which had been predicted of that nature were to fall upon that generation. But the clearest proof of all is to be found by simply reading, side by side, the three accounts which God has given us of this great prophecy. It never occurred to the writer to do this until a few months before these papers were written (it was in the summer of 1921). But when he did so he was beyond measure astonished that he had been for so long a time blinded to a fact which lies plainly revealed upon the surface of the Scriptures.

Briefly stated, what the writer found, and what anyone can see by making the same comparison, is:

1. That the words of Luke 21:20–24, beginning, "And WHEN YE SHALL SEE Jerusalem encompassed with armies, then know

that THE DESOLATION thereof is nigh," refer to the destruction of Jerusalem by the Roman armies under Titus (no expositor would dispute this);

2. That the words found in the corresponding part of Matthew's account, beginning with the words, "WHEN THEREFORE YE SHALL SEE" (Matthew 24:15–22; see also Mark 13:14–20) refer to precisely the same event as that spoken of in (Luke 21:20–24.)

We have said that, so far as we know, it is agreed by all expositors that the words recorded by Luke refer to the then approaching destruction of Jerusalem by Titus. But a careful examination of the account given by Matthew will show that, not only does it manifestly refer to the same destruction of Jerusalem, but it contains details which clearly show that our Lord was speaking of an event then close at hand. We will refer later on to those details.

And now, in order that our readers may readily make the comparison we have spoken of, we here print, in parallel columns, the three accounts of our Lord's great prophecy.

CHRIST'S OLIVET DISCOURSE		
The Question		
Matthew 24 (Matthew 24:1–44): And Jesus went out and departed from the temple, and His disciples came to Him for to show Him the buildings of the temple. And Jesus said unto them, See ye not all these things? Verily I say unto you, there shall not be left here one stone upon another, that shall not be thrown down. And as He sat upon the Mount of Olives, the disciples came unto Him privately, saying, Tell us when shall these things be? And what shall be the sign of Thy coming, and of the end of the world?	**Mark 13** (Mark 13:1–35) And as He went out of the temple one of His disciples saith unto Him, Master, see what manner of stones and what buildings are here! And Jesus answering said unto him, Seest thou these great buildings? there shall not be left one stone upon another, that shall not be thrown down. And as He sat upon the Mount of Olives, over against the temple, Peter and James and John and Andrew asked Him privately, Tell us when shall these things be? And what shall be the sign when all these things shall be fulfilled?	**Luke 21** (Luke 21:5–30) And as some spake of the temple, how it was adorned with goodly stones and gifts, He said, As for these things which ye behold, the days will come in the which there shall not be left one stone upon another, which shall not be thrown down. And they asked Him, saying, Master, but when shall these things be? And what sign shall there be when these things shall come to pass?
Warnings Against Being Deceived		
Matthew 24 (Matthew 24:1–44): And Jesus went out and departed from the temple, and His disciples came to Him for to show Him the buildings of the temple. And Jesus said unto them, See ye not all these things? Verily I say unto you, there shall not be left here one stone upon another, that shall not be thrown down. And as He sat upon the Mount of Olives, the disciples came unto Him privately, saying, Tell us when shall these things be? And what shall be the sign of Thy coming, and of the end of the world?	**Mark 13** (Mark 13:1–35) And as He went out of the temple one of His disciples saith unto Him, Master, see what manner of stones and what buildings are here! And Jesus answering said unto him, Seest thou these great buildings? there shall not be left one stone upon another, that shall not be thrown down. And as He sat upon the Mount of Olives, over against the temple, Peter and James and John and Andrew asked Him privately, Tell us when shall these things be? And what shall be the sign when all these things shall be fulfilled?	**Luke 21** (Luke 21:5–30) And as some spake of the temple, how it was adorned with goodly stones and gifts, He said, As for these things which ye behold, the days will come in the which there shall not be left one stone upon another, which shall not be thrown down. And they asked Him, saying, Master, but when shall these things be? And what sign shall there be when these things shall come to pass?

Outline of The Olivet Prophecy

Persecutions Predicted and Instructions What to Do

Matthew 24	Mark 13	Luke 21
(Matthew 24:1–44) 9. Then shall they deliver you up to be afflicted, and shall kill you; and ye shall be hated of all nations for My name's sake. And then shall many be offended, and shall betray one another, and shall hate one another. And many false prophets shall rise and shall deceive many. And because iniquity shall abound, the love of many shall wax cold. 13. But he that shall endure unto the end, the same shall be saved (Mark 13:13). 14. And this gospel of the kingdom shall be preached in all the world for a witness unto all nations; and then shall the end come. [Note: Matthew's reference to the persecutions of the disciples is relatively brief. He omits the instructions as to premeditating, etc. Luke omits the statement that the gospel must first be preached. His "not a hair perish," and "by your patience" (i.e. endurance), are the equivalent of "He that shall endure unto the end."]	(Mark 13:1–35) 9. But take heed to yourselves; for they shall deliver you up to councils; and in the synagogues ye shall be beaten; and ye shall be brought before rulers and kings for My sake, for a testimony against them. 10. And the gospel must first be published among all nations. 11. But when they shall lead you and deliver you up, take no thought beforehand what ye shall speak, neither do ye premeditate; but whatsoever shall be given you in that hour, that speak ye: for it is not ye that speak but the Holy Ghost. 12. Now the brother shall betray the brother to death, and the father the son; and children shall rise up against their parents, and shall cause them to be put to death. 13. And ye shall be hated of all men for My name's sake; but he that shall endure unto the end, the same shall be saved.	(Luke 21:5–30) 12. But before all these, they shall lay their hands on you, and persecute you, delivering you up to the synagogues and into prisons, being brought before kings and rulers for My name's sake. And it shall turn to you for a testimony. 14. Settle it therefore in your hearts not to meditate before what ye shall answer. For I will give you a mouth and wisdom which all your adversaries shall not be able to gainsay nor resist. 16. And ye shall be betrayed both by parents and brethren, and kinsfolk, and friends; and some of you shall they cause to be put to death. And ye shall be hated of all men for My name's sake. But there shall not an hair of your head perish. 19. In your patience possess ye your souls.

The Destruction of Jerusalem. The Sign to the Disciples. "When Ye Shall' See."

Matthew 24	Mark 13	Luke 21
(Matthew 24:1–44) 15. When ye therefore shall see the abomination of desolation spoken of by Daniel the prophet, stand in the holy place (whoso readeth let him understand); Then let them which be in Judea flee into the mountains; Let him which is on the housetop not come down to take anything out of the house; neither let him which is in the field return back to take his clothes. 19. And woe unto them that are with child, and to them that give suck in those days! 20. But pray ye that your flight be not in the winter, neither on the Sabbath day. 21. For then shall be great tribulation, such as was not since the beginning of the world to this time, no, nor ever shall be. 22. And except those days should be shortened, there should no flesh be saved; but for the elect's sake those days shall be shortened. 23. Then if any man shall say unto you, Lo, here is Christ, or there; believe it not. For there shall arise false Christs, and false prophets, and shall show great signs and wonders; insomuch that, if it were possible, they shall deceive the very elect. Behold, I have told you before. 26. Wherefore, if they shall say unto you, Behold he is in the desert; go not forth; behold he is in the secret chambers; believe it not. 27. For as the lightning cometh out of the east, and shineth even unto the west; so shall also the coming of the Son of man be. For wheresoever the carcass is, there will the eagles be gathered together.	(Mark 13:1–35) 14. But when ye shall see the abomination of desolation spoken of by Daniel the prophet, standing where it ought not (let him that readeth understand), then let them that be in Judea flee to the mountains; and let him that is on the housetop not go down into the house, neither enter therein to take anything out of his house. And let him that is in the field not turn back again for to take up his garment. 17. But woe to them that are with child, and to them that give suck in those days! 18. And pray ye that your flight be not in the winter. 19. For in those days shall be affliction, such as was not from the beginning of the creation which God created unto this time, neither shall be. 20. And except that the Lord had shortened those days, no flesh should be saved; but for the elect's sake, whom He hath chosen, He hath shortened the days. 21. And then if any man shall say to you, Lo, here is Christ; or lo, he is there; believe him not. 22. For false Christs and false prophets shall rise, and shall show signs and wonders, to seduce, if it were possible, the very elect. 23. But take ye heed; behold, I have foretold you all things.	(Luke 21:5–30) 20. And when ye shall see Jerusalem compassed with armies, then know that the desolation thereof is nigh. Then let them which are in Judea flee to the mountains; and let them which are in the midst of it depart out; and let not them that are in the countries enter thereinto. 22. For these be the days of vengeance, that all things which are written may be fulfilled. 23. But woe unto them that are with child, and to them that give suck in those days! For there shall be great distress in the land, and wrath upon this people. 24. And they shall fall by the edge of the sword, and shall be led away captive into all nations; and Jerusalem shall be trodden down of the Gentiles, until the times of the Gentiles be fulfilled. [Note: The special warning to beware of false Christs and false prophets at the time of the siege of Jerusalem is omitted from Luke's account.] Luke alone gives the statement that, after the destruction of the city, the Jews should be led away captives into all nations; and that Jerusalem should be trodden down of the Gentiles until the times of the Gentiles be fulfilled. The statements of Matthew 24:27 are found in Luke 17:24, 37.]

After the Tribulation of Those Days

Matthew 24	Mark 13	Luke 21
(Matthew 24:1–44) 29. Immediately after the tribulation of those days, shall the sun be darkened, and the moon shall not give her light, and the stars shall fall from heaven, and the powers of the heavens shall be shaken; And then shall appear the sign of the Son of man in heaven; and then shall all the tribes of the earth mourn; and they shall see the Son of man coming in the clouds of heaven with power and great glory. 31. And He shall send His angels with a great sound of a trumpet, and they shall gather together His elect from the four winds, from one end of heaven to the other.	(Mark 13:1–35) 24. But in those days, after that tribulation, the sun shall be darkened and the moon shall not give her light. And the stars of heaven shall fall, and the powers that are in heaven shall be shaken. 26. And then shall they see the Son of man coming in the clouds with great power and glory. 27. And then shall He send His angels, and shall gather together His elect from the four winds, from the uttermost part of the earth to the uttermost part of heaven.	(Luke 21:5–30) 25. And there shall be signs in the sun, and in the moon and in the stars; and upon the earth distress q of nations with perplexity; the sea and the waves roaring; men's hearts failing them for fear, and for looking after those things which are coming on the earth; for the powers of heaven shall be shaken. 27. And then shall they see the Son of man coming in a cloud with power and great glory. 28. And when these things begin to come to pass, then look up, and lift up your heads; for your redemption draweth nigh.

The Parable of the Fig Tree		
Matthew 24 (Matthew 24:1–44) 32. Now learn a parable of the fig tree; when his branch is yet tender and putteth forth leaves, ye know that summer is nigh; so likewise ye, when ye shall see all these things, know that it is near, even at the doors. 34. Verily I say unto you, This generation shall not pass till all these things be fulfilled. Heaven and earth shall pass away, but My words shall not pass away.	**Mark 13** (Mark 13:1–35) 28. Now learn a parable of the fig tree. When her branch is yet tender, and putteth forth leaves, ye know that summer is near. So ye in like manner, when ye shall see these things come to pass, know that it is nigh, even at the doors. 30. Verily I say unto you that this generation shall not pass till all these things be done. Heaven and earth shall pass away, but My words shall not pass away.	**Luke 21** (Luke 21:5–30) 29. And He spake unto them a parable: Behold the fig tree, and all the trees, when they now shoot forth, ye see and know of your own selves that summer is now nigh at hand. So likewise ye, when ye see these things come to pass, know ye that the Kingdom of God is nigh at hand. 32. Verily I say unto you, This generation shall not pass away, till all be fulfilled. Heaven and earth shall pass away, but My words shall not pass away.
No Sign of That Day. The Lord's People Must Always "Watch" and "Be Ready".		
Matthew 24 (Matthew 24:1–44) 36. But of that day and hour knoweth no man, no, not the angels of heaven, but My Father only. 37. But as the days of Noah were, so shall also the coming of the Son of man be. For as in the days that were before the flood they were eating and drinking, marrying and giving in marriage, until the day that Noah entered into the ark, and knew not until the flood came, and took them all away; so shall also the coming of the Son of man be. 40. Then shall two be in the field; the one shall be taken and the other left. Two women shall be grinding at the mill; the one shall be taken and the other left. 42. Watch therefore, for ye know not what hour your Lord doth come. But know this, that if the goodman of the house had known in what watch the thief would come, he would have watched, and would not have suffered his house to be broken up. 44. Therefore be ye also ready; for in such an hour as ye think not the Son of man cometh.	**Mark 13** (Mark 13:1–35) 32. But of that day and that hour knoweth no man, no, not the angels which are in heaven, neither the Son, but the Father. Take ye heed, watch and pray, for ye know not when the time is. 34. (For the Son of man is) as a man taking a far journey, who left his house, and gave authority to his servants, and to every man his work, and commanded the porter to watch. 35. Watch ye therefore, for ye know not when the master of the house cometh, at even, or at midnight, or at the cock crowing, or in the morning: lest coming suddenly he find you sleeping. And what I say unto you, I say unto all, Watch.	**Luke 21** (Luke 21:5–30) 34. And take heed to yourselves, lest at any time your hearts be overcharged with surfeiting and drunkenness, and cares of this life, and so that day come upon you unawares. For as a snare shall it come on all them that dwell on the face of the whole earth. 36. Watch ye, therefore, and pray always, that ye may be accounted worthy to escape all these things that shall come to pass, and to stand before the Son of man. (Luke's account ends here, but the Lord's words concerning the days of Noah, and the days of Lot are found in Luke 17:26–30.) [Note: Each account has an ending different from the others; yet the lesson is the same in each, namely that no definite "sign" would be given to show when the Lord was about to come again, but on the contrary His return would be entirely unexpected, as was the coming of the flood, and as is the coming of a thief. Hence the great importance to the Lord's people that they should always "watch," and "be ready also." Mark and Luke add "and pray." Luke mentions the things which are to be feared, and against which the saints are to watch "surfeiting and drunkenness, and cares of this life."] "WHEN YE SHALL SEE"

The reader will be well repaid for whatever time and effort he may expend in a diligent study and comparison of these three accounts of our Lord's prophecy. (It is the only utterance of any length whereof three separate accounts have been given us; and there must be a special reason for this.) But what we would emphasize at this point is that the section beginning "When ye shall see" (Matthew 24:12; Mark 13:14; Luke 21:20) manifestly refers, in each account, to one and the same event the approaching destruction of Jerusalem. "The abomination of desolation standing in the holy place" (Matthew and Mark) means the same thing as do the words "Jerusalem" the holy city "encompassed with armies" (the armies being the "abomination" which was to make the place a "desolation," Luke 21:20). We will return to this interesting point.

The "great tribulation, such as was not since the beginning of the world," etc. (Matthew 24:21), is the same as the "affliction" (the same word in the original as "tribulation") "such as was not since the beginning of the creation which God created" (Mark 13:19), and as "the days of vengeance, that all things which are written may be fulfilled," the "great distress in the land", and wrath "upon this people" (Luke 21:22–23).

In all three accounts are mentioned the same woes, "to them that are with child, and to them that give suck in those days," and the same directions for instant flight are given. But in Matthew's account only we have the Lord's instruction to His disciples to pray that their flight be not in the winter nor on the Sabbath day. Those words show clearly that He was speaking of a time when the stringent Rabbinical rules concerning the distance that might be traversed on the Sabbath day would be still in force. That remark fixes the time with certainty as previous to the destruction of Jerusalem. Those strict Rabbinical rules have not been in force for centuries; and there is no reason to suppose that they will ever be revived. The words do not, of course, imply that Christ's own disciples would be bound by those rules even then; but so long as they were in Judea they would have been hampered by them in their flight, should that take place on the Sabbath.

Self-inflicted Sufferings

In the light, therefore, of this comparison of scripture with scripture, we think it plain that the "great tribulation" of Matthew 24:14 was that unparalleled calamity, with its unspeakable sufferings, which befell the city and people in AD 70.

In the history of "The Wars of the Jews", by Josephus, we have a detailed account, written by an eye witness, of the almost unbelievable sufferings of the Jews during the siege of Jerusalem. To this account we will refer later on; but we wish to state at this point that the distresses of those who were hemmed in by the sudden appearance of the Roman armies were peculiar in this respect, namely, that what they endured was mainly self-inflicted. That is to say, they suffered far more from cruelties and tortures inflicted upon one another, than from the common enemy outside the walls. In this strange feature of the case it was surely "a time of trouble such as never was since there was a nation, even to that same time" (Daniel 12:1).

What went on within the distressed city calls to mind the words of Isaiah:

> "Through the wrath of the Lord of hosts is the land darkened, and the people shall be as the fuel (the food) of the fire. No man shall spare his brother. And he shall snatch on the right hand and shall be hungry; and he shall eat on the left hand and not be satisfied; they shall eat every man the flesh of his own arm. Manasseh, Ephraim; and Ephraim, Manasseh. For all this His anger is not turned away, but His wrath is poured out still" (Isaiah 9:19–21).

CHAPTER 14

Such As Never Was

It is needful that close attention be paid to the inspired words whereby the distresses attendant upon the destruction of the Jewish nation and their holy city are described in the several prophecies wherein they are foretold. For it is quite a common mistake to assume that the great tribulation was to be a calamity of unexampled magnitude as regards the number of the slain, and the amount of property destroyed. Thus we have had it said to us that the late world war exceeded the tribulation of the Jews during and resulting from the siege of Jerusalem, in that more lives were lost, more towns devastated. But the Scriptures do not speak of it as a calamity that should exceed all others in magnitude. In fact that could not be, for there has been no calamity to compare in magnitude with that of the flood, and will be none till the heavens and earth which now are shall be destroyed by fire (2 Peter 3:6–7). The prophecies we are studying speak not of a tribulation greater in magnitude or extent, but different in kind; and moreover, they speak of one which was to come as a judgment from God upon the Jewish nation. Thus, in Jeremiah 30:6 we read, Alas! for that day is great, so that none is like it; it is even the time of Jacob's trouble. Here are both of the limitations to which we have referred. The first is in the words none like it, which suggest troubles of a peculiar sort; and the second is in the words Jacob's trouble. The words of

Daniel 12:1 are equally explicit: And there shall be a time of trouble such as never was since there was a nation, etc. The words such as point to troubles of a special kind, and the words since there was a nation mean a nation of Israel, as the context shows. Finally our Lord's words are great tribulation such as was not since the beginning of the world, etc.; and again the context shows that the calamity He spoke of was to come upon that generation of Israelites. The peculiar character of those self-inflicted sufferings of the Jews during the siege will be clearly seen from the extracts given below from the history of Josephus; but there is also to be taken into consideration the fact that, at the termination of the siege, the whole nation was sold into bondage and scattered to the ends of the earth. Such a thing had never happened before (though Jerusalem had been often besieged); and the words of Christ make it sure that nothing like it will happen again.

The apostle Paul, who is the chief revelator of the second coming of Christ, speaks definitely and frequently of the wrath to come, but is absolutely silent as to any great tribulation in connection with the second advent. Thus, he says explicitly that it is a righteous thing .with God to recompense tribulation to them that trouble you; and to you that are troubled, rest with us; when the Lord Jesus shall be revealed from heaven with His mighty angels, in flaming fire taking vengeance on them that know not God, and that obey not the gospel of our Lord Jesus Christ; who shall be punished with everlasting destruction…When He shall come to be glorified in His saints, and to be admired in all them that believe…in that day (2 Thessalonians 1:6–10). This passage speaks plainly of the vengeance that is to fall, when Christ comes again, upon all who reject the gospel; but neither here nor elsewhere in the writings of Paul is there any mention of a special period of tribulation (the last of the seventy weeks of Daniel 9, as some say) preceding the revelation of Jesus Christ. What Paul distinctly foretells in this passage, and refers to in other passages (as 1 Thessalonians 1:10 5:2–3) is in agreement with the words of Christ, Who, speaking of the time of His coming again in glory with His angels, said, And then shall all the tribes of the earth mourn (Matthew 24:30–31).

We are aware that many in our day have so settled it in their minds that the appearing of Christ in glory is to be preceded by a definite period, the great tribulation so called, that it is difficult for them even to consider the idea that the period to which our Lord applied that expression is now long past. Nevertheless we are confident that all who are disposed to examine with open minds the testimony of the Scriptures will be constrained to agree with the conclusion we have reached, which is that of practically all the great commentators of bygone days, and of many in our own day. That view is well and concisely stated by Wiston in his preface to Josephus' *Wars of the Jews*, where he says:

> "That these calamities of the Jews, who were our Savior's murderers, were to be the greatest that had ever been since the beginning of the world, our Savior had directly foretold, (Matthew 24:21; Mark 13:19; Luke 21:23–24) and that they proved to be such accordingly, Josephus is here a most authentic witness."

Mark's Account of the Olivet Prophecy

Let us now, with the help thus gained, examine more closely the entire discourse. For this purpose we select the account given by Mark as the basis of our study. This we do because it is the most concise and straightforward. Since it gives the Lord's answer to the same question of the four disciples, we must assume that it is complete, in the sense of containing everything said by the Lord that relates directly to that question. Additional statements found in Matthew and Luke would be merely details, or matters collateral to the main subject.

The question—put to the Lord privately by Peter, James, John and Andrew (Mark 13:3–4)—was this: "Tell us when shall these things be? and what shall be the sign when all these things shall be fulfilled? The expression these things (or these events) is important for identification. It meant the terrible overthrow which the Lord had just announced to them, the completeness whereof was indicated by the fact that there should "not be left one stone upon another that should not be thrown down" (verse 2).

The Lord's reply begins very significantly with the words, "Take heed lest any man deceive you." These, and the words which follow to the end of verse 8, seem to be not in response to the question put to Him. But they are all the more important for that very reason; for they show that what the Lord deemed most essential was to correct the erroneous thought in their minds that the time of the happening of "these things" was to be the time of His coming again in power and glory to set up His visible Kingdom, whereof He had previously spoken to them (Matthew 16:27; 19:28). He was therefore most explicit in warning them to beware of false Christs, who would arise and deceive many at the time of the siege of Jerusalem. Furthermore, He warned them not to be disturbed by wars or rumors of wars, earthquakes, famines and the like; for such things must occur, but they were not signs of the end. Thus the subject of His own coming again at the end of the age was introduced, as we have said, in a purely negative way, and solely in order to inform the disciples that His second coming was in no way connected with the events whereof He was then forewarning them.

In this connection the Lord also informed them of the treatment they were to receive, and the sufferings they were to endure (Mark 13:9–13); and He instructed them what they were to do when summoned before tribunals for His Name's sake (Mark 13:11).

The one great thing they were to keep in mind in respect to the unmeasured period that was to elapse before His coming again was that "the gospel must first be published among all nations" (Mark 13:10). In like manner after His resurrection, when they brought up the same question concerning the restoring of the kingdom to Israel, He turned their minds from that subject, and said, But...ye shall be witnesses unto Me, both in Jerusalem, and in all Judea, and in Samaria, and unto the uttermost part of the earth (Acts 1:6-8). The end of the age will come when, and only when, the work of the Gospel shall have been finished. Thus He made the work of the Gospel to be the matter of supreme importance.

This reply to their thoughts concerning His second coming is found (with additional details) in (Matthew 24:4-14, and Luke 21:8-19. We need not refer at this point to those passages. For what we wish just now to impress upon our readers is that the Lord was not, in this part of His reply, speaking of events that were to happen just prior to His second advent, but on the contrary, was warning them not to take such things as wars, famines, pestilences, etc....as indications that His advent was near.

Obviously that warning applies throughout the entire age; for if commotions of the sort mentioned by the Lord were not indications of the nearness of His coming at the beginning of the age, they would not be indications thereof at any later period.

The Sign. At this point (Mark 13:14) the Lord changes the subject, as indicated by the word But; and He now specifies a definite sign—impossible to be misunderstood—whereby they and all the saints of that generation should know with absolute certainty that the predicted desolation was about to take place, He says: But when ye shall see the abomination of desolation, spoken of by Daniel the prophet, standing where it ought not (let him that readeth understand), then let them that be in Judea flee to the mountains, etc.

We have already shown by the corresponding passage in Luke 21:20 that the abomination of desolation was the invading army which was about to encircle Jerusalem and accomplish the desolation thereof. That abomination, when it was encompassing

Jerusalem, was standing where it ought not. A comparison of the two passages leaves no room for any uncertainty as to the Lord's meaning. What has mainly caused certain modern expositors to go astray at this point is a curious mistake in regard to the expression used by Matthew, standing in the holy place. This point is so important that we reserve it for special comment later on. In view of the very general misunderstanding concerning this particular point, the Lord's words, let him that readeth understand, are very significant.

In this part of the Lord's answer (Mark 13:14–23) He gave explicit directions to His people how to secure their own safety; and furthermore He indicated that the complete investment of the city would be so swiftly accomplished that, after the appearance of the armies, their only safety would be in instant flight. We call attention once more to the exceedingly practical character of this prophecy.

It is important to notice that the word affliction in Mark 13:19, is the same as that rendered tribulation in verse 24, and in (Matthew 24:7, 21).

In verse 20 is the promise that those days—referring to the horrors of the siege—would be shortened; and we have already shown, in discussing Daniel 12, that the time was shortened, and in a manner evidently providential, so that the Romans obtained sudden, and most unexpected, possession of the last stronghold of the city.

At this point the Lord renews the warning against expecting His return at that time. He speaks with great definiteness, saying, Then, that is during those days of siege, if any man shall say to you, Lo, here is Christ; or lo, He is there; believe him not (Mark 13:21). Moreover, He gives the reason for this explicit warning, saying, For false Christs and false prophets shall rise, and shall show signs and wonders, to seduce, if it were possible, even the elect. But take ye heed: behold, I have foretold you all things (Mark 13:22-23). These words become very clear and plain when it is seen that the Lord is speaking of false Christs, and false prophets, who would seduce (or deceive) many into the belief that He was about to appear at that time and save Jerusalem from the invading armies. Similarly in the days of Zedekiah, when the city was besieged by Nebuchadnezzar, there were false prophets who deceived the people by telling them that the enemy would not capture the city (Jeremiah 27:14). In view of the many interventions by the Lord on behalf of His people, and of the many promises given to them, it was very easy indeed to persuade the Jews to expect a miraculous deliverance. Hence it was exceedingly important that Christ should make His own disciples understand that there was to be no deliverance in this case.

In the corresponding part of Matthew's Gospel (Matthew 24:15-28) it is plain that we have another account of identically the same future events. Mark says in those days—i.e., in the days of the siege of Jerusalem—shall be affliction (great tribulation), such as was not from the beginning. Matthew says, For then shall be great tribulation, such as was not from the beginning, etc.

Matthew 24:27-28 tell what will be the manner of the Lord's appearing when He does come (as the lightning cometh out of the east). Those words are not in Mark. This further goes to show that Christ's second coming was not the main subject of His discourse here, but was a collateral matter. Obviously in this place also it was mentioned merely to give emphasis to the warning not to heed the reports which would be current at that time, that He was in the desert, or in the secret chambers.

The corresponding part of Luke's account is found in Luke 21:20-24. This account is valuable mainly for the very definite statements of verse 24, which tell how the siege was to end: And they—the people of verse 23—shall fall by the edge of the sword, and shall be led away captive into all nations; and Jerusalem shall be trodden down of the Gentiles, until the times of the Gentiles be fulfilled. These few words give a concise and accurate description of the conditions of the city and people down to the present day. They made it plain to the disciples that there was to be no deliverance for Jerusalem at that time.

It is particularly to be noted that Luke, having spoken in detail of a coming destruction of Jerusalem, which everyone admits is that which came to pass in AD 70, says not a word of any other tribulation after that one. This forbids the idea that there is yet another tribulation (and even a worse one) in store for the Jews. Their worst enemies could hardly desire it, no reason for it can be conceived, the Scriptures do not reveal it, and we should be very slow to believe that such a thing could be.

Here are three evangelists, selected by God for the special purpose, and inspired by the Holy Spirit, each of whom gives us an account of one and the same utterance of the Lord Jesus Christ. That utterance has mainly to do with an affliction of unparalleled severity, which soon was to fall upon Jerusalem and Judea, to the complete desolation of the city and the extinction of the nation, but concerning the approach whereof Christ's own people were to receive a timely warning and an opportunity to escape. If now it be indeed the case (as some modern expositors affirm) that the affliction whereof Matthew and Mark have preserved a record was not the nearby destruction of the city, but one that was not to happen until the very end of this dispensation, and only after Israel had been nationally exterminated, scattered for an entire age, and regathered in their land and city again (of all which things, however, neither Matthew nor Mark says a single word), how can we possibly account for the fact that Luke, though he speaks most impressively of the nearby destruction of Jerusalem by Titus, and of the world wide dispersion of the Jews, makes no reference at all to that far worse tribulation which is the prominent feature of the accounts given by Matthew and Mark as interpreted by certain modern expositors? Manifestly that could not be. And on the other hand, in view of the prominence given by Luke to the approaching destruction of Jerusalem, and in view also of the identical instructions given to the disciples, as recorded by all three evangelists, it is not supposable that Matthew and Mark would absolutely ignore that unspeakable affliction, and describe—in identically the same context—another tribulation that lay in the far off future.

The statement found in (Luke 21:22), "For these be the days of vengeance, that all things which are written may be fulfilled", calls for attentive consideration. The expression the days of vengeance indicates a definite period of judgment; and this is emphasized by the words, that all things which are written, which means, of course, all the threats of judgment, recorded in the law and the prophets, might be fulfilled. Manifestly, if all things of that nature were fulfilled at the destruction of Jerusalem in AD 70, then there could not be after that a further (and a worse) tribulation for Israel."[4]

As a help to the understanding of these words, let us turn to the earliest prophecy which speaks of the days of vengeance that were to come upon the faithless people. It is found in (Deuteronomy 28:49–59,) where God gave, through Moses, an outline of the future history of His people, telling how they would depart from Himself, and how He would punish them by bringing against them a nation which should besiege them in their cities. The description fits very accurately the Romans, and the desolations wrought by them. We quote a part of the passage:

> "The Lord shall bring a nation against thee from far, from the end of the earth, as swift as the eagle flieth; a nation whose tongue thou shalt not understand; a nation of fierce countenance, which shall not regard the person of the old, nor show favour to the young: …And he shall besiege thee in all thy gates, until thy high and fenced walls come down, wherein thou trustedst. …And thou shalt eat the fruit of thine own body, the flesh of thy sons and of thy daughters, which

the Lord thy God hath given thee, in the siege, and in the straitness wherewith thine enemies shall distress thee: So that the man that is tender among you and very delicate, his eye shall be evil toward his brother, and toward the wife of his bosom, and toward the remnant of his children which he shall leave; so that he will not give to any of them of the flesh of his children whom he shall eat; because he hath nothing left him in the siege, and in the straitness, wherewith thine enemies shall distress thee in all thy gates. The tender and delicate woman among you, which would not adventure to set the sole of her foot upon the ground for delicateness and tenderness, her eye shall be evil toward the husband of her bosom, and toward her son and toward her daughter, and toward her young one that cometh forth from between her feet, and toward her children which she shall bear: for she shall eat them for want of all things secretly in the siege and straitness wherewith thine enemies shall distress thee in thy gates.

The prophecy goes on to declare that the people of Israel were to be greatly diminished in numbers, were to be plucked off the land, and were to be scattered among all people, from one end of the earth even to the other, where they were to find no ease.

These predictions—terrible in their nature beyond all comparison—were fulfilled with appalling exactness and literalness in the siege of Jerusalem, and in the dispersion which followed it, and which has lasted until now. As we come to realize the character of these awful distresses, we shall surely be thankful that all things which were written, concerning the afflictions of the people of Israel, have now been fulfilled. We can but rejoice that there is no support whatever for the view that a time of distress, exceeding in severity the horrors of the siege of Jerusalem, yet awaits that much afflicted people.

It should be noticed that the nation whereof Moses speaks in this prophecy was to come from far, and was to be one whose tongue the Jews did not understand. Those specifications fit the Romans, but not the Assyrians or Chaldeans. Furthermore, in the tribulation foretold by Moses the people were to be plucked off the land and scattered among all nations from one end of the earth even to the other. This describes the result of the capture of Jerusalem by Titus, and not that of its capture by Nebuchadnezzar.

Prominent among the things that were written aforetime, and which our Lord said were to be fulfilled at the approaching destruction of Jerusalem, was that time of trouble foretold in Daniel 12:1, at which time some of Daniel's people were to be delivered, even such as should be found written in the book. This latter expression had come to mean, since the days of Moses (Ex 32:32) those who were accepted by God and owned as His. Such (i.e., believers in the Lord Jesus Christ) were delivered at that time through giving heed to His warnings.

The Abomination of Desolation

There is need that special attention be given to the words, When ye therefore shall see THE ABOMINATION OF DESOLATION, spoken of by Daniel the prophet, stand in the holy place (whoso readeth let him understand); then let them which be in Judea flee into the mountains, etc. (Matthew 24:15–16). The passage is the same it, Mark except that, instead of stand in the holy place, we read, standing where it ought not. In Luke the corresponding passage reads, And when ye shall see JERUSALEM COMPASSED WITH ARMIES, then know that THE DESOLATION thereof is nigh. Then let them which are in Judea flee to the mountains, etc.

This passage was, to the Lord's disciples then in Jerusalem and Judea, the most important of the entire prophecy; for it gave the sign whereby they were to know that the desolation, predicted in Daniel 9:26, was at hand, and upon seeing which they were to flee. Luke describes the sign in plain language. The encompassing of Jerusalem by armies was to be the warning that its desolation was nigh. But Matthew (for a reason which can be discerned) uses terms such that others than the disciples would not readily understand the meaning. To us, however, it should be clear, upon a mere comparison of the passages, that the armies which were to accomplish the desolation of the city were the abomination of desolation. But we will look further into the matter.

We have already pointed out that the word abomination means any hateful or detestable thing. It would most fittingly apply to the Roman armies on their mission of destruction. Indeed the descriptive words, of desolation, fix the meaning definitely. Yet, according to an interpretation that is widely accepted at this time, it means the setting up of an idol for worship in a Jewish temple which (it is supposed) will be built at Jerusalem in the days of Antichrist. But, in that case, the words of desolation would be quite out of place; for no one will contend that Jerusalem is to be again made a desolation. Another insuperable objection to that view is that God would not regard or speak of any part of such a temple as the holy place.

Our modern expositors have been misled by this expression (used by Matthew) the holy place. They have assumed that it meant the holy of holies in the temple. But it does not mean that at all. Anyone, with the help of a concordance (as Young's or Strong's) or a Greek dictionary, can see for himself that the word used for place in Matthew 24:15 (Matthew 24:15) is topos, which means simply a locality (we derive from it the words topical, topography, etc.). It is used in expressions like a desert place, dry places. The holy land, Judea, is therefore the holy place, where the heathen armies, with their idolatrous standards and pagan sacrifices, were to stand. Mark puts it simply as standing where it ought not. On the other hand, the term hagios topos is never used of the holy of holies of the temple. (See original text of Hebrews 9:12, 24–25.)

The Lord was referring to the particular abomination of desolation spoken of by Daniel the prophet, and at this point occurs the exhortation, Whoso readeth let him understand. The expression abomination of desolation is found only in the Septuagint version of Daniel 9:27. What then was it that is referred to in that verse? Clearly it is that which was to be God's instrument in bringing about the predicted desolation. The Hebrew text, of which our AV is a translation, reads and for the overspreading of abominations, he shall make it desolate. If instead of for, we read, by the overspreading of abominations, we have a very good indication of the spreading abroad of the Roman armies.

In Daniel 11:31 and 12:11 is a slightly different expression which makes the meaning more clear, namely, abomination that maketh desolate. That the words When ye see the abomination of desolation stand in the holy place do not mean the setting up of an idol in the inner sanctuary, further appears by consideration of the fact that it was when the disciples should see the thing referred to, that they were to know it was time for them to flee. Manifestly the setting up of an idol in the inner sanctuary could not be a Sign to the Lord's people to flee. That would be a thing which only the priests could see. And it could not possibly be a sign to them that be in Judea. Whereas the invading armies would be a sight which all could see.

Furthermore, the setting up of an idol in the sanctuary is a thing which could not be done until the city and temple were taken by the enemy, which would be at the end of the siege. Hence it could not possibly serve as a sign to the disciples to save themselves from the horrors of the siege by timely flight.

The difference between the way Matthew describes this sign to flee, and the way Luke describes it, is accounted for by the fact that Matthew's Gospel was written primarily for circulation among the Palestinian Jews. We can understand, therefore, why the Holy Spirit inspired him to use an expression which would not be understood except by the disciples. But no such reason would exist in the case of Luke's Gospel, he being the companion of Paul in his journeys through the Greek provinces, and his Gospel having been written primarily for Gentile converts. Matthew and Mark have the significant admonition, Whoso readeth let him understand. But in Luke, where the meaning is stated in clear words, that admonition is not found.

In confirmation of our view as to the abomination of desolation, we quote the following from a sound and standard work, *Smith's Bible Dictionary*:

> "Abomination of Desolation, mentioned by our Savior (Matthew 24:15), as a sign of the approaching destruction of Jerusalem, with reference to (Daniel 9:27; 11:31; 12:11.) The prophecy referred ultimately to the destruction of Jerusalem by the Romans, and consequently the abomination must describe some occurrence connected with that event...Most people refer it to the standards or banners of the Roman army."

We believe, however, that it is not the standards carried by the armies, but the armies themselves that constituted the abomination of desolation, or that maketh desolate. This conclusion is fully supported by the facts, (1) that where Matthew says when ye see the abomination of desolation, Luke says when ye see Jerusalem encompassed with armies, then know that the desolation thereof is nigh; and (2) the armies were the agency whereby the desolation was accomplished.

In further confirmation of our view as to this point we quote also from Farquharson the following clear passage:

> "Christ expressly names it (the abomination of desolation) as one of the previous signs, whereby those whom He then addressed would become aware of the immediate approach of that destruction of Jerusalem which He Himself foretold, and which, He said, would occur before the generation contemporary with Himself on earth passed away (Mt 24:34). Besides, Christ, by the term 'abomination of desolation' did not mean any temple built to a strange god, or any profane sacrifices. These are indeed abominable; but they are not desolators. Luke has preserved the explanation which Christ Himself gave of those terms ('when ye see Jerusalem compassed with armies,' etc. Luke 21:20), as we shall

have occasion afterwards more particularly to show; and Bishop Newton, in his illustration of Christ's own prophecy, refers to the explanation furnished by Luke and admits that the abomination of desolation signifies the heathen armies."

Also from the same author we quote the following passage, which occurs in the course of his comments upon Daniel 12:1, "And at that time thy people shall be delivered, every one that shall be found written in the book": —

> "The prediction of the prophet then, in this latter part of the first verse, was fulfilled in that part of Daniel's people who, obeying the call of the Savior to faith in Him, and repentance and new obedience, obtained through His blood eternal redemption. Although the Jewish rulers and the greater part. of the nation would not have Him to be their King, but delivered Him up to the Gentiles, yet says Paul, 'God hath not east away His people which He foreknew,' but, as in the days of Elias He reserved to Himself seven thousand men who had not bowed the knee to the image of Baal, even so now, 'at this present time also, there is a remnant according to the election of grace' (Romans 11:2–5). Within a short time after Christ's ascension this 'remnant' amounted to several thousands (Acts 2:41; 4:4); and afterwards 'believers were added to the Lord, multitudes of men and women' (Acts 5:14). These were at that time 'delivered.' ...But there was added to the eternal deliverance they thus obtained a temporal deliverance also, in that 'time of trouble,' 'during which their unbelieving countrymen perished by sword and famine. For He in Whom they believed had taught them the signs that should precede the approaching calamities, and had warned them to escape from them by a timely flight (Matthew 24:15–16). Of His warnings they availed themselves. We learn from ecclesiastical histories,' says Bishop Newton, 'that at this juncture (the approach of the siege of Jerusalem) all who believed in Christ departed from Jerusalem, and removed to Pella and other places beyond the River Jordan; so that they all marvellously escaped the general shipwreck of their countrymen; and we do not read anywhere that so much as one of them perished in the destruction of Jerusalem.' Thus, in every sense, 'at that time Daniel's people were delivered, all who were found written in the book.'

Luke's Account. Is it the Same Discourse?

We would notice at this point an idea which has been advanced by a few commentators (not any of prominence so far as we are aware) namely that the account found in Luke 21 is that of a different utterance of Christ from that reported in the corresponding parts of Matthew and Mark. This idea is really a confirmation of what we have been seeking to prove; for those who suggest it must have recognized that, if Luke 21 gives us an account of the same utterance as is reported by the other two gospel writers, then it must be that the great tribulation of the latter is the fall of Jerusalem described by the former, and the abomination of desolation is the armed Roman force.

But the idea referred to above is utterly untenable. According to each of the three writers the discourse occurred just after Christ left the temple for the last time; and according to each it began with the same words (not one stone shall be left upon another); and moreover the prophetic part was spoken in reply to the question of the disciples (tell us, etc.). And not only so, but the account by Luke follows the same order as the others, and uses in many passages precisely the same words. It is simply an impossibility that there should have been two distinct discourses on the same day, arising out of the same incident, and in response to the same question, from the same disciples.

It is nothing to the purpose that Matthew and Mark state the place where the conversation took place (the Mount of Olives) whereas Luke omits mention of that detail. There would be as much ground to argue that Christ endured two different agonies on the night of His betrayal, in two different places, because, while Matthew and Mark give Gethsemane as the place, Luke does not specify the name of the locality where what he describes (with differences of detail from the others) took place.

The proof is conclusive that the three accounts refer to one and the same discourse, and that what Luke plainly identifies as the then approaching destruction of Jerusalem, the other two evangelists spoke of under the general term "great tribulation."

Israel's Last Probation

We have sought to impress upon our readers the fact that the destruction of Jerusalem, and the final breakup of the Jewish nation, was a matter of immense importance in the history of the world, as divinely viewed and written. We would now, in closing this chapter, call attention to the fact that God, in marvelous forbearance and goodness, did not execute His righteous judgment upon the nation at once, but gave them a final period of probation, which lasted just 40 years, from AD 30, when the Lord was crucified, to AD 70, when the city was destroyed and the nation exterminated.

The number 40 appears to be the measure of full probation. The Israelites were tested for 40 years in the wilderness at the beginning of their national career. That was under the Law. And at the end thereof, God gave them another probation of 40 years, under the Gospel. Other periods of full probation are found in the Scriptures, as when Moses left the people to themselves, while he was in the mountain 40 days. The first three kings of Israel (Saul, David and Solomon) reigned the full period of 40 years. And finally our Lord was tested for 40 days in the wilderness, with the wild beasts, and tempted of the devil.

The Time of Jacob's Trouble

The reference to the time of Jacob's trouble is found in (Jeremiah 30:5–7). From what appears in Chapter 29:1, as well as from the immediate context, it is evident that the prophecy concerning Jacob's trouble was spoken after the captivity in Babylon had begun; so it was not the punishment inflicted by Nebuchadnezzar that the prophet was foretelling. This is made very plain by the verses immediately preceding the prophecy of Jacob's trouble, in which God says that He will bring again the captivity of His people and cause them to return to the land of their fathers. So the predicted order of events was the return of the captivity from Babylon, and after that the time of Jacob's trouble, which is foretold in these striking words:

> "For thus saith the Lord; We have heard a voice of trembling, of fear, and not of peace. Ask ye now and see whether a man doth travail with child? Wherefore do I see every man with his hands on his loins, as a woman in travail, and all faces are turned into paleness? Alas! for that day is great, so that none is like it; it is even the time of Jacob's trouble; but he shall be saved out of it" (Jeremiah 30:5–7).

The destruction of Jerusalem by the Romans is a complete fulfillment of this prophecy. Why then should we ignore a conspicuous historical fulfillment and surmise a fulfillment in the future, for which there is no proof?

The words none is like it establish the fact hat the time of Jacob's trouble, foretold by Jeremiah, is the same as the time of trouble such as never was, foretold to Daniel by the man clothed in linen, and the same as the great tribulation such as was not since the beginning of the world to this time, nor ever shall be, foretold by the Lord as then about to come upon the people. For there cannot be two such times of trouble.

Likewise the words of Jeremiah, But he shall be saved out of it, agree with the words, Thy people shall be delivered, every one that shall be found written in the book (Daniel 12:1); and with the words of Christ, But he that shall endure unto the end, the same shall be saved (Matthew 24:13). The agreement is striking.

Jeremiah, after prophesying the time of Jacob's trouble (of the particulars whereof he gives no description) proceeds to speak of another captivity for the nation, and of God's purpose to gather His people out of it, and to restore them again to their own land

(Jeremiah 30:10-11). This confirms the view that the captivity referred to in verse 3 is that in Babylon. Moreover, the terms used in describing the captivity spoken of in verses 10–11 show that it was a worldwide dispersion. For God says, 'I will save thee from afar... and Israel shall return and be at rest, and be quiet, and none shall make him afraid.' So here we have a captivity in distant lands, to be followed by a restoration and blessing—not by another tribulation. Further, we read 'For I am with thee, saith the Lord, to save thee though I make a full end of all nations whither I have scattered thee, yet will I not make a full end of end of thee' (Jeremiah 30:11).

Thus, according to all these three great prophecies which we have been studying and comparing, there was to be a time of unequaled trouble for Israel, followed by a world wide scattering of the survivors, and with this, history is in perfect agreement; for the time of trouble, such as never was either before or since, came within the generation specified by Christ, and was immediately followed by a world wide dispersion of the Jews, which has lasted until now; yet God has not made a full end of them.

All this is completely reversed by a current system of interpretation of prophecy, which makes the dispersion of the people of Israel come first, and the time of trouble such as never was to be reserved for them afterward, when God shall have brought them again, and finally, to their own land.

The Great Tribulation of Revelation 7

In Revelation 7:9–17 is described the vision of a great multitude which no man could number, of all nations and kindreds, and people, and tongues, of whom it is said that These are they which came out of great tribulation (or out of the great tribulation) and have washed their robes and made them white in the blood of the Lamb. There is nothing in this passage to show that the tribulation referred to is yet future, or to justify the expression, commonly heard in some quarters, tribulation saints. What John is here permitted to see is, not a future tribulation, but the future blessedness of those who, while on earth, were in great tribulation. The time when the tribulation occurred is not indicated at all.

We do not identify the tribulation of Matthew 24:21 with that of Revelation 7:14. The former is a specific event in history, and one that pertained strictly to the Jewish people The latter is general and indefinite.

There were people out of every nation, kindred, tongue and tribe, involved in it. The probability is (though at present we cannot express a decided opinion about it) that the company referred to (whose blessedness is precisely the same as that of all the redeemed as described in (Revelation 21:3-4) embraces all those who have suffered for the truth's sake, during all the centuries of persecution under imperial Rome and papal Rome. That tribulation, being of quite a different sort from the concrete tribulation which befell Jerusalem in AD 70, does not come into comparison with it. There was to be nothing of that sort to exceed it.

There is no good reason for doubting that the AV gives the true sense in saying, These are they which came out of great tribulation, which words do not specify a special class of sufferers, who passed through some special period of affliction. We utterly reject the idea of a separate company of tribulation saints, segregated from the main company of the redeemed, and appointed to some inferior sphere of blessing.

CHAPTER 15

The Siege of Jerusalem As Described by Josephus

In bringing now to the attention of our readers some of the things recorded by Josephus in his well known history of the last days of Jerusalem and the Jewish nation, it will be understood that we do not cite that work as evidence whereby we are to interpret the Scriptures; for we interpret the Word of God by comparing scripture with scripture. In fact we did not consult Josephus, or any other human writer, until after our conclusions as to the meaning of these prophecies (as stated in the foregoing pages) had been reached. We cite his work simply for what it is recognized on all hands to be, a trustworthy recital by an eyewitness of things which he had personal knowledge of, which things show that the word of Christ was fulfilled in the most literal way.

Farquharson quotes the following tribute to Flavius Josephus by Bishop Porteus:

"The fidelity, the veracity, and the probity of the writer are universally allowed; and Scaliger in particular declares, that not only in the affairs of the Jews, but even of foreign nations, he deserves more credit than all the Greek and Roman writers put together."

It is a matter of common knowledge that Jerusalem is, up to the present time, trodden down of the Gentiles, even as the Lord said; and that the Jews are still scattered among all nations. This is enough in itself to assure us that the Lord's prophecy in Luke 21 (and hence every other prophecy concerning the same event) has been, and is being, fulfilled. But surely it is a matter of deep interest to know how, when, and under what circumstances, those prophecies were fulfilled. The history of Josephus fully satisfies this legitimate desire; and we reiterate our belief that his account of those great events has been preserved providentially. Moreover, since Josephus was not a disciple of Christ at the time of writing his history, he cannot be suspected of having written his account of the destruction of Jerusalem with a view to supplying a fulfillment of the Lord's prophecy. His account was published in the year 75, so that it was written while the things he described were fresh in his memory. Their publication at a time when the truth of the matters related by him was known to thousands then living, is a further reason for our having confidence in the narrative.

Josephus describes the troubles which began under Pilate, the Roman governor, especially when he sent by night those images of Caesar which are called ensigns into Jerusalem (Bk. II ch. 9, sec. 2). Those ensigns or images of Caesar were particularly hateful to the Jews; and inasmuch as they were conspicuously carried in the Roman armies, we have here a reason why the latter were termed the abomination of desolation.

In the days when Cumanus was Roman Governor began the troubles, and the Jew's ruin came on (II 12:1). At that time Herod Agrippa II (the Agrippa before whom Paul appeared) was reigning as king over Galilee. He was by far the best of the Herod family; but we have no record that he was ever fully persuaded to accept Christ. At that time various calamities and disturbances began to take place. Bands of robbers infested the country, and in the city there arose an organized company of assassins called Sicarii, who slew men in the daytime, and in the city. This they did chiefly at festivals, when they mingled with the multitudes and, by means of daggers concealed under their garments, they stabbed those who were their enemies. The high priest Jonathan was one of their victims (II 13, 3).

Another class of trouble makers were certain men who, though not thieves or murderers, yet laid waste the happy state of the city no less than did those murderers. These were such men as deceived and deluded the people under pretense of Divine inspiration. It is easy to recognize in these men the false prophets whereof the Lord warned His disciples. Continuing, Josephus says' These prevailed with the multitude to act like madmen and went before them into the wilderness, pretending that God would there show them the signals of liberty (II 13:4).

There was also an Egyptian false prophet, who got together thirty thousand men that were deluded by him. These he led about from the wilderness to the mount which is called the mount of Olives. This, according to Josephus, was in the days when Felix was governor. Consequently it was at the time of Paul's last visit to Jerusalem, which calls to mind that the chief captain before whom Paul was taken after the disturbance in the Temple, supposed that he was that Egyptian, which before these days madest an uproar, and leddest out into the wilderness four thousand men that were murderers ((Acts 21:38). It also brings to mind the definite warning of Christ, Wherefore, if they shall say to you, Behold, He is in the desert, go not forth (Matthew 24:26).

Josephus likens the social conditions at that time to those of a body which is thoroughly diseased, in that when trouble subsided in one place it broke out immediately in another. For, says he, a company of deceivers and robbers got together, and persuaded the Jews to revolt, and exhorted them to assert their liberty (id. 6).

About this time Felix was succeeded by Festus (as is also recorded in (Acts 24:27), and he by Florus, who was the most wicked of all the Roman governors, and the immediate occasion of the war. This was in the twelfth year of Emperor Nero, AD 66. Josephus relates that when Cestius Gallus came to Jerusalem at the Passover season the people came about him not fewer in number than three millions (II 14:3). This shows the immense numbers which gathered in Jerusalem at that season.

Josephus relates with much detail the atrocities and barbarities which the people suffered at the hands of the soldiers, and describes their agonies and lamentations. On one occasion the soldiers, after plundering the citizens, crucified many of them, the number of those slain (including women and children) being about 3600 on that single occasion. It appears to have been the deliberate purpose of Florus to goad the Jews into a revolt, so that thereby his own acts of plunder and other crimes might be covered up (II 14, 9).

In Chapter 16 (Bk. II) Josephus gives a speech by Herod Agrippa, in which he used every persuasion and argument to restrain the Jews from the madness of revolting against the Romans. He eloquently pictured the vast power and extent of the Roman dominion as stretching from east to west, and from north to south. Indeed, said Agrippa, they have sought for another habitable earth beyond the ocean, and have carried their arms as far as the British Isles, which were never known before (II 16, 4). It seems strange to us that one of whom we read in the Bible should have spoken to the Jews in Jerusalem about the British Isles.

King Agrippa, as a final argument, attributed the world wide success of the Roman arms to the providence of God, for which reason he urged the Jews that it was vain for them to contend against them, and he concluded his speech with this strong appeal:

> "Have pity therefore, if not upon your children and wives, yet upon this your Metropolis and its sacred walls! Spare the Temple and preserve the Holy House, with its holy furniture! For if the Romans get you under their power they will no longer abstain from

(destroying) them, when their former abstinence shall have been so ungratefully requited. I call to witness your Sanctuary, and the holy angels of God, and this country, common to us all, that I have not kept back anything that is for your preservation. Josephus adds that, When Agrippa had spoken thus, both he and his sister (Bernice) wept, and by their tears repressed a great deal of the violence of the people."

Soon after this, however, the priests were persuaded that they should refuse to receive any gift or sacrifice for any foreigner. And this was the true beginning of our war with the Romans; for they (the temple authorities) rejected the sacrifice of Caesar on this account (II 17, 2).

There were at that time two parties in Jerusalem. One turbulent faction advocated immediate revolt against the Romans. The other party, led by the priests and the chief of the Pharisees, realizing the madness of the proposal, sought to restrain the seditious element; but finding they would not listen to argument or persuasion, they sent to the governor Florus, and also to Agrippa, for troops to quell the revolt. From that time the fighting began; but the Jews killed one another in numbers far greater than those slain by the soldiers. The Roman garrison was about that time besieged in the fortress of Antonia (in the temple area), and was taken and either slain or dispersed (II 17, 7). A little later another Roman garrison, besieged at Masada, which had been Herod's stronghold, surrendered under promise that their lives would be spared, but they were treacherously slain after they had laid down their arms (II 17, 10). These actions, of course, aroused the Roman authorities, who began to make preparations to subdue the revolters. In the city of Caesarea (built by Herod the Great), above 20,000 Jews were killed in one hour, and all Caesarea was emptied of its Jewish inhabitants; for Florus caught such as ran away, and sent them to the galleys. This enraged the whole Jewish nation, so that they laid waste the villages of Syria and elsewhere, burning some cities to the ground.

"But," says Josephus, "the Syrians were even with the Jews in the multitude of the men they slew. The disorders in all Syria were terrible. Every city was divided into two armies, and the preservation of the one party was in the destruction of the other. So the daytime was spent in shedding of blood, and the night in fear, which was, of the two, the more terrible...

"It was then common to see cities filled with dead bodies, still lying unburied; those of old men mingled with infants, all scattered about together. Women also lay among them without any covering. You might then see the whole province full of inexpressible calamities."

In some places the horrors were worse because Jews fought against Jews. In Scythopolis alone above 13,000 were slain at one time (II 18:1–2). Josephus relates the case of one prominent man who, because of the terrible things happening all around, and in order to save his family from a worse fate, killed first his father and mother with the sword they willingly submitting and afterwards his wife and children, finally taking his own life (II 18:3). This incident will give us at least a faint idea of the awful conditions of those 'days of vengeance, and of wrath upon this people.

Many pages are filled with accounts of the slaughter of the Jews in various places. Reading them we are impressed with the Savior's saying that except those days should be shortened there should no flesh be saved (Matthew 24:22). The calamities were beyond description. Thus, at Alexandria, where the Jews had enjoyed the greatest privileges for centuries, they were incited to rise in revolt by the seditious element, and were destroyed unmercifully, and this, their destruction, was complete. Houses were first plundered of what was in them, and then set on fire by the Romans. No mercy was shown to the infants, and no regard had to the aged; but they went on with the slaughter of persons of every age, till all the place was overflowed with blood, and fifty thousand of them lay dead in heaps (II 18:8).

The Strange Retreat of Cestius

The Roman general, Cestius, now led his army from Syria into Judea, destroying widely, and laid siege to Jerusalem. He made such rapid progress that the city was on the point of being captured. The seditious element fled in large numbers, and the peaceable inhabitants were about to throw open the gates to the Romans, when a remarkable thing took place, so unaccountable from any natural standpoint that it can only be attributed to the direct intervention of God, and for the fulfilment of the word of Christ. Josephus tells how the people were about to admit Cestius as their benefactor, when he suddenly recalled his soldiers and retired from the city without any reason in the world. Had he not withdrawn when he did, the city and the sanctuary would, of course, have been spared; and Josephus says it was, I suppose, owing to he aversion God already had towards the city and the sanctuary that he (Cestius) was hindered from putting an end to the war that very day (II 19:6).

But the translator of the history, William Whiston, adds a note at this point, which we quote in full:

> "There may be another very important and very providential reason assigned for this strange and foolish retreat of Cestius, which, if Josephus had been at the time of writing his history a Christian, he might probably have taken notice of also; and that is the opportunity afforded the Jewish Christians in the city, of calling to mind the prediction and caution given them by Christ that 'when they should see the abomination of desolation' (the idolatrous Roman armies, with the images of their idols in their ensigns) ready to lay Jerusalem desolate, 'stand where it ought not,' or 'in the holy place'; or 'when they should see Jerusalem encompassed with armies,' they should then 'flee to the mountains.' By complying with which, those Jewish Christians fled to the mountains of Perea, and escaped this destruction. Nor was there perhaps any one instance of a more unpolitical, but more providential conduct, than this retreat of Cestius visible during this whole siege of Jerusalem, which (siege)

was providentially such a 'great tribulation as has not been from the beginning of the world to that time; no, nor ever should be.'"

It was very apparent to this learned translator, and must be apparent, we should think, to all who are acquainted both with the three inspired records of our Lord's Olivet prophecy, and also with the historical facts so wonderfully preserved in this history by Josephus, that the three accounts refer to the same event, that the abomination of desolation was the armies of imperial and pagan Rome, and that the unparalleled sufferings of the Jews during those five years of terror, were the great tribulation foretold by the Lord in Matthew 24:21.

The Days of Vengeance

Josephus devotes nearly two hundred large pages (they would fill upwards of four hundred ordinary size) to the account of the events of' those 'days of vengeance', which l (as we have seen) involved not only the Jews in Palestine, but Jews all over the world. We can refer to but a very few of those tragic events; but, inasmuch as not many of our readers have access to the history of Josephus, we believe we are rendering them a service in giving the best idea we can, in small compass, of the happenings of those times.

After the retreat of Cestius, there was a slaughter of about 10,000 Jews at Damascus; and then, it being evident that war with the Romans was inevitable, the Jews began making preparations to defend Jerusalem. At that time Josephus, the writer of this history, was appointed general of the armies in Galilee. He seems to have had great ability and success as a soldier, though he was finally overpowered and captured by the Romans. Concerning one of his military operations his translator says' I cannot but think this stratagem of Josephus to be one of the finest that ever was invented and executed by any warrior whatsoever.

At this point the emperor Nero appointed Vespasian, a valiant and experienced general, to the task of subduing the Jews; and

The Seige of Jerusalem

Vespasian designated his son Titus to assist him. They invaded Judea from the north, marching along the coast, and killing many 18,000 at Askelon alone. Thus Galilee was all over filled with fire and blood; nor was it exempt from any kind of misery or calamity (III 4:1). Josephus opposed the Roman invasion with such forces as he had, but one by one the cities were taken and their inhabitants slain. Finally, Josephus himself was driven to take refuge in Jotapata, which, after long and desperate resistance, was taken by Vespasian. The incidents of this siege were terrible; and among them were events which forcibly recall the Lord's words, But woe to them that are with child, and to them that give suck in those days. The Romans were so enraged by the long and fierce resistance of the Jews that they spared none, nor pitied any. Many, moreover, in desperation, killed themselves. The life of Josephus was spared in a manner which seems miraculous (III 8:4–7), and he was taken captive to Vespasian, to whom he prophesied that both he and Titus his son would be Caesar and emperor...From that time till the end of the war Josephus was kept a prisoner; but he was with Titus during the subsequent siege of Jerusalem, in which the atrocities and miseries reached a limit impossible to be exceeded on earth. Only the state of the lost in hell could be worse.

After Jotapata fell, Joppa was taken, and then Tiberias and Taricheae on Lake Gennesaret. Thousands were killed, and upwards of 30,000 from the last named place alone were sold into slavery. Having now completely subdued Galilee, Vespasian led his army to Jerusalem.

For a right understanding of Matthew 24:15–21 it is important to know that the Roman armies were, for more than a year, occupied with the devastation of the provinces of Galilee and Judea, before Jerusalem was besieged. It should be noted also that Christ's first warnings to flee were to them which be in Judea (Matthew 24:16). This makes it perfectly certain that the abomination of desolation standing in the holy place, which was the appointed signal for them which be in Judea to flee into the mountains, was not an idol set up in the inner sanctuary of the Temple. For the desolation of Judea was completed long before Jerusalem and the Temple were taken.

At the time Vespasian led his armies to Jerusalem, that doomed city was in a state of indescribable disorder and confusion insomuch that, during the entire siege, the Jews suffered far more from one another inside the walls than from the enemy outside. Josephus says there were disorders and civil war in every city, and all those that were at quiet from the Romans turned their hands one against another. There was also a bitter contest between those that were for war, and those that were desirous for peace (IV 3:2).

Josephus further tells of the utter disgrace and ruin of the high priesthood, the basest of men being exalted to that office; and also of the profanation of the sanctuary.

The most violent party in the city was the Zealots. These called to their aid a band of blood thirsty Idumeans, who set upon the people who were peaceably inclined, and slaughtered young and old until the outer temple was all of it overflowed with blood, and that day they saw 8500 dead bodies there. Among the slain was Ananias, formerly high priest, a venerable and worthy man, concerning whom Josephus said:

> "I should not mistake if I said that the death of Ananias was the beginning of the destruction of the city, and that from this very day may be dated the overthrow of her wall, and the ruin of her affairs; that being the day whereon they saw their high priest, and the procurer of their preservation, slain in the midst of their city... And I cannot but think it was because God had doomed this city to destruction, as a polluted city, and was resolved to purge His sanctuary with fire, that He cut off these, their great defenders, while those that a little before had worn the sacred garments and presided over the public worship, were cast out naked to be the food of dogs and wild beasts...

"Now after these were slain the Zealots and the Idumeans fell upon the people as upon a flock of profane animals, and cut their throats."

Josephus also tells of the terrible torments inflicted upon nobles and citizens of the better sort who refused to comply with the demands of the Zealots. Those, after being horribly tortured, were slain, and through fear, none dared bury them. In this way 12,000 of the more eminent inhabitants perished (IV 5:3). We quote further:

"Along all the roads also vast numbers of dead bodies lay in heaps; and many who at first were zealous to desert the city chose rather to perish there; for the hopes of burial made death m their own city appear less terrible to them. But those zealots came at last to that degree of barbarity as not to bestow a burial either on those slain in the city or on those that lay along the roads; as if...at the same time that they defiled men with their wicked actions they would pollute the Deity itself also, they left the dead bodies to putrefy under the sun." (IV. 6. 3).

About this time above 15,000 fugitive Jews were killed by the Romans, and the number of those that were forced to leap into the Jordan was prodigious. ...The whole country through which they fled was filled with slaughter, and Jordan could not be passed over, by reason of the dead bodies that were in it (IV. 8. 5, 6).

Vespasian Recalled—Titus Placed in Charge

At this point Vespasian was called to Rome by reason of the death of the emperor Nero, and the operations

against the Jews devolved upon Titus. Vespasian himself was soon thereafter made emperor.

Meanwhile another tyrant rose up, whose name was Simon, and of him Josephus says: Now this Simon, who was without the wall, was a greater terror to the people than the Romans themselves; while the Zealots who were within it were more heavy upon them than both the other. Those Zealots were led by a tyrant named John; and the excesses of murder and uncleanness in which they habitually indulged are indescribable (see Bk. IV, ch. 9, sec. 10).

In order to overthrow John, the people finally admitted Simon and his followers. From that time onward the civil warfare within the city became more incessant and deadly. The distracted city was now divided into three factions instead of two. The fighting was carried even into the inner court of the temple; whereupon Josephus laments that even those who came with sacrifices to offer them in the temple were slain, and sprinkled that altar with their own blood, till the dead bodies of strangers were mingled together with those of their own country, and those of profane persons with those of priests, and the blood of all sort of dead carcases stood in lakes in the holy courts themselves (V 1:3).

Surely there never were such conditions as these in any city before or since.

Among the dire calamities which befell the wretched people was the destruction of the granaries and storehouses of food; so that famine was soon added to the other horrors. The warring factions were agreed in nothing but to kill those that were innocent. Says Josephus:

> "The noise of those that were fighting was incessant, both by day and by night; but the lamentations of those that mourned exceeded the noise of the fighting. Nor was there ever any occasion for them to leave off their lamentations, because their calamities came perpetually, one upon another....But as for the seditious bands themselves, they fought against each other while trampling upon the dead bodies which lay heaped one upon another, and being filled with a mad rage from those dead bodies under their feet, they became the more fierce. They, moreover, were still inventing pernicious things against each other; and when they had resolved upon anything, they executed it without mercy, and omitted no method of torment or of barbarity" (V. 2. 5).

At the time described in the preceding paragraphs, the Roman armies had not yet reached the city, and inasmuch as the

The Seige of Jerusalem

Passover season now came on, and things seemed to quiet down momentarily, the gates were opened for such as wished to observe the great feast. The translator, in a footnote, says:

> "Here we see the true occasion of those vast numbers of Jews that were in Jerusalem during this siege by Titus and who perished therein. For the siege began at the feast of Passover, when such prodigious multitudes of the Jews and proselytes were come from all parts of Judea, and from other countries. ...As to the number that perished during this siege, Josephus assures us, as we shall see hereafter, they were 1,100,000, besides 97,000 captives."

This is notable as the last Passover. That joyous feast of remembrance of God's great deliverance of His people out of Egypt ended in an orgy of blood. The tyrant John took advantage of this opportunity to introduce some of his followers, with concealed weapons, among the throngs of worshippers in the temple, who slew many, while others were rolled in heaps together, and trampled upon, and beaten without mercy.

And now, though the Roman armies were at their gates, the warring factions began again to destroy one another and the innocent inhabitants."

> "For", says Josephus, "they returned to their former madness, and separated one from another, and fought it out; and they did everything that the besiegers could desire them to do. For they never suffered from the Romans anything worse than they made each other suffer; nor was there any misery endured by the city which, after what these men did, could be esteemed new. It was most of all unhappy before it was overthrown; and those that took it did it a kindness. For I venture to say that the sedition destroyed the city, and the Romans destroyed the sedition. This was a much harder thing to do than to destroy the walls. So that we may justly ascribe our misfortunes to our own people" (V. 6. 2).

This is the most astonishing feature of this great tribulation; for surely there never was a besieged city whose inhabitants suffered more from one another than from the common enemy. In this feature of the case we see most clearly that it is one of judgment; and that, as the apostle Paul said, the wrath is come upon them to the uttermost.

At this point the siege began in earnest. Titus, however, sent Josephus to speak to the Jews, offering them clemency, and exhorting them to yield. Josephus made a most earnest plea to them not to resist the might of Rome, pointing out that God was no longer with them. But it was to no purpose. So the siege proceeded outside, and the famine began to rage inside, insomuch that children pulled out of their parents' mouths the morsels they were eating, and even mothers deprived their infants of the last bits of food that might have sustained their lives.

The fighters, of course, kept for their own use what food there was, and it seems that they took a keen delight in seeing others suffer. It was a species of madness. They invented terrible methods of torments, such as it would not be seemly for us to describe. And this was done, says Josephus, to keep their madness in exercise (V 10:3). The most horrible and unbelievable torments were inflicted upon all who were suspected of having any food concealed. The following passage will give an idea of the conditions:

> "It is impossible to give every instance of the iniquity of these men. I shall therefore speak my mind here at once briefly: that neither did any other city suffer such miseries, nor did any age ever breed a generation more fruitful in wickedness than this was, from the beginning of the world. (This forcibly brings to mind the Lord's own words.) Finally they brought the Hebrew nation into contempt, that they might themselves appear comparatively less impious with regard to strangers. They confessed, what was true, that they were the scum, and the spurious and abortive offspring of our nation, while they overthrew the city themselves, and forced the Romans, whether they would or no, to gain a melancholy reputation by acting gloriously against them; and did almost draw that fire upon the temple which they seemed to think came too slowly" (V. 10. 5).

Under pressure of the famine many Jews went out at night into the valleys in search of food. These were caught, tortured and crucified in sight of those on the walls of the city. About five hundred every day were thus treated. The number became finally so great that there was not room enough for the crosses, nor crosses enough for the victims. So several were oftentimes nailed to one cross.

A little later the Roman armies encompassed the entire city, so that there was no longer any egress therefrom.

> "Then," says Josephus, "did the famine widen its progress and devour the people by whole houses and families. The upper rooms were full of women and children dying by famine; and the lanes of the city were full of the dead bodies of the aged. The children also and the young men wandered about the marketplaces like shadows, all swelled with the famine, and fell down dead, wheresoever their misery seized them" (V. 12. 3).

Thus did the miseries of Jerusalem grow worse and worse every day....And indeed the multitude of carcasses that lay in heaps, one upon another, was a horrible sight, and produced a pestilential stench which was a hindrance to those that would make sallies out of the city and fight the enemy (VI. 1. 1).

The number of those that perished by famine in the city was prodigious, and their miseries were unspeakable. For if so much as the shadow of any kind of food did anywhere appear, a war was commenced presently, and the dearest friends fell a fighting one another about it.

In this connection Josephus relates in detail the case of a woman, eminent for her family and her wealth, who, while suffering the ravages of famine, slew her infant son and roasted him, and having eaten half of him, concealed the other half. When presently the seditious Jews came in to search the premises, and smelt the horrid scent of this food, they threatened her life if she did not show them what food she had prepared. She replied that she had saved for them a choice part, and withal uncovered what was left of the little body, saying, Come, eat of this food; for I have eaten of it myself. Do not you pretend to be more tender than a woman, or more compassionate than a mother. Even those desperate and hardened men were horrified at the sight, and stood aghast at the deed of this mother. They left trembling; and the whole city was full of what the woman had done. It must be remembered that all this time the lives of all in the city would have been spared and the city and temple saved, had they but yielded to the Romans. But how then should the Scripture be fulfilled? (see Deuteronomy 28:56–57) Soon after this the temple was set on fire and was burned down, though Titus tried to save it. Josephus says:

But as for that house, God had for certain long ago doomed it to the fire; and now that fatal day was come, according to the revolution of ages. It was the tenth day of the month Ab, the day upon which it was formerly burnt by the king of Babylon (VI. 4. 5).

Further Josephus says:

> "While the holy house was on fire everything was plundered that came to hand, and ten thousand of those were slain. Nor was there commiseration of any age, or any reverence of gravity; but children, old men, profane persons, and priests were all slain in the same manner....Moreover many, when they saw the fire, exerted their utmost strength, and did break out into groans and outcries. Perea also did return the echo, as well as the mountains round about Jerusalem, and augmented the force of the noise."

Yet was the misery itself more terrible than this disorder. For one would have thought that the hill itself, on which the temple stood, was seething hot, as if full of fire on every part, that the blood was more in quantity than the fire, and that the slain were more in numbers than they who slew them. For the ground did nowhere appear visible because of the dead bodies that lay upon it (VL 5. 1).

In describing how a number were killed in a certain cloister, which the soldiers set on fire, Josephus says:

"A false prophet was the occasion of the destruction of those people, he having made a public proclamation that very day that God commanded them to get upon the temple and that they should receive miraculous signs of their deliverance. There was then a large number of false prophets suborned by the tyrants to impose on the people, who announced to them that they should wait for deliverance from God" (VI. 5. 2).

In this detail also the Lord's Olivet prophecy was most literally fulfilled.

When at last the Romans gained entrance into the city, the soldiers had become so exasperated by the stubborn resistance of the Jews, that they could not be restrained from wreaking vengeance upon the survivors. So they indulged in slaughter until weary of it. The survivors were sold into slavery, but at a very low price, because they were so numerous, and the buyers were few. Thus was fulfilled the word of the Lord by Moses, And there ye shall be sold unto your enemies for bondmen and bondwomen, and no man shall buy you (Deuteronomy 28:68).

Many were put into bonds and sold to slavery in the Egyptian mines, thus fulfilling several prophecies that they should be sold into Egypt again, whence God had delivered them (Hosea 8:13; 9:3).

In concluding this part of his history Josephus gives the number of those who perished (a million one hundred thousand) and of those sold into slavery (ninety seven thousand), and explains, as we have already stated, that they were come up from all the country to the feast of unleavened bread, and were on a sudden shut up by an army. And he adds:

> "Now this vast multitude was indeed collected out of remote places, but the entire nation was now shut up by fate as in prison,

and the Roman army encompassed the city when it was crowded with inhabitants. Accordingly the multitude of those that perished therein exceeded all the destructions that either men or God ever brought upon the world" (VI. 9. 4).

Thus ended, in the greatest of all calamities of the sort, the national existence of the Jewish people, and all that pertained to that old covenant which was instituted with glory (2 Corinthians 3:7, 9, 11), but which was to be done away.

Here may be seen an example of the thoroughness of God's judgments, when He arises to do His strange work. Judgment must begin at the house of God; and in view of what is brought to our notice in this history of Josephus, how impressive is the question, And if it begin at us, what shall the end be of them that obey not the gospel of God? (1 Peter 4:17).

CHAPTER 16

Concluding Comments

Edersheim on Matthew 24

We find that reliable commentators of earlier days have pointed out (treating it as a matter too evident to require argument) that when Christ warned His disciples of the great tribulation that was to come, He meant the distresses which would attend the then approaching destruction of Jerusalem. Alfred Edersheim, who was one of the very ablest of commentators, has thus expounded the Lord's Olivet prophecy. We attach special weight and authority to his expositions, for the reason that there is probably no man of modern times who possessed such an extensive and accurate knowledge as he of the customs, manners, habits of thought, writings, and traditions of the Jews and of their leaders, in the days of Christ. *His Life and Times of Jesus the Messiah* gives a marvelously full, detailed and accurate picture of Judea and its inhabitants Jews, proselytes, priests, rabbis, scribes, Pharisees, Sadducees, Herodians, Greeks and Romans at the beginning of our era. If one were to read but half a dozen books, in addition to the Bible, Edersheim's great work should be one of the six.

Edersheim sees four divisions in the Lord's Olivet prophecy, as recorded in Matthew 24; and it will be instructive to follow his analysis of that Chapter.

1. The *first* division comprises verses 6-8, (Matthew 24:6-8) which contain warnings to the disciples that they are not to regard the sorrows He was foretelling (the wars, famines, pestilences and earthquakes) as the judgments which would usher in the Advent of their Lord; in other words, they were not to regard wars, famines, as the signs of His second coming. Those warnings have been needed throughout the age. For the sorrows foretold by Christ, especially when they happened in connection with the appearance of some supposed Antichrist from Nero down to Napoleon and more recently to the German Kaiser have frequently, says Mr. Edersheim, misled Christians into an erroneous expectancy of the immediate advent of Christ. It is really surprising that the Lord's people should so persistently take to be signs of His coming the very things He warned them were not to be regarded as such.

2. The *second* division of the prophecy embraces Matthew 24:9-14. It contains warnings broader in scope than those of the first section. Two general dangers are here specified; (a) internal, from heresies ('false prophets') and decay of faith; (b) external, from persecutions. But along with those two dangers, two consoling facts are also pointed out. The first is that, notwithstanding the fierce persecutions they were to undergo from those high in authority, Divine aid would be given them, and by the presence and power of the Holy Spirit they would be enabled to testify before kings, rulers and tribunals (Mark 13:9). The second consoling fact, as pointed out by Edersheim, is that despite the persecutions by Jews and Gentiles, before the end cometh 'this gospel of the kingdom' shall be preached in all the inhabited earth for a testimony to all nations. This then is really the only sign of 'the end' of this present age.

3. The *third* division of the prophecy is contained in Matthew 24:15-28. Concerning this division Mr. Edersheim says "The Lord proceeds, in the third part of this discourse, to advertise the disciples of the great historic fact immediately before them, and of the dangers which would spring from it. In truth we have

here His answer to their question 'when shall these things be?' And with this He conjoins the (then) present application of His warning regarding false Christs (given in verses 4–5). The fact of which He now advertises them is the destruction of Jerusalem. It will be observed that the question, When shall these things be? is directly answered by the words, When ye shall see (Matthew 24:15 Luke. 21:20). Mr. Edersheim further says: This, together with tribulation to Israel, unparalleled in the terrible past of its history, and unequaled even in its bloody future was about to befall them. Nay, so dreadful would be the persecution that, if Divine mercy had not interposed for the sake of the followers of Christ, the whole Jewish race that inhabited the land would have been swept away. There should have been no flesh saved. We endorse, and heartily commend, this simple and satisfactory explanation of the Lord's words, And except those days should be shortened there should no flesh be saved (Matthew 24:22). We have already shown, from the records of Josephus, how those awful days were shortened.

4. The *fourth* division of the prophecy is contained in Matthew 24:29–31. As to this portion Mr. Edersheim says, "The times of the Gentiles, 'the end of the age', and with it the new allegiance of His then penitent people Israel, 'the sign of the Son of man in heaven' perceived by them, ...the coming of Christ, the last trumpet, the resurrection of the dead such, in most rapid sketch, is the outline which the Lord draws of His coming and the end of the world (age)."

This finishes the prophetic part of the Chapter; and now at Matthew 24:32–33 the Lord speaks a parable to impress upon the minds of His disciples the importance and the application of the sign He had given them, whereby they might know that the destruction of the holy city was near. We quote further from Edersheim:

> "From the fig tree, under which on that spring afternoon they may have rested, they were to learn a parable. We can picture Christ taking one of its twigs, just as its softening tips were bursting into

young leaf. Surely this meant that summer was nigh not that it had actually come. The distinction is important; for it seems to prove that 'all these things' which were to indicate to them that 'it' was 'near, even at the doors', and which were to be fulfilled ere 'this generation' had passed away, could not have referred to the last signs connected with the advent of Christ, but must apply to the previous prediction of the destruction of Jerusalem and of the Jewish commonwealth. This too is a very simple and satisfactory explanation of the words, This generation shall not pass till all these things be fulfilled. If those words be taken as His answer to the question, When shall these things be? (verse 3), they are easy of interpretation; but if their application be postponed to the far off future they present much difficulty. For example, thus to postpone their application would make the Lord contradict His positive and most emphatic statement that no signs would precede and give warning of His second advent."

Edersheim further points out in this connection that the bursting of the fig tree into leaf is not the sign of harvest, which is the end of the age, but of summer, which precedes the harvest. This is significant.

The Beginning of Sorrows

In describing the wars and other commotions which were to characterize this age from the very start, the Lord used an expression which calls for special notice. All these, He said, are the beginning of birth pangs (Matthew 24:8). This word pictures to us the present age as one of pains and sorrows such as accompany childbirth. But there is a decidedly hopeful character to such pains; for they eventuate in that which causes joy. This present age is the period of the birth pangs of the new era, which will be that of the manifestation of the sons of God.

The word birth pangs connects this part of our Lord's prophecy with that of Paul in (Romans 8:22, where the same word occurs in its verb form, "For we know", says the apostle, "that the whole creation groaneth and travaileth in pain together until now". But the verses which precede tell what the joyful outcome will be, namely, the manifestation of the sons of God, also called the adoption, at which time the creation itself also shall be delivered from the bondage of corruption into the glorious liberty of the children of God.

The word *travail-in-birth* is found again in a similar connection in (1 Thessalonians 5:3,) where (speaking of the coming of the day of the Lord) Paul says: For when they shall say, Peace and safety; then sudden destruction cometh upon them, as travail upon a woman with child.

From these and other passages of Scripture we may gather that woes and pains of the sort specified by the Lord in Matthew 24:6–8 will visit the earth with intensified force at the very time of the end (although the frequency of such occurrences throughout the age would prevent them from serving as signs). The wars and other woes whereof the Lord spake were the beginning of birth pangs; and it is pertinent to recall that birth pangs, after the first intense ones, are intermittent until, at the very end, occur the most severe of all. Thus, no doubt, it will be at the end of this present age, as is clearly predicted in the Book of Revelation.

We would also point out in this connection that the word birth pangs connects the prophecy likewise with Jeremiah 30:5–7, which we have already discussed. In that passage the prophet foretells the return of the Jews from Babylon (Jeremiah 30:3) and then he speaks of the time of Jacob's trouble, concerning which he says: Ask ye now and see whether a man doth travail with child? Wherefore do I see every man with his hands on his loins, as a woman in travail, etc.

If then we regard this entire age as a period of birth pangs (as we have warrant to do from the scriptures cited above) we may consider the time of Jacob's trouble as lasting from the destruction of Jerusalem until now. In that view, the words but he shall be saved out of it seem to be now upon the eve of fulfillment.

An Illuminating Contrast

We would now call attention to a strong and pointed contrast in our Lord's Olivet discourse, the which, if we give due heed thereto, will afford us much aid in the interpretation of this prophecy, and in the interpretation of all prophecies which relate to the end of this present age.

If we examine carefully the entire discourse (as given for example by Mark) we will see that our Lord divides the future into two distinct periods. The first of these extended from the time then present to the destruction of Jerusalem, the second from that event to His own second advent. Beginning at verse 14 with the words, But when ye shall see the abomination of desolation, spoken of by Daniel the prophet, standing where it ought not, down to the end of verse 23, (Mark 13:14–23) Christ is speaking to His disciples concerning the invasion of Judea and the siege of Jerusalem by the Roman armies. As to all those things (whereof the utter demolition of the magnificent temple was the most prominent) His purpose manifestly was to give them explicit information; for those things were to happen in that generation.

Therefore, as regards that period He says: "But take ye heed; behold, I have foretold you all things" (Mark 13:23).

At that point He begins to speak of the second period, saying: "But in those days after that tribulation" (Mark 13:24). Concerning this second period, however, instead of imparting definite information, and giving a sign whereby His people might be warned of the approaching end thereof, He speaks only in the most general terms, and He makes plain only one thing, namely, that no immediately preceding signs would be given whereby His people would know that His advent was near. This feature of His coming again its unexpectedness is stated in so many different ways, and is so emphatically applied and illustrated (see Mark 13:32–37) that we are absolutely controlled by it in the interpretation, not only of the Mount Olivet discourse, but of every other prophecy relating to the second coming of Christ. Here is a great contrast: one event whereof the Lord was speaking was then close at hand; it was to happen within that generation, and it would be immediately preceded by a sign, which His disciples could not fail to recognize. But the other event (His own coming) would be at a time unknown even to Himself, and moreover there should be no sign to appraise His people of its approach, for which reason He impressed it upon them that they were to watch at every season (Luke 21:36, Greek). Concerning the first event He said, Behold, I have foretold you all things; but of the second He said, But of that day and hour knoweth no man, no, not the angels which are in heaven, neither the Son, but the Father (Mark 13:32).

We are aware that it is often attempted to escape the force of this verse by saying that it is only the precise day and hour of the Lord's coming that is left in uncertainty, and that His words do not forbid us to compute (as many attempt to do) the year of His return. But we think that is not treating the Lord's words fairly, or giving them their proper force; for He plainly meant to declare emphatically that the time of His coming was a matter of uncertainty. Moreover, the very next verse says, Watch and pray; for ye know not when the time is, so it is not merely a question of the day and hour, but of the time in general. And finally, the teaching of verses 33–37, with the parable by which the Lord illustrated it, makes it plain that the uncertainty as to His return was to extend through the entire period of His absence.

For, just as He spoke a parable to illustrate and to settle the meaning of His teaching concerning the period before the destruction of Jerusalem (the parable of the fig tree), so likewise He spoke a parable to illustrate and to settle the meaning of His teaching concerning the period we are now in, which He designates simply as those days after that tribulation, but which, in Luke's account, is called the times of the Gentiles.

The point of the first parable is that just as the budding of the fig tree was a sure sign of the nearness of summer, so the presence of the Roman armies in Judea would be a sure sign of the nearness of the destruction of Jerusalem.

The second parable speaks with equal clearness. It is in these words, (For the Son of man is) "...as a man taking a far journey, who left his house, and gave authority to his servants, and to every man his work, and commanded the porter to watch. The Lord Himself has applied this parable, saying, "Watch ye therefore, FOR YE KNOW NOT WHEN THE MASTER OF THE HOUSE COMETH at even, or at midnight, or at the cock crowing, or in the morning' lest coming suddenly He find you sleeping. And what I say unto you, I say unto all, Watch".

So this parable teaches exactly the reverse of the other. The night was divided, according to the custom of that time, into four watches. So the Lord speaks of His absence as being like a night, in any one of the four watches whereof He might return. Thus the question of the time of His return was purposely left from the very beginning in uncertainty, insomuch that, after the destruction of Jerusalem, the only way for His people to insure themselves against being taken unawares was to watch. He was coming suddenly, and hence there was always the possibility that His people might be found sleeping.

Thus Mark's account gives the Lord's teaching on this subject in a positive way, showing the possibility that He might come at any watch of the night. In Matthew's account (and also in Luke 17:24–30) the converse is declared, namely, that the Lord's coming would not be preceded by any sign whatever. It would be as in the days that were before the flood when the ordinary incidents of life continued until the day that Noah entered into the ark (Matthew 24:37–38); and also as it was in the days of Lot, when the overthrow of Sodom and Gomorrah came suddenly and unexpectedly, there being no warning, but the same day that Lot went out of Sodom, it rained fire and brimstone from heaven, and destroyed them all. Even thus shall it be in the day when the Son of man is revealed (Luke 17:28–30). Words could not be plainer.

From these sayings of the Lord Jesus Christ we can see that it is, and always has been, an impossibility to calculate, from any figures given in the Bible, the year, or even the approximate year, of the Lord's return. For if that was unknown even to Christ Himself when He spoke those words, then there was certainly no information in the Scriptures from which it could be computed.

Furthermore we can see how contrary to the teaching of Christ is the idea, which is accepted by so many at the present time, that He will be revealed at the end of a supposed great tribulation of determinate length (seven years, according to some, or three and a half years, according to others). Those who locate the revelation of the Lord Jesus Christ at the end of the great tribulation of current teaching, do plainly contradict His own teaching, in that they make the supposed tribulation a sure sign that His coming is at hand.

Mr. H. Grattan Guinness, in his Light for the Last Days, speaking of signs of the Lord's second coming, says:

> "If such signs as are imagined by some were to precede the advent, the state of society predicted in these passages could not by any possibility exist. If monstrous, unheard of, supernatural, portentous events were to transpire, would they not be telegraphed the same day all over a startled world, and produce such a sense of alarm and expectation that buying, and selling, planting and building, marrying and giving in marriage, would all be arrested together, and 'peace and safety' would be far from anyone's lips or thoughts? ...No, there was nothing special to alarm the antediluvians before the day that Noah entered into the ark; nothing special to startle the men of Sodom ere the fire from heaven fell; and like as it was in those days, so will it be in these. All going on just as usual, no stupendous sign to attract the world's attention."

Signs in the Sun, Moon and Stars

There remains for consideration a passage which is undeniably difficult. We refer to the Lord's saying about signs in the sun, moon and stars, which, as given by Mark, is as follows:

> "But in those days after that tribulation, the sun shall be darkened, and the moon shall not give her light, and the stars of heaven shall fall, and the powers that are in heaven shall be shaken. And then shall they see the Son of man coming in the clouds with great power and glory."

This passage might be taken to mean that the signs in the physical sun, moon and stars, were the immediate precursors of the revelation of the Son of man; but the teaching of Christ which we have just been considering absolutely forbids that interpretation; and to that extent it helps us in our search for the true meaning.

Looking closely at the passage we will see that it is very indefinite. All it tells us is that in those days after that tribulation the commotions in sun, moon and stars will occur; but there is nothing to indicate at what part of those days (which now have lasted over eighteen hundred years) the described commotions would take place. Then which may mean any indefinite period in the future Christ Himself would be seen coming in the clouds.

Inasmuch as what we have learned from the latter part of the Chapter forbids us to take celestial disturbances here foretold as premonitory signs of the Lord's coming, the question arises, for what purpose then did He mention them? And this raises another question, namely, are we to take these words literally, as do the Adventists and some others? or are they to be taken as figurative, and as referring to the political heavens (i.e., the sphere of governments) as understood by some able expositors, among whom one of the most prominent is Sir Isaac Newton? We know of nothing at present whereby this question can be so definitely settled

Concluding Comments

as to put the matter beyond all doubt; but we will offer some further suggestions which may perhaps contribute towards its solution.

In the first place, seeing we are debarred by the Lord's plain teaching from taking these commotions to be physical signs, visible to the eye, preceding and heralding His coming, or as having any special connection with that event, it would seem almost imperative that we give the words a figurative meaning. For it is not conceivable that, in speaking of this long age which was to be so full of important happenings, Christ would single out for mention nothing but a few isolated phenomena of nature in the physical heavens. This consideration practically compels us to find a meaning for the words which would make them descriptive of some distinguishing characteristic of the age, or at least of the latter part of it.

When we turn to Luke's account we find strong confirmation of this view. This confirmation appears in two particulars, first in the manner in which the reference to the sun, moon and stars is introduced; and second in the fact that it is directly coupled with certain general characteristics of the age, such as we should expect in a brief utterance of this kind. For Luke gives it thus (we put the salient part in italics):

For there shall be great distress in the land and wrath upon this people. And they shall fall by the edge of the sword, and shall be led away captive into all nations; *and Jerusalem shall be trodden down of the Gentiles, until the times of the Gentiles be fulfilled.* And there shall be signs in the sun, and in the moon, and in the stars, and upon the earth distress of nations with perplexity, the sea and the waves roaring: Men's hearts failing them for fear, and for looking after those things which are coming on the earth; for the powers of heaven shall be shaken (Luke 21:23–26).

According to this account the Lord does not break off His predictions abruptly at the capture and destruction of Jerusalem, but follows the Jews in their dispersion unto all nations, and also foretells the treading down of Jerusalem by the Gentiles until the times of the Gentiles be fulfilled. Thus we are carried into the period which follows after the tribulation of those days, and are informed that that period is divinely designated the times of the Gentiles.[5] And now immediately follows (in Luke's account) the passage we are examining, And there shall be signs in the sun, and in the moon, and in the stars. But here we have also the further statement, and on the earth distress of nations with perplexity, the sea and the waves roaring, men's hearts failing them, etc. From these words it is clear that the Lord is giving (which, as we have pointed out, is what we should expect) some very broad and general characteristics of our age, with an eye especially upon the closing part thereof. Moreover, in speaking of the unsettled state of the nations He uses a familiar figurative expression, namely, the sea and the waves roaring. This figure represents the turbulence of the peoples of the earth (see Revelation 17:15, Isaiah 8:7), just as the sun, moon and stars represent rulership, governments, and authorities. Thus we find good reason for concluding that the Lord is here speaking figuratively of unusual happenings in the political firmament, that is to say, in the sphere of governments, or what Paul calls the higher powers (Romans 13:1).

In Isaiah 13:7–10 we have an example of the use of this figure. It occurs in connection with a description of the day of the Lord. We quote verse 10: "For the stars of heaven and the constellations thereof shall not give their light; the sun shall be darkened in his going forth, and the moon shall not cause her light to shine". Taking these words in connection with Genesis 1:16–18, and with Joseph's dream about the sun, moon and stars (which his father and brethren had no need of one to interpret for them, (Genesis 37:9–10), and in connection also with (Ezekiel 32:7; Joel 2:31, 3:15; Revelation 12:1) we get the idea that the sun stands for authority on earth in the broadest sense, and the moon for lesser authority, and the stars for prominent persons in the sphere of government.

Further reason in support of the view that the Lord used the sun, moon and stars as symbols in this passage, is found in the fact that, throughout the Scriptures, the prediction of political changes of this era are given in a veiled form, that is to say, by figures and symbols. Thus, in Daniel the successive powers are indicated first as parts of a huge metallic image, and then as great beasts, following one after another. In Revelation the last of these beasts reappears, in its ten-horned (that is its latter) stage of development, which is the state it will be in when destroyed by the coming of Christ. Individual powers are represented by horns, and notable personages in the political heavens by stars. That the sun, moon and stars are used in a figurative sense in Revelation is proved by the words, "And there appeared a great wonder in heaven; a woman clothed with the sun; and the moon under her feet, and upon her head a crown of twelve stars" (Revelation 12:1). From this we may safely infer that the sun stands for supreme governmental authority over the earth, the moon for lesser dominion, and the stars for notable rulers or potentates.

Turning now to (Revelation 6:12) we read, and the sun became black as sackcloth of hair, and the moon became as blood, and the stars of heaven fell unto the earth, which words are suited to present, symbolically, the complete overthrow of governmental authority, the bloody character of that which for the time takes its place, and the downfall of all rulers and magistrates.

The reasons for speaking thus in veiled language of political changes in the world in this dispensation, are not hard do discern; for this is an era in which God's people are strangers and pilgrims on earth, having no affiliations with the powers that be, but are taught to be in subjection to them. Hence, our Lord Himself would, of course, use the same form of utterance in forecasting the political happenings of these times of the Gentiles. Therefore it may reasonably be taken that when the Lord spake of the sun, moon and stars in terms strikingly similar to those found in Revelation, He meant to say that the darkening of the sun (i.e., the decay of supreme authority in the world), would begin immediately after the destruction of Jerusalem; and putting the two passages together, we would conclude that this figurative darkening of the sun was to become more and more pronounced until, at the climax of the dispensation, it would become total darkness, while at the same time the rulers would all fall together, as a fig tree casts her figs when shaken by a mighty wind.

Some such interpretation of the Lord's words seems almost a necessity when we consider His express declaration that physical signs were not to be given in this age in respect to the one and only event for which His people were to wait and watch.

A gradual weakening of authority on earth in the hands of those with whom it has been lodged, such as we have indicated above, has been a characteristic of this age; and it is such a pronounced feature of our own days, that the decay of authority and the spirit of lawlessness are themes upon which men in public life often dilate at the present time, and in words which betray the most serious apprehensions as to the outcome. In the moon's not giving her light, we may see the weakening of authority in a narrower sphere, such as national governments, which are all changing from monarchies to democracies. And in the stars' falling from heaven, we may see the downfall of notable personages, as the German Kaiser, the imperial family of Austria (the Hapsburgs), the Romanoffs for centuries rulers of Russia, the kings of Greece and Bulgaria, and lesser personages in the political sphere (see Revelation 9:1).

These happenings are not sufficiently definite to serve as signs of the Lord's coming, nor do they stand in any given time relation to that event. But they do serve admirably to the furtherance of the one practical object which the Lord had in view in speaking this part of His discourse, and which He has made quite plain, namely, that His people should be kept constantly in a state of expectancy of His coming again. So, without giving them any sign of His coming, or making any definite statement about it, He could say, And when these things begin to come to pass, then look up, and lift up your heads, for your redemption draweth nigh (Luke 21:28).

One further point is to be noted: In connection with the reference to the sun, moon and stars, Luke says, for the powers of the heavens shall be shaken; and the same words occur, in the same connection, in both Matthew and Mark. These words are explanatory of what the Lord said about the sun, moon and stars, and show that He did not mean physical commotions. There is no power (of this sort) but from God (Romans 13:1). Peter uses the same word when, speaking of Christ's having ascended on high, he said, angels and authorities and powers being made subject unto Him (1 Peter 3:22). We have seen in the course of these studies that there is a mysterious connection between the several powers that rule in the world and certain mighty angelic beings. But these powers have been all made subject to Christ, Whose prerogative it is to shake them at His pleasure. And surely there has been a great shaking of these powers in our day,[6] reminding us of what is written in another place' But now He hath promised, saying, Yet once more I shake not the earth only, but also heaven (Hebrews 12:26). This is in close agreement with the words found in Matthew's account, And the powers of the heavens shall be shaken (Matthew 24:29).

It should not be overlooked that, in Matthew's account, we have the word immediately; for he says Immediately after the tribulation of those days shall the sun be darkened, etc. (Matthew 24:29); and no doubt this word is what has led many expositors to suppose that the great tribulation was to be at the very end of this present age, followed immediately by signs in the physical heavens, and by the visible coming of Christ. But whatever be the force of the word which our translators have rendered immediately, it cannot be permitted to displace the tribulation foretold by Christ as coming (and which did come) in that generation, and to remove it away off to the end of this age. Nor can it be permitted to make the tribulation and the commotions in the heavens a sign of His second coming, in contradiction of His plain teaching as to that event. Rather, must we assume, in harmony with all that Christ has said on that subject, that the fulfillment of this particular part of the prophecy began from the destruction of Jerusalem, and is to be seen in all of God's dealings in judgment with the higher powers (Romans 13:1), from that time onward.

The word immediately used by Matthew (not found in the corresponding part of Mark or Luke) signifies merely that the destruction of Jerusalem would be followed immediately by a period (of unmeasured length) which would be characterized by commotions of the sort described. Such disturbances have been, as we have seen, one of the outstanding characteristics of the age, and are a special mark of our own times.

Finally, in bringing these studies to a close, we would say again that we do not in the least question that there will be much tribulation for mankind, and many distresses and woes, in the end time of this present age, to be followed by the outpouring of the vials in which is filled up the wrath of God (Revelation 15:1). All we assert is that, regardless of the nature and severity of the afflictions which are yet to come, that particular tribulation whereof the Lord spake as the great tribulation, and as the days of vengeance (Matthew 24:21; Luke 21:22) was the execution of Divine judgment upon Daniel's people and his holy city, for which God used the Roman armies under Titus in AD 70.

APPENDIX

In the course of my revision of this book for the printing of a new edition (just twenty years after the first edition) I have found less need than might have been expected for corrections and additions. For the then existing conditions of the world, political and industrial, afforded warrant for the belief that the great and final shaking of The heavens, the earth, the sea, the dry land, and all nations, foretold by the Prophet Haggai (Haggai 2:6-7) and quoted in substance in Hebrews (Hebrews 12:26-27) was even then in progress. But now, as these lines are being written, the whole world is in the throes of a convulsion so violent and so widespread that it seems well nigh impossible there should ever be a greater.

However that may be (as to which I make no prediction) there is certainly one conspicuous feature of this present outpouring of divine judgments, which comes within the scope of the purpose of this book, and is well worthy of additional discussion. I have in mind the distresses, cruelties and persecutions, unprecedented in violence and extent, now being visited upon that people scattered and peeled, the sorely afflicted survivors of the Jewish race, which persecutions in themselves constitute a tribulation unsurpassed in all previous history.

It is impossible, however, that the present day affliction of the Jews should be taken as the great tribulation of the futurist scheme of interpretation of prophecy. For, according to the basic assumptions of that system, the great tribulation will not (and indeed cannot) come to pass until the surviving Jews shall have been reconstituted as a nation, shall have regained possession of Palestine, and shall have rebuilt the temple at Jerusalem, reestablished the Mosaic sacrifices and ordinances, made a covenant with

Antichrist for the absurdly brief period of one week, and until that covenant shall have been broken in the midst of the week. For the futurist system requires that all these great events shall take place in the week (seven years) which immediately precedes the second coming of Christ.

On the other hand, however, and directly to the contrary, the unparalleled distress of nations, now in progress, and especially the bloody persecutions of the widely dispersed survivors of the Jewish race, which have now reached a degree of intensity (in the fiendish cruelties devised by Adolph Hitler) unequalled hitherto in the annals of mankind, do accord perfectly with that interpretation of prophecy, to which nearly all evangelical commentators have adhered from the days of the Protestant Reformation until a recent date; and which is advocated in this book. From current news sources (October, 1943) we learn that the estimated Jewish population of Europe ten years ago was 8,300,000; and that has been reduced by 5,000,000. So that in the whole of continental Europe occupied by the Axis, only 3,000,000 Jews remain alive. Surely we have here a harrowing item of a tribulation which is immeasurably great. Is it supposable that a tribulation of even greater severity is yet in store for that sorely afflicted race, and the mouth of the compassionate Savior has declared it? Impossible.

In view of these things I welcomed the opportunity now presented for calling attention to certain features of the great subject we are studying (the great tribulation of the Olivet prophecy) which lend additional support to the view of that subject presented in this book.

It is manifest that, in order to arrive at a fairly correct estimate of the magnitude of that great tribulation (which was to be such as was not since the beginning of the world...nor ever shall be), due weight must be given to the words: "And they shall be led away captive into all nations, and Jerusalem shall be trodden down of the Gentiles until the times of the Gentiles be fulfilled". It is likewise manifest that this part of verse 24 (Luke 21:24)) deals with the very same topics (Jerusalem and the Jewish people) as the preceding clause of the verse. Moreover, it is now evident that the period of trials and sufferings, which the survivors of the destruction of Jerusalem were to endure during their age long dispersion throughout the nations of the world, constitutes by far the major part of the predicted tribulation, which was to be without parallel in the history of the world. This is more clearly seen when the history of the Jews of the dispersion is viewed in the light of the prophecy of Moses in his last words to that nation whereof he was the founder and the nursing father. Those words are recorded in the concluding chapters of Deuteronomy. In that final message he faithfully warned his beloved people, and in the clearest words, of the consequences of departure from the commandments of the Lord. A long Chapter (Deuteronomy 28) is occupied with the details of this vital subject. He had previously reminded them of the great features, which distinguished in a remarkable way the beginnings of their history from those of all other nations. Those differences are notable indeed (See Deuteronomy 4:7–12). But we will not comment upon them now. It is sufficient for our present purpose to refer to verse 34, where it is forcefully implied (in the form of a rhetorical question) that never, in any case save that of Israel, had God assayed to go and take Him a nation out of the midst of another nation. What is, however, comparable to this, and is foreshadowed by it, is that God is now visiting all nations of the world to take out of them a people for His Name (Acts 15:14).

Thus, taking Chapter 4 of Deuteronomy with the Olivet prophecy of our Lord, we have His word for it that, like as God visited Egypt (the greatest of all nations of that era) to take out of it a people for His Name (His old covenant people) so likewise, in this era of the fulfilment of all the types and shadows of the law, He would visit ALL nations, to take out of them a chosen generation, a royal priesthood, an holy nation, a peculiar people (1 Peter 2:9). Thus we are given to know that, like as Israel was unique as a nation in its beginning, in that it was taken as an entirety—men, women and children, with all their possessions and much spoil—out of the midst of another nation, in which they had been captives, even so its end was to be unique, in that its survivors were to be led away captive into all nations. Furthermore, their holy city was to be given into the hands of their enemies for the duration of the entire times of the Gentiles.

One of the most remarkable facts connected with the ending of the history of Israel as an earthly nation, and the age long condition of its city and its surviving people, as we behold them today preserving their racial identity despite the most cruel and contemptuous treatment to which a people were ever subjected was clearly foretold by the great founder of their nation, in what were almost his last words to the people he so dearly loved. We quote:

And the LORD shall scatter thee among all people from the one end of the earth even unto the other; and there thou shalt serve other gods, which neither thou nor thy fathers have known, even wood and stone. And among those nations shalt thou find no ease, neither shall the sole of thy foot have rest: but the LORD shall give thee there a trembling heart, and failing of eyes, and sorrow of mind. And thy life shall hang in doubt before thee; and thou shalt fear day and night, and shalt have none assurance of thy life: In the morning thou shalt say, Would God it were even! and at even thou shalt say, Would God it were morning! for the fear of thine heart wherewith thou shalt fear, and for the sight of thine eyes which thou shalt see (Deuteronomy 28:64–67).

Thus ends the history of the natural Israel as seen and foretold by its founder. It is a dark picture indeed. But there is nevertheless a brighter side, whereof we may get a satisfying glimpse in our

Lord's Olivet prophecy. For He Who, when He beheld the city, wept over it, foreseeing its approaching doom (Luke 19:41–44) spake a gracious word of promise, wherein is an assurance of mercy and salvation that was to follow that people and to be accessible to them in all their wanderings throughout this long day of salvation. For God has not cast away His people which He foreknew. And this is to be seen in the fact that, while decreeing that they should be led away captive into all nations, He also decreed that This gospel of the Kingdom shall be preached in all the world for a witness to all nations, before the end shall come.

Therefore, in whatever nation they may be throughout the times of the Gentiles, they are within reach of the life saving sound of the gospel of God, which is the power of God unto salvation to everyone that believeth; to the Jew first (Romans 1:16). Moreover, through the gracious providence of God there are now in all the principle countries of the world special agencies for the evangelization of the people of Jewish descent.

What shall we then say to these things? Let us be zealous to take up the unfinished business of the great apostle to the Gentiles, preaching the Kingdom of God (Acts 28:31) with special efforts at reaching the lost sheep of the house of Israel, to the end that they, the natural branches, may be grafted into their own olive tree. For God is able to graft them in again; and He will do so, if they abide not still in unbelief. For SO—and not in any other way—ALL ISRAEL SHALL BE SAVED.

ENDNOTES

1. This Josephus was a priest who was born about four years after the death of Christ. He was a God-fearing man, highly gifted, and is regarded as a remarkably able and trustworthy historian. He was an eye-witness and an active participator in the *Wars of the Jews* which culminated in the destruction of Jerusalem by Titus. We believe the annals of Josephus have been providentially preserved, whereby we have authentic records of the fulfilment of prophecy by an eyewitness who, at the time he wrote, was not a Christian. We shall have occasion to quote largely from this writer later on.

2. See *Wonders of Bible Chronology* by P. Mauro. Daniel stood trembling; and then the angel further said: "Fear not, Daniel, for from the first day that thou didst set thy heart to understand, and to chasten thyself before thy God, thy words were heard…Now I am come to make thee understand what shall befall thy people in the latter days" (Daniel 10:2–14).

3. Also God's two witnesses (Revelation 11:3) are to prophecy a thousand two hundred and threescore days (the same period stated in terms of days): and of the ten-horned Beast it is said that power would be given unto him to continue forty and two months. (Re 13:5.)

4. The stones of the Temple were of huge dimensions. Edersheim says: According to Josephus the city was so upheaved and dug up that it was difficult to believe it had ever been inhabited. At a later period Turnus Rufus had the plowshare drawn over it. In regard to the temple walls, notwithstanding the massiveness of the stones,

there was nothing left in place, with the exception of some corner or portion of wall—left almost to show how great had been the ruin and desolation.

5. The times of the Gentiles are commonly taken as beginning when Nebuchadnezzar carried the Jews into captivity. But there is nothing in the Scripture to support this idea, so far as we are aware. If the times of the Gentiles were the captivity in Babylon, then they would have ended when that captivity ended. But God did not then turn away from the Jews to the Gentiles. For He sent them His prophets, Haggai, Zechariah and Malachi. John the Baptist's ministry was to Israel; the Lord Himself was sent to the lost sheep of the house of Israel, and His apostles were charged to preach the gospel to the Jew first, which they were faithful to do. But from the destruction of Jerusalem down to the present time, the work of God's Word and Spirit has been among the Gentiles. In view of all this we are inclined to the opinion that, although there was a brief period when the preaching of the gospel to the Gentiles overlapped the preaching of Peter and other apostles to the Jews, yet the times of the Gentiles may be said to have fully begun from the destruction of Jerusalem. It is, of course, a matter of comparatively slight importance when the times of the Gentiles began, since it is agreed on all hands that they are in continuance at the present time, and that they will extend to the second coming of Christ.

6. And now (in April, 1944) a far greater shaking is in progress than that referred to above.

For a comprehensive guide to all end-times prophecy—

Available at
www.greatchristianbooks.com

THE MISSION OF GREAT CHRISTIAN BOOKS

The ministry of Great Christian Books was established to glorify The Lord Jesus Christ and to be used by Him to expand and edify the kingdom of God while we occupy and anticipate Christ's glorious return. Great Christian Books will seek to accomplish this mission by publishing Gospel literature which is biblically faithful, relevant, and practically applicable to many of the serious spiritual needs of mankind upon the beginning of this new millennium. To do so we will always seek to boldly incorporate the truths of Scripture, especially those which were largely articulated as a body of theology during the Protestant Reformation of the sixteenth century and ensuing years. We gladly join our voice in the proclamations of— Scripture Alone, Faith Alone, Grace Alone, Christ Alone, and God's Glory Alone!

Our ministry seeks the blessing of our God as we seek His face to both confirm and support our labors for Him. Our prayers for this work can be summarized by two verses from the Book of Psalms:

"...let the beauty of the LORD our God be upon us, And establish the work of our hands for us; Yes, establish the work of our hands." —Psalm 90:17

"Not unto us, O LORD, not unto us, but to your name give glory." —Psalm 115:1

Great Christian Books appreciates the financial support of anyone who shares our burden and vision for publishing literature which combines sound Bible doctrine and practical exhortation in an age when too few so-called "Christian" publications do the same. We thank you in advance for any assistance you can give us in our labors to fulfill this important mission. May God bless you.

For a catalog of other great Christian books including additional titles on End Time Prophecy.

contact us in any of the following ways:

write us at:
Great Christian Books
160 37th Street
Lindenhurst, NY 11757

call us at:
(631) 956-0998

find us online:
www.greatchristianbooks.com

email us at:
mail@greatchristianbooks.com

www.ingramcontent.com/pod-product-compliance
Lightning Source LLC
LaVergne TN
LVHW041540070426
835507LV00011B/835